*Rudyard Kipling and Sir Henry Rider Haggard
on Screen, Stage, Radio and Television*

Rudyard Kipling and Sir Henry Rider Haggard on Screen, Stage, Radio and Television

by
PHILIP LEIBFRIED

McFarland & Company, Inc., Publishers
Jefferson, North Carolina, and London

Cover, clockwise from top: Rudyard Kipling; Henry Rider Haggard; John Richardson and Ursula Andress in the 1965 Hammer production of *She* (courtesy Collectors Book Store); Sabu in *Jungle Book* (1942).

Library of Congress Cataloguing-in-Publication data are available

Leibfried, Philip, 1948–
Rudyard Kipling and Sir Henry Rider Haggard on screen, stage,
radio and television / by Philip Leibfried
p. cm.
Includes bibliographical references and index.
ISBN 0-7864-0707-7 (illustrated case binding : 50# alkaline paper)

1. Kipling Rudyard, 1865–1936 — Film and video adaptations.
2. Haggard, H. Rider (Henry Rider), 1856–1925 — Film and video adaptations.
3. Haggard, H. Rider (Henry Rider), 1856–1925 — Adaptations.
4. Adventure stories, English — Film and video adaptations.
5. Fantasy fiction, English — Film and video adaptations.
6. Kipling, Rudyard, 1865–1936 — Adaptations.
7. Adventure stories, English — Adaptations.
8. Fantasy fiction, English — Adaptations. I. Title.

PR4858.F55 L45   2000   791.43'6 — dc21   99-49415 CIP

British Library Cataloguing-in-Publication data are available

Manufactured in the United States of America

McFarland & Company, Inc., Publishers
Box 611, Jefferson, North Carolina 28640
www.mcfarlandpub.com

For all the Allan Quatermains
and Gunga Dins of the world

Acknowledgments

Non-fiction books being a collaborative effort, thanks must be meted out to those who selflessly give of their valuable time to assist the author.

To Madeline Matz, Reference Librarian of the Library of Congress' Motion Picture, Broadcasting and Recorded Sound Division, goes much gratitude for her supplying me with vital data concerning the films herein listed.

To my one-time fellow adventurer, long time friend and historical artist extraordinaire Gary Zaboly, I extend my deepest gratitude for all the material he sent me immediately upon learning of my contract for this book; I hope his armchair is as comfortable as mine.

To my dear friend Annette M. D'Agostino, Keeper of the Flame for Harold Lloyd aficionados worldwide, go my heartfelt thanks not only for her continued moral support, but for apprising me of certain obscure information regarding Rudyard Kipling's connection with filmmaking. Two of her books, *An Index to Short and Feature Film Reviews in* The Moving Picture World: *The Early Years, 1907–1915* and *Filmmakers in* The Moving Picture World: *An Index of Articles, 1907–1927,* proved invaluable in facilitating my search for necessary data.

To Greta Dunn of Hallmark Entertainment, Malcolm Willits of Collectors Bookstore, Roger Hill of Nothing's New, Ned Thanhouser of the Thanhouser Company, Annette Fern, Reference Librarian of the Pusey Library at Harvard University, the late Robert Douglas, and the late John D. Roles, Michael F. Blake, John Cocchi, Anthony Slide, Roger Allen of the Rider Haggard Appreciation Society, Ed Hurley, Ray Schnitzer, Thom Sciacca of Schlock Cinema and George Rackus go my sincerest thanks for providing me with useful data and material.

My thanks to Andrew Luff, Head of Sales at London Films, for furnishing me with valuable data on that company's production of *Kim*, and also to Susan Wilkinson for her kindness in supplying stills from that production.

I am also grateful to Sally Dumaux for generously sharing data on *The City of Terrible Night*, from her forthcoming book on early film star King Baggot.

Special thanks to Claire of Eddie Brandt's Saturday Matinee for going the extra mile and to Carol Walsh for her generous assistance.

Thanks also to Stephen Cleary of the BBC Sound Archives for providing me with the British radio program adaptations.

To all of the following, my continued thanks for your moral support: Ed Bielcik, Kelly Brown, David Busch, Bill Eggert, Garen Ewing, Pierre Guinle, Estella Johnson, Rick Levinson, Tsuyoshi Minamoto, Franklin Santana, Brian Taves, Richard Whalen, Frances Whalen, Michael Whalen, Gene Vazzana and Fred Yannantuono.

Philip Leibfried
New York
September 1999

Table of Contents

Acknowledgments   vii
Introduction   1

Rudyard Kipling Filmography   13
H. Rider Haggard Filmography   95
Rudyard Kipling Stage Adaptations   191
H. Rider Haggard Stage Adaptations   195
Rudyard Kipling Radio Adaptations   202
H. Rider Haggard Radio Adaptations   204
Rudyard Kipling Television Adaptations   205

Bibliography   207
Index   209

Introduction

Among the most popular writers of the late Victorian era were two men whose outputs were of very different stripes, yet who were the best of friends. Their physical appearances and personalities were also dissimilar. Rudyard Kipling was short, slender, extremely myopic and shy. Henry Rider Haggard was tall, handsome, well-built and gregarious.

Both became enamored of faraway lands, writing of exotic locales in timeless prose and poetry. One trumpeted the glory of the British Empire in India, usually through the eyes and tongue of the common soldier, while the other created fantasy lands and strange peoples in the heart of Africa, a continent which was then still being explored and charted by Europeans. Of course, neither author wrote exclusively in those areas, but they became inextricably linked with them. Haggard actually did write very little else since his fictional works were so enormously popular, bringing him a steady and healthy income. Of his 67 books, 57 were novels, and most of those were set somewhere in Africa.

Rudyard Kipling and Henry Rider Haggard created their stories and characters in a time far removed from our own, when the world situation was very different (both geographically and politically) from today's. Imperialism was rampant, especially on the part of Great Britain, which controlled territory on almost every continent. Kipling's and Haggard's outlooks must therefore be taken in context.

These were heady times for lovers of adventure fiction. The 1880s saw the publication of *Treasure Island* and *Kidnapped* by Scotsman Robert Louis Stevenson; G. A. Henty was still turning out historical novels for boys after 20 years. The 1890s brought Anthony Hope and his Ruritanian romances, beginning with *The Prisoner of Zenda* (1894). To top all that, the most famous fictional character of all made his first appearance in 1887, when a novella entitled *A Study in Scarlet* was published. The lead character, a brilliant detective called Sherlock Holmes, became a household name and brought literary immortality to his creator, a burly Irish doctor by the name of Arthur Conan Doyle.

The influence of Haggard and Kipling has been great down through the years. While not the first to conjure up lost races in his books, Haggard epitomized that genre, being the inspiration

Rudyard Kipling

for such twentieth century exponents of the field as Edgar Rice Burroughs, C. S. Lewis and J. R. R. Tolkien. Kipling's "Jungle Books" also inspired Burroughs' most famous creation, the seemingly indestructible Tarzan of the Apes. Kipling remains a major literary figure, despite the imperialistic slant of much of his work. Haggard has fallen by the wayside, apparently bound forever to the late Victorian period, although there is a society in Britain dedicated to his memory and works (as there is for Kipling).

The son of a professor of architectural sculpture, Joseph Rudyard Kipling entered the world on December 30, 1865. The place was Bombay, India, a thriving port on a peninsula off the west coast of India, the "Jewel in the Crown" of Great Britain's vast empire. He owed his unusual middle name to his aunt Louisa, who suggested it after Lake Rudyard in Staffordshire, where the boy's parents first met.

At the age of five, he was sent to England to begin his formal education. For almost six years he resided in the home of a retired merchant naval officer in Southsea. This period was the most miserable of his life: after the officer's passing, Kipling was physically abused by the man's widow. Finally Kipling's mother returned to Britain and enrolled him at the United Services College at Westward Ho, on Bideford Bay in Devon, where the faculty allowed him full rein in his gluttonous reading and writing habits.

In 1882, Kipling returned to India, where he worked as an assistant editor for the *Civil and Military Gazette* in Lahore. He remained in the sub-continent as a journalist for seven years, during which time he secured a well-deserved reputation as a relator of the British experience in India. He was exposed to much of this type of life first-hand, and was once shot at in the Khyber Pass.

Kipling's earliest work also appeared in the *Weekly News* and *Pioneer*. In 1887, the 21-year-old journalist moved over to the *Pioneer*, a national paper published in Allahabad. While there, he did much traveling around India and also created his three most popular characters — Privates Mulvaney, Ortheris and Learoyd, the "Soldiers Three." In January 1888, *Plain Tales from the Hills*, a collection of his columns from the *Gazette*, was published.

In late 1888, the publishing house A.H. Wheeler and Co., which had an exclusive contract for the Indian railway book stalls, devised the idea of issuing inexpensive reprints of popular works for reading on the trains. Kipling's latest short stories filled the first six numbers of the series. These booklets, priced at one rupee each, gave the fledgling author the exposure he needed, as they were carried all over the world by readers. They appeared later in the volumes known today as *Soldiers Three* and *Wee Willie Winkie*, the latter including the story considered Kipling's finest, *The Man Who Would Be King*.

In early 1889, Kipling returned to England, traveling eastward through the Orient and America. In New York, he found a pirated edition of his *Plain Tales from the Hills* and myriad reviews of his railway stories.

Arriving in London in October, he was introduced to the members of the fashionable Savile Club by Andrew Lang, a reader for the publishing firm of Sampson Low. There he met the novelist Henry Rider Haggard for the first time. Lang also arranged for young Rudyard to meet with his employer, resulting in the publication of *Soldiers Three* for the English market early in 1890.

The next few years saw the publication of his first novel, *The Light That Failed*, and the ever-popular *Barrack-Room Ballads*, a collection of poems which includes *Mandalay* and *Gunga Din*, both of which were later adapted for the screen (as was the novel). Kipling's popularity at this time was such that his works were being pirated on a larger scale than before. With no international copyright agreement with the United States existing, the author had no legal recourse to combat this injustice. It was during this troublesome period that Kipling met a young man who would prove most influential in correcting this problem. (An international copyright agreement was reached in 1891 when the U.S. Congress voted approval on the International Copyright Act, which was already subscribed to by most of the nations of Europe.)

Wolcott Balestier, an American from Vermont working as agent for the publisher J.W. Lovell & Co., which specialized in cheap reprints of popular books, was unparalleled in his ability to attract people who were in the public eye. He proved his talent beyond question when he secured the American rights for his company from Kipling, who was no respecter of such publishers. This charming fellow also convinced Kipling to agree to collaborate on a novel, *The Naulahka*, the only such example in the famed author's canon. Balestier also introduced him to his younger sister Caroline, who later became Mrs. Rudyard Kipling.

In September 1891, Kipling embarked on another world tour, which was cut short by news of Balestier's death from typhoid fever in early December. The novel he and Kipling had written was finished save for the last installment. That was completed by Kipling on his honeymoon, aboard the S.S. *Teutonic*. The book was published in 1892.

On January 18, 1892, Rudyard and Caroline were wed. The following month the couple settled in a cottage owned by Caroline's grandmother out-side Brattleboro, Vermont. The next year, the Kiplings built a home of their own, which they named "Naulakha" (the correct spelling of that Hindi word; the *k* and the *h* had been trans-posed in the title of the novel) in honor of Caroline's late brother. There Kipling would pen his most memorable works, *The Jungle Book* and *The Second Jungle Book*, a collection of 15 fanciful animal tales, eight of which featured a feral child named Mowgli. In a letter to his friend Haggard, he revealed that the inspiration for those immortal stories had been a scene from Haggard's *Nada the Lily* and his own short story of 1893, *In the Rukh*, from the collection *Many Inventions*.

By this time, Rudyard Kipling was receiving excellent remuneration for his work, being paid at the rate of 25¢ per word. An American admirer, hear-ing of this, enclosed a quarter in a let-ter to the author requesting a word. Kipling wrote "Thanks" on the letter and returned it.

A locally celebrated court case involving Rudyard and his brother-in-law, Beatty Balestier, in the spring of 1896 brought throngs of reporters from all over New England for the hearing. To avoid what promised to be a circus atmosphere, the intensely private Kiplings left their beloved Vermont home in a hurry in August of 1896, never to return, before the case came to trial.

Back in England, the popular writer continued his prolific output of prose and poetry. The following year saw his second novel, *Captains Coura-geous*, and a short poem, *The Vampire*.

The latter was a trifle dashed off in honor of his cousin, the artist Philip Burne-Jones, whose salon painting of that year bore the same title. It depicted a tall woman in white, looming exul-tantly over the body of a young man on a bed. The poem was printed in the cat-alogue for the painting and never copy-righted, as it was a gift to the artist. The result of this oversight was a plethora of plagiarized versions of both the paint-ing and the poem, including a play upon which at least two early film adaptations were based.

In 1900, Kipling journeyed to South Africa where he viewed an actual battle of the Boer War. The inadequa-cies of the British troops there affected him so strongly that his output for the next two years dealt almost exclusively with the problem. This shift in his opinion of his country's military cost him some popularity.

The following year, Kipling's novel *Kim*, about an orphan Anglo-Indian youth who becomes involved both with a holy man and the British Secret Ser-vice, was published. *Kim* was the result of seven years of intermittent writing, during which time Kipling picked through his notes of another proposed novel, *Mother Maturin*. Kipling ex-pected this story of an Irish woman who runs an opium den in Lahore to be his masterpiece. However, his father's disapproval led to its abandonment after several hundred pages had been completed. *Kim* was to be Kipling's final work with an Indian setting.

Never one for commissioned work, Kipling twice refused a knighthood and all official honors offered him (includ-ing the Order of Merit) and was set to reject the post of poet laureate, had it been offered. As it was, Rudyard Kipling was the unofficial poet laureate in the minds of the British people. In 1907, he did accept the Nobel Prize for Literature, becoming the first British writer so honored (and, at 41, the youngest recipient of that award).

The second decade of the twentieth century was a very difficult period for Rudyard Kipling. Having already lost his mother in November 1910, he lost his father in January 1911, and his only son, John, was killed at the Battle of Loos in 1915. The 18-year-old's body was never recovered. Kipling's health, never the best, went into severe decline after this heart-wrenching loss. (The Kiplings' firstborn, Josephine, died in 1899 at age six from pneumonia; their daughter Elsie, born in 1896, was the only child to survive her parents.) His politics remained the same, but this did not affect the sales of his numerous works. Much of his post-war output dealt with that horrible conflagration, including *The Irish Guards in the Great War* (1923) and the acclaimed short story *A Madonna of the Trenches* (1924).

Kipling's poetry has given the world many frequently quoted phrases, among them "a rag and a bone, and a hank of hair" (*The Vampire*) and "You're a better man than I am, Gunga Din!" (*Gunga Din*). In the minds of many, he is a major pro–Imperialist figure, but his genius transcended mere politics.

The oft-quoted writer died at his home in Sussex of a perforated duodenum on January 18, 1936, his forty-fourth wedding anniversary. His ashes

Henry Rider Haggard

were placed among those of many other noted British men of letters in the Poets Corner of Westminster Abbey in London. A few years after his passing, a destroyer, the H.M.S. *Kipling*, was commissioned, seeing action in the Mediterranean during World War II.

In the late nineteenth century, when the term "romance" referred to stories of exotic adventure rather than those of passion, no novelist was more popular than Henry Rider Haggard. More than any other writer, he popularized the "lost race" novel at a time when much of the earth remained uncharted, allowing much conjecture as to conditions in those unknown realms.

A country squire's son, he was born at Bradenham, Norfolk, on June 22, 1856, the eighth of ten children.

During the first three months of his life, he suffered from both jaundice and inflamed lungs. After overcoming the second illness, he grew into a robust youth.

Due to the large size of the family, young Henry was relegated to a nursery. A particularly maladjusted nurse became aware of his vivid imagination and used a wretched-looking doll which she called "She-Who-Must-Be-Obeyed" to make her charge behave. This early memory gave rise to Haggard's most famous creation, Ayesha, the title character of his best-selling novel *She*. Many of Rider's other childhood acquaintances and experiences also found their way into his books, such as the farmer William Quatermain, who became "Allan" Quatermain, Haggard's most popular character, appearing in 14 novels.

In 1875, Haggard's father arranged for his son to go to Africa as part of Sir Henry Bulwer's staff. Bulwer, nephew of the novelist Edward Bulwer-Lytton, had just been appointed Lieutenant-Governor of Natal. Haggard's duties there left him with much free time to observe the people and the environment, giving him a wealth of material for the books he was to author.

In early 1877, a treaty was signed with the Boers, the Dutch settlers of the region, and the British flag was raised over the newly annexed Transvaal. Haggard's participation in this event was a source of great pride to him in later years. Shortly thereafter he was given two official positions and soon became the youngest man to head a government department in South Africa.

Haggard returned to England in the summer of 1879 and married the former Mariana Louisa Margitson, the orphaned daughter of Major Margitson of Ditchingham House, Norfolk, on August 11, 1880. He and his new wife sailed to South Africa that October, arriving just as the First Boer War commenced. Within a year they had a son and had departed for England, fearing retribution from the Boers for his involvement in the Transvaal annexation.

Haggard had some articles published during his first tour in Africa, and again took up the pen after resettling in Britain. He wrote accounts of his African experiences for several publications. His first book, *Cetywayo and His White Neighbours*, was published in 1882, partially at his own expense, but did not sell well.

Advised by a friend to attempt writing fiction, Haggard did so. He had his first novel, *Dawn*, published in 1884, followed by a second novel in December of that year. While critically acclaimed, *The Witch's Head* had an edition of but 500 copies, so Haggard stood to earn little from its sales. He began a study of law, feeling he could earn a better living that way, although he continued to write.

With the publication (September 1885) of his third novel, *King Solomon's Mines*, written in 13 weeks earlier that year, Henry Rider Haggard joined the ranks of best-selling authors. Haggard said that this book was an attempt to create an adventure story for boys in the vein of Robert Louis Stevenson's immensely popular *Treasure Island*, published two years previously. To say he succeeded would be an understatement. As in Kipling's case, several pirated editions of this timeless tale appeared in the United States.

When his sixth novel, *She*, was published on New Year's Day 1887, Haggard's place in romance literature was solidified. Although not as critically well received as *King Solomon's Mines*, the first edition of 10,000 copies of *She* sold out within a few weeks. The tale of a lost civilization dwelling in darkest Africa and ruled by an iron-fisted and immortal queen who is herself a slave to love, *She* caught the reading public's imagination as few other works of fiction have. Besides being the most popular of his novels, it is the most frequently filmed and staged of his works.

All this success brought a flood of accusations challenging the originality of his work. (*She*, especially, came under attack from many sides.) Also in 1887, it was Haggard's misfortune to author an article entitled "About Fiction" in which he stated that, except for sculpture, romance writing was the most difficult of the arts and that 75 percent of books were worthless. As may be imagined, this caused a firestorm of criticism. He still easily weathered the attacks of controversy, secure in the ever-increasing sales of his books in regular and cheap editions. A number of parodies of his works further attested to their popularity. Among them were "He," "Pa," "Ma" and "King Solomon's Wives." Haggard's friend Andrew Lang was allegedly the author of some of them.

With his fourth novel, *Allan Quatermain*, Haggard's works had begun to be serialized in popular magazines, thus insuring a ready-made audience for the hard- and softcover editions which followed. When *Allan Quatermain* was published in July 1887 (though written before *She*, the latter was published first), it was issued in a 20,000 copy hardcover edition and an illustrated large paper edition of 112 copies. Among its readers was a 13-year-old future Prime Minister, Winston Churchill, who wrote the author that he had enjoyed *Allan Quatermain* more than *King Solomon's Mines* and hoped that Haggard would write "many more books."

Like Kipling, Haggard was championed by the noted critic Andrew Lang. Also like Kipling, he earned a very good income, in the neighborhood of several thousand pounds a year, at a time when one pound equaled five American dollars. Another correlation between the two friends was Haggard's collaboration on a novel, with Lang, entitled *The World's Desire*, which was published in 1890. It received poor reviews, but the public liked it and sales were brisk.

Convinced to visit a friend's mine in Mexico where he could study Aztec ruins and search for buried treasure, Haggard made his first trip across the Atlantic in early 1891. In both New York and New Orleans he was given celebrity treatment. Shortly after arriving in Mexico City, the Haggards received word of their only son's death from peritonitis at the tender age of nine.

Though suffering badly from shock, Haggard did some traveling about Mexico before returning home. His Mexican experiences resulted in

Montezuma's Daughter, published in 1893. He first sent the manuscript to his friend Andrew Lang for criticism. Finding Lang's negative comments too harsh, he never sent another manuscript to the critic.

By the early 1890s, Haggard had settled comfortably into the existence of a prosperous country squire at his home in Ditchingham. His desire to write had temporarily diminished; when it returned, he hired a secretary to do the pen pushing. In late 1892, his third daughter and final child was born. Named Lilias Rider, she would write a biography of her father, *The Cloak That I Left* (1951).

The popular novelist ran for Parliament in 1895, but lost by less than 200 votes. With his authorship of some books dealing with agrarian issues, such as *Rural England* (1902) and *A Gardener's Year* (1905), Haggard became acknowledged as an expert on the land. He was genuinely concerned with agricultural conditions and the plight of the poor, giving speeches and writing letters to those in power concerning land reform.

In January 1905, Haggard was made a Commissioner to the United States to inspect the Labour Colonies of the Salvation Army there. During his seven weeks in America, he met with President Theodore Roosevelt, who had been reading Haggard's book *Rural England* and agreed with its author's aims. In June his report was published, but his proposals were rejected by the government. He was given a Royal Commission on Coastal Erosion, however. This being a non-paying position, he was forced to return to writing fiction for a livelihood. He turned out seven novels during his tenure as commissioner and began his autobiography the year after the commission ended.

In 1912, the 56-year-old author became *Sir* Henry Rider Haggard. Very soon thereafter he received his second Royal Commission. Completing his autobiography, *The Days of My Life*, in September of that year, he had his publisher lock it up, not to be printed until after his death.

His work on the commission took him over half the British Empire before it was cut short by the outbreak of World War I in August 1914. In 1916, while still holding his commission, the now 60-year-old writer was made chairman of a committee to draw up a feasible plan for settling returned soldiers in the dominions. This assignment took Haggard to South Africa, Australasia and Canada. He was very well received in the latter country, which honored him by naming a mountain and a glacier after him. Sir Rider Mountain and the Haggard Glacier can both be found in the Rockies.

Haggard continued writing novels during and after the war, including new adventures for both Ayesha and Allan Quatermain. His final four works, *The Treasure of the Lake, Allan and the Ice-Gods, Mary of Marion Isle* and *Belshazzar*, as well as his autobiography, were published posthumously.

On May 14, 1925, Sir Henry Rider Haggard died at age 68 from an infected bladder. His ashes were buried in Ditchingham Church, far from the vast rolling plains of Africa which he loved so well.

While Rudyard Kipling and Rider

Haggard took an immediate liking to each other, their correspondence was sporadic until after the turn of the century. Between October 1889, when they were first introduced, until about 1902, they met frequently at the Savile Club and entertained each other in their homes on a regular basis, so there was no real need for letter writing.

Most of what survives of their correspondence is Kipling's letters to Haggard, for the former had the unfortunate habit of burning his mail once he was done with it. Many of Haggard's diary entries refer to Kipling, however, so there remains some documentation of Haggard's thoughts on his friend. Over the years, Kipling's salutation to Haggard went from "Dear Haggard" to "Dear old man."

As might be expected, the two writers discussed their common interests, which were legion, and critiqued each other's work. Kipling also helped his friend with details for his novels; most notably, he chose the name for a major character in Haggard's 1911 tale of the Black Death, *Red Eve*, and created scenes and plot devices for *The Ghost Kings* (1914) and *Allan and the Ice Gods* (1927). Kipling's last letter to Haggard was written the day before the latter's death in May 1925.

The popular authors became linked in the public eye as a result of their friendship. The attention they received caused one of their fellow Savile Club members, J.K. Stephen, to dash off the following gently kidding piece:

Will there never come a season
  Which shall rid us from the curse
Of a prose which knows no reason
  And an unmelodious verse:

Where the world shall cease to wonder
  At the genius of an Ass,
And a boy's eccentric blunder
  Shall not bring success to pass:

When mankind shall be delivered
  From the clash of magazines,
And the inkstand shall be shivered
  Into countless smithereens:
Where there stands a muzzled stripling,
  Mute, beside a muzzled bore:
When the Rudyards cease from Kipling
  And the Haggards Ride no more.

Many years later, this poem was recalled in a *Daily Herald* article about the anti–Bolshevist Liberty League, which both Kipling and Haggard sponsored. Its author contributed his own clever verse on the current situation:

Two Hearts that Beat as One…

"Every Bolsh is a blackguard,"
  Said Kipling to Haggard.
"And given to tippling,"
  Said Haggard to Kipling.

"And a blooming outsider,"
  Said Rudyard to Rider.
"Their domain is blood-yard,"
  Said Rider to Rudyard.

"That's just what I say,"
  Said the author of "They."
"I agree; I agree,"
  Said the author of "She."

That the friendship of these gentlemen endured for 36 years is proof enough of its depth; no one can deny them that.

Both authors had their works adapted as motion pictures while film was still struggling to find its identity amidst established forms of entertainment. These adaptations have continued up to the present day. Between the two, there have been a total of 62 films made from their works: 33 from Haggard's and 29 from Kipling's. Included among these totals are a number of remakes and variations on the sources, most notably in the case of Haggard's *She*, which has served as the basis for 13 motion pictures. Haggard's appeal was stronger in the silent era, when 20 films based on his works were produced. Kipling's attraction is almost evenly divided, with 13 silent and 16 sound films produced to date.

The global appeal of Haggard's works was also much broader than that of Kipling's, the latter being limited to Great Britain and the United States, while the former were adapted as far afield as India and South Africa. Oddly, Kipling has had but three film adaptations in his native country. This is unusual for a man who was so honored by his own people as a standard-bearer of British imperialism. It also seems strange that relatively few of Haggard's African romances have been filmed. Only two of the Quatermain tales and one of the Ayesha books have been transferred to the silver screen, leaving much material to be mined, including the novel *She and Allan,* wherein Haggard's most popular creations meet.

What is not so strange is that Kipling's works have received better film treatment than Haggard's. The Bombay-born writer was unquestionably a genius with words and meter; the squire's son, while a very fine and imaginative story-teller, lacked Kipling's gift of style.

Haggard never had a personal hand in the film adaptations of any of his works, and he wrote in his diary that he was not entirely satisfied with the results of producer Horace Lucoque's attempts to adapt them for the screen.

Kipling, on the other hand, was approached by the American branch of the French company Pathé Frères to create screenplays based on his works. In 1914, Pathé had merged with the Eclectic Film Company and formed Pathé Exchange, at which point they became involved in the productions of several companies. The Kipling films were to be made at the Robert Brunton Studios. From late 1920 to mid–1921, four announcements to this effect appeared in *Moving Picture World*, a leading trade paper of the day. According to the articles, the rights to several of the British author's works were secured, with the stipulation that he would write the screenplays. No specific poems, novels or short stories were named and the only film to result from this association was the 1921 production *Without Benefit of Clergy*. Mention also was made of how quickly Kipling had learned the art of writing for the screen.

An additional note concerning several films: There are many who might think that *Sergeants Three* (1961) should be included in this index because it's based on *Gunga Din*. The true basis for the film was not Kipling's poem, but the story written by Ben Hecht and Charles MacArthur for the 1939 RKO film *Gunga Din*; in fact, the producers, Essex Productions, had to buy the rights from RKO in order to avoid a plagiarism lawsuit, as they had made the film without permission.

Kipling's 1930 novella *Thy Servant — A Dog* was given a film treatment in 1935, then withdrawn after being shown to the Trade in Britain. This film has also been excluded from the filmography.

Several filmographies include *Hidden Valley* (Pathé, 1917) as an adaptation of Rider Haggard's *She*. I have chosen not to do so. Available material suggests that the story lacks the most important elements of Haggard's novel — fantasy and magic. Further, the white woman in the picture is a captive, rather than a ruler of the native people. While the film was likely influenced by the book, these differences are too important to consider it an adaptation.

A 1975 South African release entitled *The Virgin Goddess* has sometimes been listed as an adaptation of *She*. This writer has it straight from the director-screenwriter that the film was based on the legend of a white woman who lived among the bushmen of Namibia; hence its exclusion.

Films entitled *Soldiers Three* were produced by Vitagraph in 1911 and Bison in 1913; neither was based on the Kipling short stories. The same can be said for the 1912 Vitagraph and Pathé productions bearing the title *The Light That Failed*.

Rudyard Kipling Filmography

The Ballad of Fisher's Boarding House
(poem, 1888)

SYNOPSIS: This short poem tells of a hangout populated by sailors of all nationalities — Pamba the Malay, Carboy Gin the Guinea cook, Luz from Vigo Bay — and is ruled by Anne of Austria. She is Salem Hardieker's girl, but sets her sights on Hans the blue-eyed Dane. He rejects her advances and she raises a row. Hans is stabbed to death by Salem, despite the fact that he wore "a little silver crucifix which keeps a man from harm."

Fultah Fisher's Boarding House

Fireside Productions/Pathé Exchange, Inc.; Released April 2, 1922; one reel; Based on the poem *The Ballad of Fisher's Boarding House*; DIRECTOR: Frank Capra; SCREENPLAY: Frank Capra, Walter Montague; PHOTOGRAPHY: Roy Wiggins

CAST: Mildred Owens (Anne of Austria), Olaf Skavlan (Hans), Ethan Allen (Salem Hardiecker), Gerald Griffin (British Sailor), Oreste Seragnoli (Luz)

This was the first film directed by Italian emigré Frank Capra (1897–1991), who later helmed such classics as *Mr. Smith Goes to Washington* (1939) and *It's a Wonderful Life* (1946). The only professional performer among the cast was Mildred Owens, a chorus girl. The rest were the dregs of society culled from the waterfront of San Francisco, where the picture was filmed in a former gymnasium at Golden Gate Park.

The one-reel format was ideally suited for adapting such a short poem. Capra did an acceptable job, beginning with a wide shot of the barroom and introducing the characters one by one. Although the print viewed by this writer was rather dark, it would seem that the succeeding action faithfully follows that of the poem.

Motion Picture News, April 15, 1922 (Laurence Reid):

> Rudyard Kipling's graphic poem of a sailor's boarding house has been transferred to the screen with remarkable fidelity. A dramatic epic, it releases a volume of interesting action, stirring at all times and unusually rich in characterization. The vivid figures are all there in their places from Hans, the blue-eyed Dane, who wears the silver crucifix to keep himself from harm, to Anne of Austria and the rest of the motley throng. The lines of the poem are used in their entirety and as subtitles certainly embroider the picture with realism.

The crew gathers about the table. They are resting preparatory to sailing forth again on the briny deep. And they all have eyes for Anne. The scenes are laid in a waterfront retreat and it is filled with these interesting figures who sail under various flags. The girl is a sailor's sweetheart, but Hans scorns her. And this means a fight to the death. Overcome with fury to find herself repulsed she precipitates the bloody battle. And Hans lies dead upon the floor. She searches his body for souvenirs and comes across the "little silver crucifix that keeps a man from harm." Straightaway her redemption begins. She repulses the other sailors, places the crucifix next to her heart and finds spiritual consolation. Thus Anne of Austria rises from the depths of degradation through the death of a sailor.

The little drama is marked for its intensity of scene and the players enter into the atmosphere of the poem with splendid enthusiasm. They are all wonderful types. The picture is a masterpiece of realism, carrying dramatic value and a spiritual flavor. You can catch the suspense by merely watching the expressions of the sailors who lived their elemental lives with complete abandon...

Captains Courageous
(novel, 1897)

SYNOPSIS: Harvey Cheyne is the spoiled adolescent son of a tycoon with interests in railroad, lumber, shipping and mines. On a voyage to Europe with his mother, Harvey becomes seasick while smoking a cigar and is swept overboard at the Grand Banks. He is rescued by a Portuguese fisherman of the schooner *We're Here,* out of Gloucester.

When he awakes, the captain's son, Dan Troop, checks him for injuries and gives him food and coffee. Harvey tells Capt. Troop he will be well paid if he returns him to New York City. The boy is informed that the fishing season has just begun, so he will have to wait until September to return to New York. In the meantime, he can earn $10.50 a month by working aboard the boat. Harvey throws a tantrum, renews his financial offer and accuses Troop of having stolen his wallet. For this he is decked by the captain. After talking with Dan, he realizes that his wallet may have been lost at sea, so he apologizes to Capt. Troop.

The fishermen return in their dories with their catches and are introduced to Harvey. They include Long Jack, Penn, Uncle Salters, Tom Platt and a black cook named Brown, who speaks Gaelic.

Young Cheyne quickly gets into the swing of things. His first time out fishing with Dan, he catches a 100-pound halibut. He learns that Penn lost his mind after seeing his entire family swept away in the great Johnstown Flood. Long Jack takes the lad under his wing, teaching him everything about the various ropes.

The *We're Here* has a brief encounter with one Uncle Abishai, who captains a wretched-looking ancient trawler. Abishai is a jonah who is not allowed into any port, so he makes his living by trading bait. When his boat suddenly disappears into the sea, Capt. Disko Troop goes to his aid. When the schooner reaches the spot where Abishai went down, only a few items are found floating about. The crew was drunk and made a serious error in sailing, resulting in an explosion.

Harvey later goes fishing with Manuel a few times and learns how to steer the *We're Here*.

Meeting a French boat one day, Harvey shows his proficiency in that tongue, but Tom outdoes him with sign language because he and the Frenchmen are Freemasons.

The *We're Here* crew hears a loud cracking sound and finds the remains of a fishing boat. They pick up the captain, who appears to be the only survivor. He does not wish to leave, believing that his son is dead. Penn prays with him and the son is found alive soon thereafter.

A few days later, they come upon a "town"—a gathering of some 100 fishing boats in one area. There is much greeting among friends, and inquiries after Harvey, who is already known about among the fleet. Then begins a fierce competition among the boats to see who can catch the most cod. That night, the shoals become choppy and the boats are tossed about. The next morning, after everything is sorted out, it is discovered that three men have drowned and many are badly bruised. One man dies aboard ship later. One of the dead men was a Frenchman whose belongings are auctioned off after his burial at sea. Dan gets his knife, which he gives to Harvey, because they are dory mates. While fishing, Harvey hooks something that takes the strength of both boys to haul in. It is the corpse of the Frenchman. They cut it adrift, but not without some difficulty. They throw their catch overboard, believing it cursed. The cook comes to get them, because they have been gone a very long time. Aboard the *We're Here*, the cook covers for the boys' indiscretion with a story so that they are regaled instead of beaten.

The next day, the *We're Here* goes one-on-one in a fishing contest which lasts from dawn until dark. By noon the next day they have left the Virgin Shoals. The schooner docks in Gloucester and Mrs. Troop comes aboard to greet her men. Harvey sends a telegram to his father apprising him of his situation.

All this time Harvey's mother has been frantic, believing her son drowned. Her husband tried everything to ease her mind, to no avail. He takes her to San Diego, where Harvey's telegram arrives. He tells his wife and immediately orders a private train car, mapping a route to Boston. Just under four days later, they arrive in Boston to find their son awaiting them.

Over dinner, Harvey tells his parents everything that transpired after he fell off the ship. The next day Harvey returns to Gloucester, for he is to be the tally man for the *We're Here*. His father tests him by offering him alternatives, but the boy sticks to his promise to the fishermen.

Without revealing his identity, Cheyne Sr. questions Capt. Troop about Harvey Jr. He and his wife visit the schooner. Satisfied at the answers he receives, Mr. Cheyne tells Troop that Harvey is his son. Capt. Troop and his crew finally believe Harvey's stories of his family's wealth. Mr. Cheyne thanks the crew and invites them to his private railroad car, where the men are fed a sumptuous meal. He then makes an offer to Troop to have Dan work on his Pacific Clipper ship line for two years. They discuss the matter with Mrs. Troop, who agrees, for she has always feared losing her son in the rough Atlantic Ocean. Mrs. Cheyne offers money to Manuel for his having rescued Harvey Jr., but he takes only five dollars to buy a gift for his girl. He asks Mrs. Cheyne to give any other money to the sailors' widows of Gloucester. With their free time, Harvey Sr. finally gets to know his son, telling him his life story.

The Cheynes attend a memorial service for the fishermen lost at sea during the past year. Harvey Jr. sits with the crew of the *We're Here*. An actress from Philadelphia recites a poem, followed by Capt. Bart Edwardes, who reads his own composition, which elicits a shout from the fishermen at its end. Young Cheyne becomes queasy after the name of a fellow crew member is announced and has to leave the church. The Cheynes go to see the *We're Here* off on its next voyage.

A brief epilogue has Dan and Harvey meeting a few years later on the West Coast. Dan is to be second mate on his next trip and learns that Harvey will be taking over management of the clipper line the following fall.

Captains Courageous

MGM; Released May 1937; 116 minutes; DIRECTOR: Victor Fleming; PRODUCER: Louis D. Lighton; SCREENPLAY: John Lee Mahin, Marc Connelly, Dale Van Every; PHOTOGRAPHY: Harold Rosson; MUSIC: Franz Waxman, Clifford Vaughan; EDITOR: Elmo Vernon; ART DIRECTORS: Cedric Gibbons, A. Arnold Gillespie, Edwin B. Willis; MARINE DIRECTOR: James Havens; SOUND: Douglas Shearer SONGS:

"Don't Cry Little Fish" and "Ooh What a Terrible Man!" by Franz Waxman and Gus Kahn

CAST: Spencer Tracy (Manuel), Freddie Bartholomew (Harvey Cheyne), Lionel Barrymore (Capt. Disko Troop), Mickey Rooney (Dan Troop), John Carradine (Long Jack), Melvyn Douglas (Mr. Cheyne), Charley Grapewin (Uncle Salters), Jack LaRue (Priest), Christian Rub (Old Clement), Oscar O'Shea (Cushman), Walter Kingsford (Dr. Finley), Tommy Bupp (Boy), Leo G. Carroll (Burns), Charles Trowbridge (Dr. Walsh), Billy Burrud (Charles), Billy Gilbert (Soda Steward), Murray Kinnell (Minister), William Stack (Elliott), Bobby Watson (Reporter), David Thursby (Tom), Dave Wengren (Lars), Donald Briggs (Tyler), Dora Early (Appleton's Wife), Jay Ward (Pogey), Gladden James (Secretary Cobb), Katherine Kenworthy (Mrs. Disko), Kenneth Wilson (Alvin), Norman Ainsley (Robbins), Roger Gray (Nate Rogers), Sam McDaniel (Doc), Wally Albright (Boy)

ACADEMY AWARD: Best Actor (Spencer Tracy). ACADEMY AWARD NOMINATIONS: Best Production, Best Original Screenplay, Best Editing.

Captains Courageous was Kipling's only novel with a completely American setting (*The Naulahka* was set in both America and India). The author combined research and the stories told by his best friend in Brattleboro, Dr. James Conland, who had sailed with the Gloucester fleet in the 1860s. Kipling also visited Gloucester and attended one of the annual memorial services for fishermen lost at sea, an experience he utilizes in the novel.

Filming began in the fall of 1936, with Long Beach Harbor filling in for the Grand Banks, although some footage was also shot in Newfoundland. The boat used was an authentic Gloucester schooner.

Captains Courageous (MGM, 1937). Spencer Tracy, Freddie Bartholomew. (Courtesy Collectors Book Store.)

Captains Courageous (MGM, 1937). Freddie Bartholomew, Spencer Tracy, John Carradine. (Courtesy Collectors Book Store.)

The minor role of Manuel, the Portuguese fisherman, was magnified to accommodate Spencer Tracy's (1900–1967) star stature. For the part, he had to learn to sing passably, play the vielle (hand organ) and submit to having his hair curled and darkened. The role of Dan Troop was downplayed.

Captains Courageous has a lively, salty air about it. Despite a number of differences with the novel, it is a fine evocation of the fisherman's life, especially during the "town" sequence and a race between two schooners.

Harvey Cheyne is only ten years old here, and motherless. He is given an extended background, showing his life at a private school. He believes anyone can be bought with money and favors. When a particular escapade is brought to his father's attention, the parent decides to take him on an ocean cruise so he can get to know the boy better.

After downing six ice cream sodas, Harvey is unwell and goes on deck to be sick. He trips, falls overboard and is picked up by a Portuguese fisherman named Manuel, as in the book. On board the *We're Here*, when he demands to be returned to either Europe or New York, he is told that neither is possible and that he must work with the crew, for which he will be paid $3 a month (this was during the Great Depression, remember). Capt. Disko Troop makes him Manuel's responsibility, since Manuel brought him aboard.

Harvey begins to fit in. When Manuel takes him out fishing for the first time, though, the boy deliberately tangles the lines of Long Jack, with whom Manuel had a wager. The boy confesses when Long Jack threatens Manuel. The latter is pleased, but the former is unfriendly towards the boy and does not teach him about ropes, as in the book.

Manuel's example finally impresses Harvey, and he becomes one of the crew. When the schooner nears Gloucester, Manuel tells the boy what he will do ashore, and learns that the boy only wants to be with him.

After the town sequence, the *We're Here* races another schooner to Gloucester. Their overextended lines snap, causing some of the masts to break and fall into the sea. Manuel was aloft in one of them and has his legs severed in the accident. In order to save the ship, Capt. Disko must cut the lines holding the masts, resulting in Manuel's drowning. Harvey watches in horror as his friend goes under.

Mr. Cheyne comes to pick up his son and overhears him praying for Manuel in a church. At the memorial service for lost fishermen, Cheyne tosses a wreath into the water beside Harvey's and they walk away together hand in hand.

It is odd that for Kipling's only American novel that a British actor should be given the lead role, but it worked, as Freddie Bartholomew (1924–1992) gave a moving performance. Manuel's death is not in the book. The rest of Kipling's grim material — the exploding ship, dying fishermen in the "town" and lone survivors picked up at sea — are omitted in this version. This *Captains Courageous* is still worthwhile viewing.

Variety, May 11, 1937:

> Sea stuff is stirringly impressive ... the fine photographic job credit goes to Harold Rosson and his crew.... Some excellent process work figures, but most of the shots are genuine.

Captains Courageous

ABC-TV; Norman Rosemont Productions; Air Date: December 4, 1977; 120 minutes; DIRECTOR: Harvey Hart; PRODUCER: Norman Rosemont; TELEPLAY: John Gay; PHOTOGRAPHY: Philip Lathrop; EDITOR: Jack McSweeney; MUSIC: Allyn Ferguson; PRODUCTION DESIGN: Hilyard Brown

CAST: Karl Malden (Capt. Troop), Jonathan Kahn (Harvey Cheyne), Johnny Doran (Dan), Neville Brand (Little Penn), Fred Gwynne (Long Jack), Charles Dierkop (Tom Platt), Jeff Corey (Salters), Fritz Weaver (Harvey Cheyne, Sr.), Ricardo Montalban (Manuel), Stan Haze (Cook), Redmond Gleeson (Phillips), Shay Duffin (Chief Steward), Milton Frome (Mr. Atkins), Stanja Lowe (Mrs. Cheyne), Len Wayland (McLean), Don Plumley (Capt. Olley), Orville Young (Capt. Bush), Randy Faustino (Boy)

This production has likely been aired but once, as this writer has never seen it, nor knows anyone who has. Even the producer does not have complete data regarding it.

Variety:

> The boating and fishing scenes were well produced, and the supporting cast of crew members, particularly

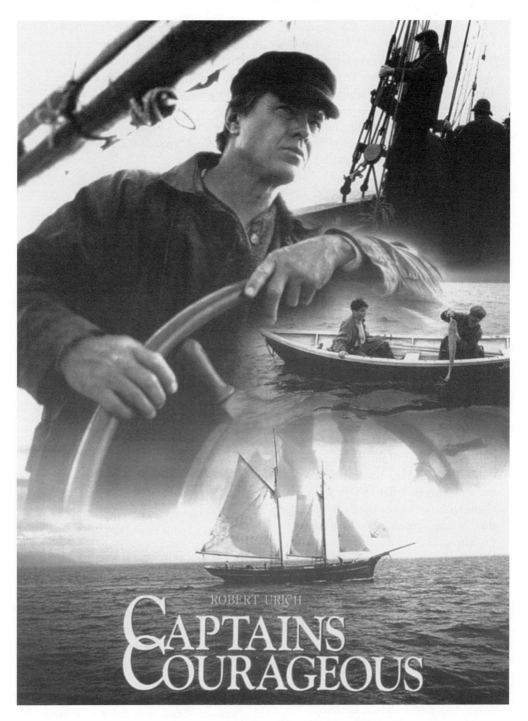

Captains Courageous (Leucadia, 1996). Poster.

Captains Courageous (Leucadia, 1996). Top: Ken Vadas, Kaj-Erik Eriksen. Bottom: Ken Vadas.

Captains Courageous (Leucadia, 1996). Ken Vadas.

Ricardo Montalban, were fine.... Despite reservations about changing the story to emphasize Malden, it's still a good yarn.

Captains Courageous

Family Channel/Hallmark Entertainment; Air Date: April 21, 1996; Distributed by Leucadia Film Corporation; 93 minutes; DIRECTOR: Michael Anderson; EXECUTIVE PRODUCERS: Tony Allard, Robert Halmi, Sr., Matthew O'Connor; ASSOCIATE PRODUCER: Lisa Towers; TELEPLAY: John McGreevey; PHOTOGRAPHY: Glen MacPherson; CAMERA OPERATOR: Randal Platt; EDITOR: Bernadette Kelly; MUSIC: Claude Desjardins, Eric N. Robertson; PRODUCTION DESIGN: Brent Thomas; COSTUME DESIGN: Karen L. Matthews; ASSISTANT EDITOR: John Cameron; MAKEUP: Rosalina De Silva; ART DIRECTOR: Helen Jarvis; SET DECORATOR: Peter Louis Lando; ASSISTANT DIRECTOR: Lee Knippleberg; HAIR STYLES: Kandace Loewen; VISUAL EFFECTS SUPERVISOR: Lee Wilson; SPECIAL EFFECTS COORDINATOR: Randy Shymkiw

CAST: Robert Urich (Capt. Matthew Troop), Kenny Vadas (Harvey Cheyne, Jr.), Kaj-Erik Eriksen (Dan Troop), Robert Wisden (Arthur Wade), Sandra Nelson (Mrs. Troop), Terence Kelly (Uncle Salter), Colin Cunningham (Manuel), Robert Thurston (Little Penn), Duncan Fraser (Long Jack), Roger R. Cross (Hannibal), Eric Schneider (Purser), Lane Campbell (Abashai), Kevin Hansen (Gino), Doron Bell (Hans), Ken Camroux (Spokesman)

Well-made but unexceptional visually, this production boasts fine performances and good casting. It adheres very closely to the novel, with the minor exception of calling Capt. Troop "Matthew" instead of "Disko," and the major exception of having Dan Troop drowned in the act of saving another fisherman. The film closes with Harvey's return to New York, omitting the scene years later with Harvey as the owner of the ship line and Dan as a captain.

Robert Urich is not as crusty as Lionel Barrymore, but then, who is? His is an underplayed performance which works just as well. This production has as many sunny scenes as the 1937 version had overcast ones. A good, straightforward filmization, with more accuracy than inaccuracy, this version is worth at least one viewing by fans of the novel. It was filmed on location in Vancouver, British Columbia, and Gloucester, Massachusetts.

The City of Dreadful Night
(short story, 1885)

SYNOPSIS: More a word-picture than a story, this piece describes the sights seen and sounds heard by a man who takes a walk one evening to the City of Dreadful Night.

The road to the City is lined with the corpses of men. At the Mosque of Wazir Khan, the man ascends a minaret and views the city from above. The rooftops are full of people trying to sleep in the stifling heat. Two muezzins recite the evening prayer. The man dozes off and awakes as the morning prayer is being recited. He leaves the mosque and arrives in the street, where he finds himself blocking the funeral procession of a woman who died from the heat in the night.

The City of Terrible Night

Imp; Released April 2, 1915; Two reels; DIRECTOR: George A. Lessey; SCREEN-PLAY: Mrs. George E. Hall
CAST: King Baggot (Jack Van Rensselaer), Ned Reardon (Boris), Frank Smith (Rudolph), Ed Duane (Jack's Valet), Arline Pretty (Olga, Rudolph's daughter)

A lost film, *The City of Terrible Night* differs greatly from its source material, utilizing only its mood. According to Charles Curry's prose version which appeared in *Photoplay* magazine, the action occurs in New York City and concerns an upper class gentleman named Stewart who becomes bored with the social whirl. He goes looking for adventure in the seamier sections of New York City.

Encountering a Russian cobbler and his daughter, he follows the girl when she goes to a social club with a friend. The man dances with her and takes her home, then lingers outside. Almost immediately he hears a scream, and the cobbler comes staggering outside. Stewart eases him to the ground as he dies. A crowd gathers and a police-man arrives. The cobbler has been stabbed and Stewart is arrested. The crowd becomes hostile, attacking Stewart and the cop. Stewart manages to escape. Returning home, his valet helps him change clothes. He escapes through a window as the cops enter and arrest the valet. Stewart goes looking for the real murderer; back at the scene of the crime he is recognized and is arrested again as he declares his innocence to the victim's daughter.

At the jail, his valet is telling the authorities that his cellmate has confessed to the crime after recovering his senses. He had sustained a blow to the head which made him groggy; thinking him drunk, a cop had arrested him. It seems that he and the victim had been members of a secret society in Russia. The cobbler had refused an order and fled the country. The killer tracked him all the way to New York, where he finally killed him. Stewart and his valet are freed, and the gentleman goes to the cobbler's daughter.

Hopefully, the film is better than Curry's poorly written *Photoplay* piece, which changed the names of the main characters.

Gunga Din
(poem, 1890)

SYNOPSIS: The tale of an Indian water-bearer serving British troops is told by a cockney private soldier. He relates how Gunga Din did his job well and was always ready when called on. One day, the soldier is hit; Din gives him water and carries him to a covered litter. Just as the private is made comfortable, the water-bearer is himself

Gunga Din (RKO, 1939). Douglas Fairbanks, Jr., Cary Grant, Victor McLaglen.

fatally shot. His last words are "I 'ope you liked your drink." The soldier says he'll meet Din in Hell, where " 'e'll be squattin' on the coals, givin' drink to poor damned souls..." He then salutes the Indian with the immortal lines:

Though I've belted you and flayed you,
by the livin' Gawd that made you,
You're a better man than I am, Gunga Din!

Gunga Din

Powers Co.; Released May 20, 1911; One reel; *DIRECTOR*: Pat Powers
CAST: Unknown
The Moving Picture World (May 20, 1911) printed one stanza of the poem along with the following promotion: "Kipling's world-famous lines on the faithfulness of the Indian regimental water carrier, is the inspiration for a picture portrayal that will prove immensely interesting."

Gunga Din

RKO; Released February 17, 1939; 117 minutes; *PRODUCER-DIRECTOR*: George Stevens; *EXECUTIVE PRODUCER*: Pandro S. Berman; *SCREENPLAY*: Joel Sayre, Fred Guiol; *STORY*: Ben Hecht, Charles MacArthur; Suggested by the poem by Rudyard Kipling; *MUSIC*: Alfred Newman; *PHOTOGRAPHY*: Joseph H. August; *ART DIRECTION*: Van Nest Polglase, Perry Ferguson; *SET DECORATIONS*: Darrell Silvera; *PHOTOGRAPHIC EFFECTS*: Vernon L. Walker; *GOWNS*: Edward Stevenson; *EDITORS*: Henry Berman, John Lockert; *RECORDED BY*: John E. Tribby, James Stewart; *SECOND UNIT CAMERA*: Frank Redman; *OPTICAL PHOTOGRAPHY*: LINWOOD Dunn; *EFFECTS PHOTOGRAPHY*: Clifford Stine; William Collins; *ASSISTANT DIRECTORS*: Edward Killy, Dewey Starkey; *TECHNICAL ADVISORS*: Sir Robert Erskine Holland, Capt. Clive Morgan, Sgt. Major William Briers; *MAKEUP*: Charles Gemora; *OPERATIVE CAMERAMEN*: Charles Burke, William Clothier, Eddie Pyle, George Diskant; *ASSISTANT*

CAMERAMEN: Charles Straumer, Joe August, Jr., Ledge Haddow, Bill Reinhold

CAST: Cary Grant (Sgt. Cutter), Victor McLaglen (Sgt. MacChesney), Douglas Fairbanks, Jr. (Sgt. Ballantine), Sam Jaffe (Gunga Din), Joan Fontaine (Emmy Stebbins), Eduardo Ciannelli (Guru), Montagu Love (Col. Weeks), Robert Coote (Sgt. Higginbotham), Abner Biberman (Chota), Lumsden Hare (Major Mitchell), Reginald Sheffield (Rudyard Kipling), Cecil Kellaway (Mr. Stebbins), Lalo Encinas (Executioner), Lee Sketchley (Corporal), Frank Levya (Native Merchant), Fulad (Olin Francis), Ann Evers, Audrey Manners, Fay McKenzie (Girls at Party), George Ducount, Jamiel Hasson, George Regas (Thug Chieftains), Bryant Fryer (Scottish Sergeant), Richard Robles (Thugee), Lal Chand Mehra (Thugee), Roland Varno (Lt. Markham), Charles Bennett (Telegrapher), Clive Morgan (Lancer Captain)

This most famous of all motion pictures derived from the works of Rudyard Kipling is on every film fan's list of favorite adventure films. A certified classic of the genre, it combines humor, crisp dialogue, sharp photography and enthusiastic performances. Among the latter, Eduardo Ciannelli's (1889–1969) stands out. As the guru, head of the fanatical sect of Thugs, his eyes burn like glowing coals as he exhorts the murderous members of the cult to "Rise and kill; kill lest ye yourselves be killed; kill for the love of killing; kill for the love of Kali; kill, kill, *kill!*"

Gunga Din (RKO, 1939). The fight at Tantrapur.

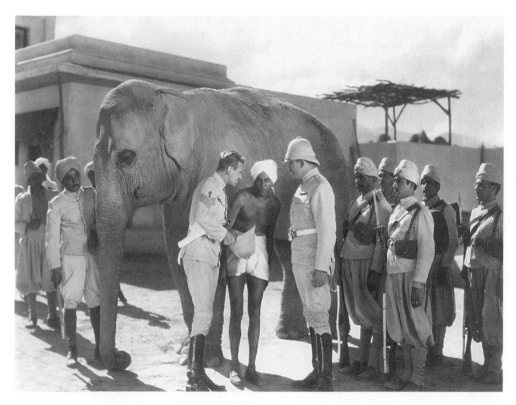

Gunga Din (RKO, 1939). Annie the elephant, Doulgas Fairbanks, Jr., Sam Jaffe, Victor McLaglen. (Courtesy Collectors Book Store.)

There is also Sam Jaffe's (1891–1984) wonderfully understated playing of the title character. He imparts real dignity to the humble water-bearer who bears the brunt of the soldiers' gibes. The producers originally sought Indian child actor Sabu for the part, but Alexander Korda, head of London Films and Sabu's employer, refused to loan him. Having had a great success with his own pro-imperialist film *The Drum* (1938), the producer was preparing for his most ambitious undertaking, a remake of *The Thief of Bagdad* (1924), and wanted Sabu for the title role.

The camaraderie among the three leads also rings true; Victor McLaglen

(1886–1959) remarked many years later that Sgt. MacChesney was the favorite among all his roles. Douglas Fairbanks, Jr., (b. 1909) at a screening of the film attended by this writer at New York's Metropolitan Museum of Art in 1989, revealed that for many years afterward, he and Cary Grant (1904–1986) called each other "Cutter" and "Ballantine."

Not all was fun and games for the cast during filming. While on location at the foot of Mt. Whitney, McLaglen and Fairbanks narrowly escaped injury when their car collided with an elephant which had been frightened by thunder. Fairbanks also sustained a broken rib and three broken fingers

performing in some of the more haz-
ardous scenes. A fire broke out at one
point and destroyed an entire block of
the village of "Tantrapur"; it was the
largest movie loss in 16 years paid off by
Lloyd's of London. A team of carpen-
ters rushed out from Hollywood completed repairs in ten days.

Alfred Newman, hired after Erich
Wolfgang Korngold bowed out, created
one of his most memorable scores for
this production. If one recites the poem
while listening to it, one will notice that
the melody fits the words very well.
(Some of Kipling's poems were set to
music, but it's not known if Newman

was aware of this or heard any of the
songs.)

Two months after Kipling's death
(January 1936), Edward Small and Harry
Goetz of the independent Reliance Pictures bought the rights to the poem from
Kipling's widow for $5,000. They hired
literary giant William Faulkner to write
a scenario based on the poem. He managed to produce a couple of treatments
and a partial script. When Reliance was
liquidated, Small became a producer at
RKO, bringing the rights to the work
with him.

Two treatments by other writers
were then completed for use by veteran

Gunga Din (RKO, 1939). Victor McLaglen, Douglas Fairbanks, Jr., Eduardo Ciannelli.
(Courtesy Collectors Book Store.)

Gunga Din (RKO, 1939). Sam Jaffe as Din.

director King Vidor. The project was turned over to Howard Hawks in late 1936. He began all over with Charles MacArthur and Ben Hecht, of *The Front Page* fame, on the script. While continuing to polish that script, Hawks also busied himself producing and directing the Cary Grant-Katharine Hepburn screwball comedy, *Bringing Up Baby* (1938), which went well over budget and schedule. This brought him into conflict with RKO's vice-president in charge of production, Sam Briskin, resulting in the termination of his contract by mutual agreement. He was replaced by George Stevens, a veteran cameraman from the Hal Roach studio. Stevens' first task was to tighten the Hecht-MacArthur treatment, which he did with the aid of a former novelist

and newspaperman Joel Sayre, and another Roach alumnus, writer-director Fred Guiol.

The characters from Kipling's collection of short stories *Soldiers Three*, which concerned the adventures of three privates (Mulvaney, Ortheris, and Learoyd) were added to help flesh out the story to feature length (the poem is only five stanzas). They were given less unusual names — Cutter, Ballantine, and MacChesney — and promoted to sergeants. Their introductory scene has them engaged in a rollicking barroom brawl, in which, of course, they are victorious. This is totally in keeping with the "Soldiers Three" stories, which are mainly reminiscences of the men's youthful adventures, although here the screenwriters devised their own exploits. The sergeants buy a map of a buried treasure from another soldier, but become involved with the revived cult of Thugee, who have been murdering Her Majesty's subjects. Gunga Din finds a gold temple and leads Cutter to it. It turns out to be the Thugs base; Cutter allows himself to be caught while Din flees to the British fort to tell the colonel. MacChesney, Ballantine and Din go on ahead and are also captured. They manage to make a hostage of the guru, leader of the Thugs, but are still trapped atop the temple. They watch helplessly as the regiment approaches, unaware of the trap set for them. Gunga Din, though seriously wounded, climbs to the top of the dome of the temple and blows a warning call on his bugle, alerting the British. He is shot as he does this and dies. The British rout the Thugs in the subsequent battle. Din is given a soldier's burial as Kipling pens his immortal poem inside a tent.

There are some who decry the "political incorrectness" of the British soldiers treatment of the Indians, but *Gunga Din*, like any historical work, must be taken in context. The poem was written by Kipling in 1890, at a time when the British Empire was in full flower. Queen Victoria still reigned, and many there were who firmly believed that "God is an Englishman." Thus, Sgt. Ballantine's referring to the guru's son as "toad face" and Sgt. MacChesney's use of the term "beggar" are right in keeping with the temper of the times. The poem is really a paean to the *bhistis*, who proved invaluable to the soldiers of the queen. Besides the famous closing lines, Din is also referred to as "the finest man I knew..."

Location shooting was done outside one Pine, California, in the High Sierra foothills, and in the Alabama Hills, near Mt. Whitney; production took ten weeks, instead of the projected six. Interiors were shot on sound stages at the Hollywood Studio of RKO and RKO-Pathé in Culver City. Principal photography wrapped on October 15, 1938.

After 104 working days and nearly half a million dollars over budget (final negative cost: $1,909,669.28), *Gunga Din* premiered on February 17, 1939, only to face one last obstacle. The Kipling family objected to the scene wherein the author composed the title poem at a battle site. RKO returned the film to their lab where a wagon was superimposed over the foreground, blocking the figure of Reginald Sheffield, who portrayed Kipling. There are prints both with and without the wagon in circulation today.

Statistics for this production are also impressive: some 200 men spent four weeks erecting tents and galleys for the cast and crew; 16 cars, 12 trucks, 10 busses and a trailer with a film lab transported the 500 technicians needed to prepare the sets. Three hundred and twenty-five actors and technicians lived at the site, while the commissary held a staff of 37. It took 14 tons of food per week to feed everyone, and 15,000 pounds of ice were necessary to refrigerate the food.

A solid box office hit, *Gunga Din* has been re-issued more than once over the years.

In 1979, it was announced that actor Stuart Whitman had procured the rights for a re-make in which he would play a missionary and three British actors, as yet unnamed, would take the roles of the soldiers. Two years later, an item appeared in *Variety* to the effect that Roger Moore had rejected being cast in a remake for Cannon International, because he had already been to India. The other two leads were to be Sean Connery and American Christopher Reeve, of *Superman* fame. This author, for one, is thankful that neither project reached fruition.

The New York Times, January 27, 1939 (B. R. Crisler):

> [*Gunga Din*] moves with all the discipline, dash and color of a vanished time ... the first 25 and last 30 minutes ... are the sheer poetry of cinematic motion. [F]or all the dash cut by the three stars ... it is the humble, ascetic, stooped, yet somehow sublime figure of Sam Jaffe that one remembers.... There's infinite humility, age-old patience and pity, in the way old Din offers water to the living and the dying....

The Jungle Book and The Second Jungle Book
(short story collections, 1894-1895)

SYNOPSIS: *The Jungle Book* and *The Second Jungle Book* are comprised of 15 short stories. They are tied together by the character of the feral child Mowgli, who appears in eight of the tales. These Mowgli stories are the only ones synopsized here, as (among the others) only *Toomai of the Elephants* has been filmed, and that is covered later.

The first tale, *Mowgli's Brothers*, tells of Mowgli's adoption by a wolf pack when, as an infant, he wanders into the cave of a family of wolves. It then skips ahead a decade and describes how Mowgli and Bagheera the Black Panther became friends. Also related is the boy's enmity with Shere Khan the Tiger, and its exacerbation at a meeting of the jungle animals. Most of the latter side with Shere Khan and drive Mowgli from the jungle.

The second, *Kaa's Hunting*, begins with Mowgli receiving a lesson in jungle lore from Baloo the Bear. He is warned against associating with the Bandar-log, the monkey people. The other jungle animals have nothing to do with them. When Mowgli is kidnapped by them, Baloo and Bagheera the Black Panther enlist the aid of Kaa, the Rock Python, in saving him. Learning from a kite that Mowgli has been taken to a dead city, they arrive there one night and by their combined strengths manage to rescue the boy.

The next, *Tiger! Tiger!*, relates Mowgli's first contact with men and his settling of his score with Shere Khan. He travels to a village far from the jungle where he is given a home by the richest woman, Messua, whose infant son had been taken by a tiger. She hopes that Mowgli might be her boy, but after close examination, she decides that he is not. She teaches him human speech and he becomes the village herd-boy. Some months later, Mowgli sees his opportunity to kill Shere Khan. With the assistance of two wolves, he maneuvers the water buffalo herd into trapping the big cat in a ravine where it is trampled to death.

How Fear Came includes the origin of the tiger's stripes and a drought which nearly destroys all the jungle flora and fauna.

In the next story, *Letting in the Jungle*, Mowgli returns to the wolf pack. One day he overhears Buldeo telling some villagers that Messua and her husband have been accused of harboring a devil-child. After Messua is beaten, the couple is tied up in their home awaiting death by fire. Mowgli frees them, then returns once more to the jungle where he organizes the animals and leads them toward the village in an effort to drive out the humans while destroying their homes and crops.

The following tale, *The King's Ankus*, relates the visit of Mowgli and Kaa the python to the treasure chamber of an ancient king of a long-dead city. Guarded by a superannuated cobra, the treasure includes an ankus (elephant prod) containing a priceless ruby and encrusted with turquoises. This is the only item Mowgli finds attractive. Warned by the cobra that the ankus will bring only death, Mowgli takes it anyway. Tiring of it later, the boy leaves it in the jungle. Wishing to see it again, though, he finds that a man has taken it. Following his trail, Mowgli discovers six dead men before finding the prod. He becomes aware that they had killed one another for possession of the ankus, but he fails to understand why they did so.

In the penultimate story, *Red Dog*, an outsider wolf brings word to Mowgli and the wolves that a pack of dholes — killer dogs — is heading their way.

Mowgli devises a plan with Kaa whereby the dholes will be led into the gorge where wild bees dwell. The boy goes ahead and taunts the dholes, leading them straight to the bees, which attack the dogs. Some of the pack jumps into the river, some are driven in. Mowgli kills many with his knife, and the remainder are dispatched by the wolves as they struggle in the water.

The final tale, *The Spring Running*, describes a ritual engaged in by the animals every spring: They run great distances for the sheer joy of experiencing the sights and smells of the new season. Mowgli, though not feeling well, sets out on his run and ends up at the house of Messua, the woman who had taken him in years before when he first encountered the "man pack." She is older, a widow with an infant son. Mowgli spends a little time with her until the wolves come and take him back to the jungle. (See also *Toomai of the Elephants*, p. 96)

Jungle Book

United Artists; Released April 3, 1942; 109 minutes; Technicolor; DIRECTOR: Zoltan Korda; PRODUCER: Alexander Korda; SCREENPLAY: Laurence Stallings, adapted from *The Jungle Books* by Rudyard Kipling; PHOTOGRAPHY: Lee Garmes; ASSISTANT PHOTOGRAPHER: W. Howard Greene; PRODUCTION DESIGNER: Vincent Korda; MUSIC: Miklos Rozsa; ART DIRECTORS: Jack Okey, J. MacMillan Johnson; EDITOR: William Hornbeck; SECOND UNIT DIRECTOR: Andre de Toth; ASSISTANT DIRECTOR: Lowell Farrell; SPECIAL EFFECTS: Lawrence Butler; PRODUCTION MANAGER: Walter Mayo; INTERIOR DECORATION: Julia Heron; PRODUCTION ASSISTANT: Charles David; TECHNICOLOR DIRECTOR: Natalie Kalmus

CAST: Sabu (Mowgli), Rosemary DeCamp (Messua), Joseph Calleia (Buldeo), John Qualen (The Barber), Frank Puglia (The Pundit), Patricia O'Rourke (Mahala), Ralph Byrd (Durga), John Mather (Rao), Faith Brook (English Woman), Noble Johnson (Subarah)

ACADEMY AWARD NOMINATIONS: Art Direction (Color), Cinematography (Color), Special Effects, Musical Score

This initial filmization of Kipling's most enduring works remains the definitive one. In his final picture for Alexander Korda, Indian actor Sabu (1924-1963) at last got to play the role for which he was born, that of Mowgli, the Indian child raised by wolves.

Laurence Stallings, co-author of the famed anti-war play *What Price Glory?* and creator of a number of screenplays, fashioned his scenario from five of the Mowgli tales: *Mowgli's Brothers, Tiger! Tiger!, How Fear Came, Letting in the Jungle* and *The King's Ankus*. He also borrowed one line of dialogue from *The Spring Running* and one from *Red Dog*. Besides closely following Kipling's storylines, Stallings also retained the language of the animals, such as "red flower" for fire and "man pack" for humans. Buldeo, a character who appears only in the second and fourth of the aforementioned stories, is utilized as an on-screen narrator in the picture's framing segments. He is an old man who tells stories for a living, here relating the legend of Mowgli to an audience of Indians and a young Englishwoman.

The screenwriter used the beginning of the first tale up to the point where Mowgli reaches his pre-teen years and vows to kill Shere Khan. He drew upon all of *Tiger! Tiger!*, with a few alterations. In the film, Messua is widowed early on, her husband being killed by a tiger as he searches for their infant son in the jungle. Buldeo has a daughter who becomes Mowgli's platonic love interest. Mowgli kills Shere Khan with a knife after luring the cat into a river, but not until much later in the film. Little is taken from *How Fear Came*; Buldeo's opening narration tells how the tiger got its stripes, and the drought becomes a fire occurring near the end of the movie. Here the screenplay alternates events from the last two stories, while making other changes. Buldeo's daughter, rather than Kaa the Snake, accompanies Mowgli to the dead city, and Mowgli heeds the old cobra's warning, and takes no treasure. The girl does take a gold coin, however. When her father sees it, she tells him of the treasure chamber. Buldeo begins scheming, but is forced to confide in a pundit and the village barber. This trio stands in for Kipling's faceless men of greed.

Mowgli then gets his chance to settle his score with Shere Khan, going off alone after the tiger. A frantic Messua trusts in Buldeo and his cohorts to find her son. Mowgli kills Shere Khan and Buldeo tries to force him to reveal the location of the dead city. With Bagheera's aid, the boy makes the hunter believe he can change into a panther at will, and chases the men back to the village. There Buldeo has Mowgli bound and whipped for being a witch. He then allows Messua to help the boy escape so that he and his cronies can follow him to the treasure chamber. First he ties up Messua and a friendly villager named Durga as Mowgli's accomplices. Mowgli deliberately leads the men to the lost city, remembering the old cobra's words.

After the three men have loaded themselves with treasure, they head back to the village; on the way, the pundit kills the barber and is himself eaten by a crocodile. Buldeo, the sole survivor, returns to the village. As Mowgli heads for the village leading a herd of elephants, Buldeo drives a wagon full of flaming hay into the jungle in an attempt to burn out the boy and the jungle creatures. The wind shifts and the fire heads toward the village, forcing the villagers to flee. Informed of Messua's peril by Mahala, Buldeo's daughter, he rescues her, then begins aiding animals trapped by the fire. Messua watches him from an island in midstream. She calls to her son to come to her, but he elects to return to the jungle.

Jungle Book was Sabu's last film for the Kordas, and also the last film on which all three Korda brothers worked together—Alex as producer, Zoltan as director and Vincent as art director. The final product shows the great care which was the hallmark of London Films. Alex spent almost $50,000 on tropical plants as well as

Jungle Book (United Artists, 1942). Mowgli (Sabu) learns about money from Messua (Rosemary De Camp).

Jungle Book (United Artists, 1942). Mowgli (Sabu) kills Shere Khan.

buying 70,000 gold coins which had been struck for the 1939-40 Golden Gate Exposition held in San Francisco. The latter were strewn over the dusty floor of the treasure chamber. Miklos Rozsa's score made musical history, being the first commercial recording of a Hollywood film score when it was released by RCA Victor in 1943, with narration by Sabu.

Jungle Book, like many films of the 30s and 40s, was dramatized on radio. Sabu journeyed to New York in the spring of 1942, where he appeared on *Rainbow House With Bob Emery*, which broadcast over the Mutual Network. (See Radio Adaptations.)

The picture was nominated for four Academy Awards — Art Direction (Color), Cinematography (Color), Special Effects and Musical Score, but lost in all four, which says a lot for its competition. A better filimization of Kipling's most popular work seems unlikely.

The Herald Tribune (New York), April 12, 1942 (Howard Barnes):

The chief asset of this particular literary classic on the screen ... is the presence of Sabu in the role of Mowgli. He is perfect for this motion picture *tour de force.* Whether he is communing with his friends in the jungle or coping with his enemies ... he gives a direct and unswerving portrayal which holds the production together far more than the script or the spectacular staging.

The New York Times, April 6, 1942 (Bosley Crowther):

Mr. Korda...has given [Mowgli] a proper jungle training as a foundling of the wolves. He has let him go among the human beings as a highly unappreciated waif, and ... let the human beings show their natures by making a remarkably greedy attempt to gain ... wealth ... he has sent Mowgli back ... to a world he understands.... The color is strikingly vivid and some of the individual scenes have natural charm....

The Jungle Book

Walt Disney Pictures/Buena Vista; Released October 18, 1967; 78 minutes; Technicolor; DIRECTOR: Wolfgang Reitherman; STORY: Larry Clemmons, Ralph Wright, Ken Anderson, Vance Gerry, inspired by the Rudyard Kipling "Mowgli" stories; DIRECTING ANIMATORS: Milt Kahl, Frank Thomas, Ollie Johnston, John Lounsbery; CHARACTER ANIMATION: Hal King, Eric Larson, Walt Stanchfield, Eric Cleworth, Fred Hellmich, John Ewing, Dick Lucas; MUSIC: George Bruns; ORCHESTRATION: Walter Sheets; SONGS: "I Wanna Be Like You," "Kaa's Song," "My Own Home," "That's What Friends Are For," "Colonel Hathi's March" by Robert B. Sherman, Richard M. Sherman; "The Bare Necessities" by Terry

Jungle Book (United Artists, 1942). Patricia O'Rourke, Sabu and friend.

Gilkyson; *LAYOUT*: Don Griffith, Basil Davidovich, Tom Codrick, Dale Barnhart, Sylvia Roemer; *BACKGROUND STYLING*: Al Dempster; *BACKGROUND*: Bill Layne, Art Riley, Ralph Hulett, Thelma Witmer, Frank Armitage; *EFFECTS ANIMATION*: Dan MacManus; *PRODUCTION MANAGER*: Don Duckwell; *FILM EDITORS*: Tom Acosta, Norman Carlisle; *MUSIC EDITOR*: Evelyn Kennedy; *SOUND*: Robert O. Cook

FEATURING THE VOICES OF: Phil Harris (Baloo the Bear), Sebastian Cabot (Bagheera the Panther), Louis Prima (King Louie of the Apes), George Sanders (Shere Khan the Tiger), Sterling Holloway (Kaa the Snake), J. Pat O'Malley (Col. Hathi, the Elephant), Bruce Reitherman (Mowgli, the Man Cub), Verna Felton, Clint Howard (Elephants), Chad Stuart, Lord Tim Hudson (Vultures), John Abbott, Ben Wright (Wolves), Darleen Carr (The Girl).

ACADEMY AWARD NOMINATION: Best Song ("The Bare Necessities" by Terry Gilkyson)

The Jungle Book was the final animated feature personally supervised by Walt Disney, who passed away in December 1966. His usual high artistic standards were adhered to in this production. Extremely popular, it garnered more than $13 million at the box office and the soundtrack was the first from an animated feature to be certified gold.

In this truncated, musicalized version of Kipling's most popular work, the writers had the honesty to state that it was "inspired" by "the Mowgli stories" in the credits, as the differences between the two are legion. In the film, the infant Mowgli is found in a basket (shades of Moses!) by Bagheera the panther, who takes it to a wolf family. Flash forward several years: A council of wolves decides that Mowgli must leave them, for Shere Khan the Tiger is a hater of man and will surely kill him. Bagheera offers to take him to the man village. On the way, the boy meets the other notable animal characters from the tales — Baloo the Bear, Kaa the Python, the Bandar-Log (herein called monkeys) and two original creations: Col. Hathi of the Elephants and King Louis the Orangutan. Baloo, takes to the boy and the boy to him.

At one point, Mowgli decides he does not want to go to the man village and runs away from Baloo's protection. Shere Khan sets out to find him. When he does, Mowgli shows no fear. Then, with the aid of four cockney vultures, he ties a burning branch to the tiger's tail, and the carnivore flees the scene and the film. Reunited with Baloo and Bagheera, Mowgli seems destined to remain a jungle boy until he hears a young girl's voice coming from the nearby river. Curious, he spots her as she draws water from the river, but then he falls into the latter when the branch he was on gives way. The girl starts for the village, coyly dropping her vase on the way. Mowgli picks it up and follows her; Baloo and Bagheera realize he is lost and return to the jungle.

This picture is for Disney fans only.

The New York Times, December 23, 1967 (Howard Thompson):

> Based loosely on Rudyard Kipling's "Mowgli" stories ... [this] is simple, uncluttered, straightforward fun.... The picture unfolds like an intelligent comic-strip fairy tale...."

Rudyard Kipling's "The Jungle Book"

Walt Disney Pictures/Buena Vista; Released December 25, 1994; 108 minutes; Technicolor; DIRECTOR: Stephen Sommers; PRODUCERS: Edward S. Feldman, Raju Patel; ASSOCIATE PRODUCER (India): Yash Johar; ASSOCIATE PRODUCER (U.S.): Eric Angelson; *Screenplay:* Stephen Sommers, Ronald Yanover, Mark D. Geldman STORY: Ronald Yanover, Mark D. Geldman, based on characters from *The Jungle Book* by Rudyard Kipling; PHOTOGRAPHY: Juan Ruiz-Anchia; EDITOR: Bob Ducsay; MUSIC: Basil Poledouris; PRODUCTION DESIGNER: Allan Cameron; COSTUMES DESIGNER: John Mollo; SET DECORATOR: Crispian Sallis; CAMERA OPERATOR: Ian Fox; FIRST ASSISTANT DIRECTOR: Artist Robinson; SECOND ASSISTANT DIRECTOR: Christian P. Della Penna; PRODUCTION SUPERVISOR: Carl Griffin; MAKEUP: Cindy Williams, Mustaque Ashrafi, Noriko Watanabe; HAIR STYLISTS: Vera Mitchell, Deanna Yacullo; VISUAL EFFECTS SUPERVISOR: Peter Montgomery; MUSIC EDITOR: George A. Martin; HEAD ANIMAL TRAINER: Steve Martin; TREASURE ROOM SNAKE CREATED BY: Animated Extras-London; ORCHESTRATIONS: Greig McRitchie; MUSIC CONDUCTED BY: David Snell; Interiors photographed at Mehboob Studios, Bombay, India; Filmed on location at Jodhpur, India; Falls Creek State Park and Cumberland Mountain State Park, Tennessee; and Fripp Island, South Carolina

CAST: Jason Scott Lee (Mowgli), Cary Elwes (Boone), Lena Headey (Kitty), Sam Neill (Bryden), John Cleese (Dr. Plumford), Jason Flemyng (Wilkins), Stefan Kalipha (Buldeo), Ron Donachie (Harley), Anirudh Agrawal (Tabaqui), Faran Tahir (Nathoo), Sean Naegeli (Mowgli, Age 5), Joanna Wolff (Kitty, Age 5), Liza Walker (Alice), Rachel Robertson (Rose), Natalie Morse (Margaret), Gerry Crampton (Sgt. Major), Amrik Gill (Butler), Rick Glassey (Sgt. Claibourne), Casey the Bear (Baloo), Shadow the Panther (Bagheera), Shannon the Wolf (Grey Brother), Lowell the Orangutan (King Louis), Bombay the Tiger (Shere Khan)

Location filming added greatly to this film's visual appeal, although the jungle segments were filmed stateside. Inexplicably, in an era when non-white roles were finally being portrayed on a large scale by actors of the correct ethnicity, the part of Mowgli was given to a young *Chinese-American* actor named Jason Scott Lee instead of an Indian actor, although Mowgli as a child *was* played by an Indian boy. In the credits it is stated that this adaptation is "based on characters created by Rudyard Kipling"; such is the case, as the storyline is really more revisionist than true Kipling.

The British figure prominently in the action and are portrayed as rather a bad lot, except for the girl who falls in love with Mowgli, her officer-father and one Dr. Plumford, who is on hand to tend to both humans and animals. This is a major departure from the source material, wherein Mowgli never encounters either girls or British soldiers. Here he falls in love with the English girl, whom he had known as a child before he was carried off into the jungle by two horses panicked by a fire. As in the stories, he finds himself deep in the jungle, where he is adopted by a family of wolves. As a young man, he encounters the girl, who attempts to "civilize" him by teaching him English and etiquette. Her betrothed, a British officer, takes exception to all this and makes life rough for Mowgli. Later, by threatening to harm the girl, he forces Mowgli to take him to the treasure chamber. Naturally, he and his cronies are destroyed by their greed.

The well-trained animals retain the Kipling names, but do not speak with human voices as they did in the 1942 film. It is interesting to see the character of King Louie again, as this was an original character created for the 1967 Disney animated version, not one found in the book. The treasure chamber in the dead city is definitely impressive, although the snake which guards it is a nightmarish creature not in keeping with Kipling's ancient cobra. Shere Khan, the tiger, is a catalytic presence throughout this production, and is still alive at the conclusion, another difference from the earlier picture, and from Kipling. Jason Scott Lee gave a credible performance as Mowgli. Despite being a product of the 90s, this version of *The Jungle Book* is worth a look.

The New York Times, December 23, 1994 (Stephen Holden):

> Brashly panoramic... Jungle Book ... is absolutely clear in what it wants to say.... Mr. Lee ... is exotic enough to convince ... children ... he grew up with wolves and tigers.... The personalities of Kipling's animal characters remain undeveloped, and the book's rich layer of allegorical fantasy ... is missing.... The film's ultimate vision of the jungle ... still exerts a mystical tug.

Rudyard Kipling's "The Second Jungle Book—Mowgli and Baloo"

Tri-Star Pictures; Released May 16, 1997; 88 minutes; DIRECTOR: Duncan McLachlan; PRODUCER: Raju Patel; SCREENPLAY: Bayard Johnson, and Matthew Horton, based on the novel by Rudyard Kipling; PHOTOGRAPHY: Adolfo Bartoli; EDITOR: Marcus Manton; MUSIC: John Scott; PRODUCTION DESIGNER: Errol Kelly; COSTUMES: Ann Hollowood; Filmed in Sri Lanka

CAST: Jamie Williams (Mowgli), Bill Campbell (Harrison), Roddy McDowall (King Murphy), David Paul Francis (Chuchundra), Dyrk Ashton (Karait), Gulshan Grover (Buldeo), B.J. Hogg (Col. Reese)

This is a motion picture which should never have been produced, not even for video. Made on the cheap in an attempt to cash in on a famous literary work, it insults the intelligence of anyone over the age of three months. The screenwriters even had the unmitigated gall to suggest that it was actually based on Kipling's novel. None of the events in this production even remotely resemble those penned by the Bard of Sussex. The slapstick humor is of a pre–Mack Sennett level, and both Mowgli and his animal friends are devoid of personality. Jamie Williams is merely a grubby little brat who would be more at home in a *Gremlins* picture as one of the title characters.

Buldeo, Mowgli's uncle here, is out to kill the boy so he will not inherit his parents' estate. He is aided by an unsuspecting circus scout, who thinks he will have the boy as an attraction for the circus. With the help of the non-speaking animals and an old British soldier living in a dead city, Mowgli defeats his uncle.

Among the characters created for this misbegotten production is a bald, evil-eyed pro-wrestling wannabe who carries a trained snake around his neck. He obviously took a wrong turn on his way to Greenwich Village.

To say more would be to waste the reader's time; this film is a disaster on all counts.

Rudyard Kipling's "The Second Jungle Book—Mowgli and Baloo" (Tri-Star, 1997). Jamie Williams. (Courtesy Collectors Book Store.)

The New York Times May 16, 1997 (Lawrence Van Gelder):

> [The movie] is busy without being lively.... A P.T. Barnum talent scout who foresees big box office if he can ... capture the snarling wolf child ... innocently joins forces with Buldeo, Mowgli's evil uncle, who is determined to kill the boy to keep him from inheriting his parents' estate.... Old-fashioned adventure has fallen on hard times.

The Jungle Book—Mowgli's Story

Walt Disney Productions/Buena Vista; Released September 29, 1998 (video only); 76 minutes; Technicolor; DIRECTOR: Nick Marck; EXECUTIVE PRODUCER: Barry Bernardi; PRODUCER: Mack H. Ovitz; CO-PRODUCER: Nick Marck; PHOTOGRAPHY: Ronn Schmidt; EDITOR: Alan Baumgarten; TELEPLAY: Jose Rivera, Jim Herzfeld; MUSIC: Robert Folk; COSTUME DESIGN: Tom Bronson; PRODUCTION DESIGN: Thomas A. Walsh; FIRST ASSISTANT DIRECTOR: Scott Cameron; SPECIAL EFFECTS COORDINATOR: Eddie E. Surkin; NARRATOR: Fred Savage; STUNT CO-ORDINATOR: Dick Hancock

CAST: Ryan Taylor (Young Mowgli), Brandon Baker (Mowgli), Rajan Patel (Indian Soldier); and Featuring the Voices of: Sherman Howard (Shere Khan), Clancy Brown (Akela), Eartha Kitt (Bagheera), Marty Ingels (Hathi), Brian Doyle-Murray (Baloo), Stephen Tobokowsky (Tabaqui), Wallace Shawn (Tarzan Chimp), Peri Gilpin (Raksha), Kathy Najimy (Chil)

This straight-to-video release was made for the kiddie market. The well-trained animals are dubbed with human voices, and they speak in modern American usage (e.g., "I was like totally lost!"), yet it works as it is otherwise a reasonably direct filmization of its source material. It also contains more of the animal characters than any previous version. As in the 1994 version, the film begins with Mowgli at age five. Mowgli flees into the jungle in search of his parents after Shere Khan attacks their camp. He fails to find them and wanders into a wolf den. Adopted by the wolf family of Akela, he grows up among the jungle beasts. Shere Khan had marked Mowgli for a meal at the camp and spends the rest of the film attempting to catch him.

The boy's only contact with men are a brief view of an Indian soldier wandering about the jungle to no apparent purpose, and a short visit to the outskirts of a village. Discovering some matches in a hut, Mowgli later traps Shere Khan within a ring of fire and forces him to swear to leave the jungle forever. He had also found a copy of Kipling's *The Jungle Book* in the hut; at the end he goes off with it, as the voiceover says he found one adventure after another in it, obviously a reference to a sequel.

Kim
(novel, 1901)

SYNOPSIS: Twelve-year-old Kim (full name: Kimball O'Hara), the son of an Irish woman and a color sergeant of an Irish regiment, resides in Lahore. A very streetwise fellow, he is known as "Friend to All the World." His mother died of cholera when he was three, and his father took up with a woman who smoked opium. Being weak, the father acquired the habit and eventually died from it, leaving little Kim only his birth certificate and two other papers. The

Rudyard Kipling's "The Second Jungle Book—Mowgli and Baloo" (Tri-Star, 1997). Bill Campbell, Dyrk Ashton, Jamie Williams. (Courtesy Collectors Book Store.)

woman sewed these into a leather amulet case which she hung about the boy's neck. Sgt. O'Hara also left a prophecy: Two men will come to make things ready, and a Red Bull on a green field, a Colonel riding on his horse and 900 devils shall come for him.

One day Kim meets an old Tibetan lama who seeks a holy river which was created by an arrow shot by Buddha. The boy learns this by eavesdropping on the lama and the curator of the Museum in Lahore. Kim befriends the old man and tells him of his father's prophecy.

Kim goes to Mahbub Ali, an old horse trader who dyes his beard red to hide the gray. Ali says he will pay Kim to deliver a message to a British officer in order to establish a pedigree of a certain white stallion. Kim gets the money hidden in bread grudgingly given him by Mahbub Ali, who is really a British Secret Service agent.

Ali wishes to entrust Kim with a letter, but finds he has already departed for Benares with the lama. They board a train for Umballa, where Kim is to find the British officer. The boy finds him and delivers Ali's message, then spies on the officer as he reads it in his room. Another officer soon appears and the two discuss a punitive action to be taken immediately.

After spending a night in a temple, the lama finds Kim and they continue their journey on foot. They are joined by an old soldier who tells them of the Great Mutiny, in which he participated. They encounter a precocious child and a policeman; the soldier meets one of his sons. The son gives Kim a coin when they part company. A policeman

tries to get it as a road tax, but he is overruled by a senior officer. The pair next meets an old woman of the hills, who asks the lama to pray that she have a second son.

Farther on, Kim sees two British soldiers approaching. Hiding behind a tree, he and the lama watch as they plant camp-marking flags in the ground. Kim is amazed to see a Red Bull on a green flag. He is unaware that these soldiers belong to the Mavericks, the same regiment to which his father belonged. He continues to watch as the regiment marches up and pitches camp. Spotting a man in clerical garb among them, the lama expresses a desire to speak with him. Kim advises the lama to let the priest eat first; "Never speak to a white man till he is fed." They rejoin their party for supper. Returning to the soldiers' camp, Kim bids the lama wait while he tries to discover more about the Red Bull.

As Kim watches the soldiers at mess, he fails to hear the reverend come up behind him, and he is collared. In his struggle, his amulet string snaps off and the reverend has the case. Kim begs him, in English, to return it. The reverend asks the advice of a priest, who opens the case against Kim's protests. Surprised at finding the papers of O'Hara, the priest opens Kim's shirt and observes that he is not so dark and could be white. He asks the boy his name. "Kim." "Or Kimball?" "Maybe." "What else?" "They call me Kim Rishti ke." "What is Rishti?" "Eye-rishti — that was the regiment — my father's." The priest asks Kim to tell him his story. The boys complies, adding about the holy man who waits nearby. Kim brings the lama to the priest's tent. Kim acts as interpreter between the two, with his own ideas. He tells the lama that he is the son of a *Sahib* and the priest wishes to put him in a school. He says he will go for a day or two, then run away and rejoin him in his search. The lama departs after learning how Kim will be educated.

Kim is washed and given a suit to wear. He mentions the punitive expedition he heard about and calls it a war which will involve the Mavericks. The next morning, the regiment gets its orders to move to the front. The priest and the reverend ask Kim how he knew about this, but the boy says nothing.

Kim attends school one day, and gets himself dismissed by the schoolmaster. He hires a letter writer and sends a letter to Mahbub Ali telling what has transpired since he left Lahore. He asks Ali to come help him or send money.

Kim receives a letter from the lama, who is going to Benares. The lama promises to send money for the boy's education for one year. Mahbub Ali comes for Kim and arrangements are made to send the boy to school in Lucknow.

A letter is sent by Kim to the lama in Benares informing him of this. The colonel of the regiment at Umballa rides with Kim on the train to Lucknow. When they part, Kim takes a carriage to the school; on the way Kim sees the lama and jumps out to greet him. He finds the lama has a new disciple, but will come to see him now and then, for he will be using a certain Benares temple as his base during his search for the River.

After a semester in Lucknow, Kim runs away during the holidays and has himself coifed dark like a native. He sends a letter to Mahbub Ali stating he will return on the appointed day. A month later, Ali meets Kim on a road and the boy relates all that has happened. He goes back with Ali to Umballa. There he overhears a plot to assassinate Ali in the morning. Kim is able to warn Ali, who avoids the trap. They travel to Simla; on the way, a sudden flood takes one of the horses and almost drowns Kim.

At Simla, Kim undergoes another make-over, emerging as a Eurasian boy. Ali tells Kim he is to lodge with one Lurgan Sahib until it is time to return to school, and forget that he knows Mahbub Ali or Col. Creighton.

Kim finds a child to take him to Lurgan's dwelling. Inside he meets Lurgan, a black-bearded man, stringing pearls. He is given a place to sleep in the room, which is filled with masks and other curios. He also meets the child who led him there. The child is jealous of Kim and asks Lurgan to send him away. Lurgan explains that Kim will leave when it is time for him to return to school. He then devises a game for Kim. He gives a bag of precious stones to the child, who puts them on a tray. He tells Kim to look at them, then places a piece of paper over them and asks Kim to describe them. Of the 15 stones, Kim is able to recall 14. The child describes them all and in greater detail. The child bests Kim each time they repeat the test with different items. He then agrees to teach Kim how to observe. During the next 16 days, the boys watch everyone who enters

Lurgan's shop, observing every detail of clothing and speech. Lurgan dresses the boys in different outfits, teaching them the various details of each type of person. Kim proves adept at this and regales Lurgan with his impressions of people he knew. He meets a Babu who appears to work with Lurgan.

When he bids good bye to Kim, Lurgan tells the boy he is welcome to return if he wishes. Kim boards a train for Lucknow and school, accompanied by the Babu. The Babu gives him much useful information and leaves him a brass box with quinine and other drugs.

Kim returns to school, where he excels in math and map-making. One day he scales the gate and meets with the lama. He asks the holy man to accompany him next holiday, but the lama tells him he must get all the wisdom of the *Sahibs* first.

Three years pass; in his wanderings, the lama comes again to the village where he first met Kim, and learns that the boy has been there recently. The lama is puzzled by this, not knowing that Kim is now active in Mahbub Ali's service. Kim is also learning from Lurgan Sahib.

Col. Creighton meets with Ali and Lurgan for a report on Kim. They decide he is to be freed from school again for six months to travel with the lama and learn what he can.

Ali takes Kim to the home of a blind woman who performs an incantation over the boy to protect him from evil. The Babu reappears and assists in staining Kim's skin, which had become pale. Babu tells Kim of the amulet given him by the woman, and words used by the agents to identify themselves to each other.

Kim goes to Benares, where he meets the lama again. In the temple, Kim helps a man's sick child by giving him tablets from his brass box. The next morning, before Kim and the lama set out, the man returns to show Kim that his child has been restored to health. Kim tells him to bring food to the railway bridge, which the man does. He later joins the two on their journey.

On a train, Kim encounters a fellow agent who wears the same amulet. The agent, E23, is fleeing from some southern men; Kim changes the agent's appearance by smearing ashes over his body and putting a caste mark on his forehead.

The agent uses a clever ruse to get word to his superior of his whereabouts, and Kim and the lama visit the old woman of Kulu. She welcomes them and tells them of a man from Dacca who is a marvel with medicines. Kim meets him and engages in a verbal duel. After the man disperses the crowd which was listening, he reveals himself to Kim; he is none other than the Babu. He tells Kim that two local kings are collaborating with the Russians. They have allowed two surveyors who are disguised as hunters into the region to the north. Babu plans to ingratiate himself with them in order to spy on them. Kim wants to be in with him and says that he and the lama will be on the same road a few miles behind. Babu tells Kim to keep his eyes out for his large striped umbrella.

Passing himself off as a Rajah's agent, Babu is taken on as a guide by the two Russians. After some time, the party encounters Kim and the lama at the side of the road. Due to a misunderstanding, one of the Russians strikes the lama and causes a riot among their coolies, who are Buddhists. They pelt the Russians with stones; Kim tackles one of them and they roll down a hillside. Babu leaps on top of Kim, whispering in his ear to follow the coolies, for they have all the baggage, including the Russians' maps and documents. Kim runs after the coolies as the other Russian fires at him and misses. Babu tells the Russian that he's rescued his companion. One of the coolies prepares to fire at the Russians, but is prevented by the lama, who then collapses. He is given some whisky. The Babu tries to pacify the Russians, who are bent on vengeance on Kim and want their baggage back.

That night, Kim and the lama camp with the coolies. The next morning, a local woman gives Kim the bag containing the Russians' maps and equipment. Kim keeps only the important material, throwing the rest into a valley. He writes a letter to Babu and gives it to the woman to deliver. In it he tells Babu that he has their property, and asks what to do next. He tells the woman to have the nearby villagers feed the strangers and send them on their way peacefully.

The woman returns with Babu's reply: He will rejoin Kim after he has left the Russians in Simla. Later the woman has her husband and another man carry the lama in a litter, for he is still weak. After they leave him, Kim sends a message to the old woman of Kulu, who sends a palanquin for the lama. At her home, Kim is purged, massaged and fed, relieving him of his fatigue. Kim learns of the presence of a man who says they were blood brothers and asked after Kim's health. This turns out to be the ubiquitous Babu. Kim gives him the documents and maps. Babu then entrains for Umballa after telling Kim how he tricked the Russians, one of whom is really French.

As Kim takes a long rest, Mahbub Ali meets with the lama to inquire after the boy's well-being. Satisfied, he returns to his business.

When Kim awakes, the lama tells him of a vision he had, wherein the River he sought was revealed to him. It is nearby, thus ending his quest.

Kim

MGM; Released December 1950; 113 minutes; Technicolor; DIRECTOR: Victor Saville; PRODUCER: Leon Gordon; SCREEN-PLAY: Leon Gordon, Helen Deutsch, Richard Schayer, based on the novel by Rudyard Kipling; MUSIC: Andre Previn; PHOTOGRAPHY: William V. Skall; EDITOR: George Boemler; ART DIRECTORS: Cedric Gibbons, Hans Peters; SET DECORATORS: Edwin B. Willis, Arthur Krams, Hugh Hunt; SOUND: Douglas Shearer; Standish Lambert; COSTUMES: Valles; MAKEUP: William Tuttle, Ben Lane; HAIR STYLES: Sydney Guilaroff; SPECIAL EFFECTS: A. Arnold Gillespie; Warren Newcombe; MONTAGE SEQUENCE: Peter Ballbusch; ASSISTANT DIRECTOR: George Rhein; TECHNICAL ADVISER: I.A. Hafesjee; COLOR CONSULTANTS: Henri Jaffa, James Gooch; UNIT MANAGER: Keith Weeks

CAST: Errol Flynn (Mahbub Ali, the Red Beard), Dean Stockwell (Kim), Paul Lukas (Lama), Robert Douglas (Col. Creighton), Thomas Gomez (Emissary), Cecil Kellaway (Hurree Chunder), Arnold Moss (Lurgan Sahib), Laurette Luez (Laluli), Reginald Owen (Father Victor),

Kim (MGM, 1950). Dean Stockwell. (Courtesy Collectors Book Store.)

Richard Hale (Hassan Bey), Roman Toporow, Ivan Triesault (Russians), Hayden Rorke (Major Ainsley), Walter Kingsford (Dr. Bronson), Frank Lackteen (Shadow), Jeanette Nolan (Foster Mother), Henry Corden, Peter Mamakos (Conspirators), Rodd Redwing (Servant), Michael Ansara, Lou Krugman (Guards), Adeline DeWalt Reynolds (Old Maharanee), Lal Chand Mehra (Policeman), Movita Castaneda (Woman With baby), Wallace Clark (British General), Stanley Price (Water Carrier), Francis McDonald (Letter Writer), Robin Camp (Thorp), Danny Rees (Biggs), Keith McConnell (Master), Betty Daniels (Miss Manners), Olaf Hyt-

ten (Mr. Fairlee), Bobby Barber (Cart Driver), Mitchell Lewis (Farmer)

This production had been planned by MGM as early as 1938, as a vehicle for Freddie Bartholomew and Robert Taylor, to be filmed in India. With the beginning of World War II, it was shelved. In 1942 it was revived, with Mickey Rooney, Basil Rathbone and Conrad Veidt slated to appear in it. This time the Office of War Information advised the studio against producing it, feeling that Far Eastern nations would object to the story's depiction of white supremacy and imperialism.

Having gained its independence from Great Britain in 1947, India's government granted MGM permission to film in their country, although only Errol Flynn (1909–1959) and Paul Lukas (1894–1971), among the principals, made the trip. The rest of the cast did all their work in Lone Pine, California. An interesting sidelight is that Flynn had the choice between appearing in this film or *King Solomon's Mines* [q.v.], which was filmed simultaneously in Africa. Had he opted for the Dark Continent over the sub-continent, his career, which was just beginning to decline, might have had a temporary boost. As it was, his decline continued, as *Kim* failed to generate much business at the box office.

This film opens with an old Indian man, who becomes the narrator, seated cross-legged on the floor. He states the time to be 1885, then opens the curtains to reveal scenes of Indian life while introducing the characters of Col. Creighton, head of the British Secret Service in India, and young Kim, "who lived by his shrewdness and cunning in the streets of Lahore."

Events in the novel become scrambled in this production. Kim first gives a message from Mahbub Ali to a courtesan, instead of the one for Col. Creighton. She informs two men of Ali's coming, and asks why they don't kill him in some alley as he is only a horse trader. They believe him to be a different kind of horse trader. They tell her to look for a certain parchment which tells of the hillmen's plans in their upcoming revolt.

Mahbub Ali makes his entrance jumping down into an alley in front of Kim, who goes about as a native boy because white boys are sent to school. Kim gives Ali the woman's message. At the woman's place, Ali pretends to get drunk, allowing the woman to search him and his bag, but she finds nothing, as he had given the parchment to Kim.

Kim later spots a lama in the town square. Asking him questions, the boy learns of the River of the Arrow, which the lama is seeking. Kim begs for the lama and tells him of his quest for a red bull on a green field, showing the old man the papers in the amulet which he carries. He takes the lama to Ali, who gives the boy a message to take to Col. Creighton.

A man named Lurgan appears at Creighton's office and tells him of the planned attack of the hill men. Another man named Babu is also present. When Kim arrives, he gives Ali's message to the colonel. He also overhears a general giving mobilization plans to the colonel. This is just a slight variation from the novel. When Kim and the lama continue their journey, the encounters with the soldier, policeman and child are omitted.

The old woman is then seen briefly, and for the only time. Shortly thereafter, Kim finds the Mavericks, and his quest is over. Caught by a reverend, Kim is taken to his tent, where they are joined by a priest, and Kim is questioned. The lama enters and arrangements are made for the boy's schooling. Kim tells of the mobilization plans, but is laughed at. Just then the troops are ordered to fall in. Kim says he is a prophet when asked how he knew.

The letter writing sequence is verbatim from the novel.

Ali takes Kim to Col. Creighton, who receives money from the lama for the boy's schooling. Kim attends school in Lucknow; while there, he encounters the lama again.

During summer vacation, the boy reverts to his Indian self, having his skin stained by a young woman, rather than by an old blind woman and Babu.

Arriving at Ali's camp, he overhears a plot to assassinate the horse trader. Kim warns Ali and aids him in foiling the plot. Ali takes the boy to Lurgan's shop, where he is tested and trained as in the book. Lurgan also teaches Kim about hypnotism, warning him never to let anyone hypnotize him.

Babu, who is also an agent, appears with a note at Lurgan's and tells of two men who have followed him. The note contains important information for Col. Creighton; Kim is entrusted with it, while Babu departs to try to lose the men who followed him. Kim is also followed, but cleverly manages to shake the man with help from Col. Creighton, who gives him a message for Babu. It states that the geologists are not who they appear to be.

Kim later finds Babu strangled; in the book, Babu survives his adventures.

Kim (MGM, 1950). Errol Flynn, Dean Stockwell. (Courtesy Collectors Book Store.)

When Col. Creighton learns of this, he calls Ali to replace him. Meanwhile, Kim has disappeared. Ali finds the camp of the Russian geologists, and sees Kim working as their servant. Disguised as a goatherd, Ali meets with Kim and learns of the Russians' true plans, to smuggle arms to rebel tribesmen. One of the rebel leaders meets with them and becomes suspicious when he learns that Kim attached himself to them. The leader tries to hypnotize Kim, who pretends to go under. The tribal leader is not fooled, however. When he begins to manhandle the boy, the lama comes to his aid, but is beaten by the Russians. The rebel leader suspends Kim by a rope over a cliff until he talks. Ali sneaks up behind the rebel and throws him over the cliff and rescues Kim.

Ali confronts the Russians, as their soldiers approach. Ali shoots one of them and creates an avalanche which disperses the soldiers, crushing a few.

Kim tends the lama, who suddenly believes he sees his river. He begins walking toward it, only to collapse and die in the hills; the river was an illusion. This is a major departure from the source, wherein the lama actually found his river.

The film ends with Kim and Ali watching some British troops heading for the Khyber Pass.

Precious little music (composed by Andre Previn) is used. Considering the languid direction, more music would have helped sustain interest in the action.

The New York Times, December 8, 1950 (Bosley Crowther):

> The rich and rare atmosphere of India runs through its lush, romantic scenes.... In sticking fairly closely to Rudyard Kipling's classic yarn, the script writers have dragged out the story to a somewhat tedious length.... Victor Saville has directed the company at a suave and leisurely pace....

Kim

CBS-TV; London Films; Original air date: May 16, 1984; 141 minutes; DIRECTOR: John Davies; TELEPLAY: James Brabazon, from the novel by Rudyard Kipling; PHOTOGRAPHY: Michael Reed; PRODUCER: David Conroy; ASSOCIATE PRODUCER: Peter Manley; EXECUTIVE PRODUCER: Mark Shelmerdine; Music: Marc Wilkinson; EDITOR: John Shirley; COSTUME DESIGNER: Phyllis Dalton; PRODUCTION MANAGER: Jean Walter; CASTING DIRECTOR: Ann Fielden; PRODUCTION DESIGNER: Roger Hall; MUSIC EDITOR: Larry Richardson; ASSISTANT DIRECTOR: Gino Marotta; SPECIAL EFFECTS: Nobby Clark; HAIRDRESSER: Stephanie Kaye; ASSISTANT HAIRDRESSER: Mariam Samuel

CAST: Peter O'Toole (Lama), Bryan Brown (Mahbub Ali), Ravi Sheth (Kim), John Rhys-Davies (Babu), Julian Glover (Col. Creighton), Lee Montague (Kozelski), Alfred Burke (Lurgan), Mick Ford (Corporal Bruce), Roger Booth (Father Victor), Bill Leadbitter (Gorin), Sneh Gupta (Indra), Peter Childs (Company Sergeant-Major), Noel Coleman (Commander-in-Chief), Jalal Agha (Rajah of Bunar), Sean Scanlon (Sergeant Major), Prentis Hancock (Grogan), Phunsok Ladhakhi (Aruk), Keith Stevenson (Mohammed), Brian Badcoe (School Teacher), Nigel Lea-Jones (Monk), Ashiek Madhvani (Boy), Raj Kapoor (Policeman), Saleem Ghouse (E23), Sagarika Ghosh (Village Girl), Benita Stevenson (Flower of Delight), Reenie Kaur (Market Woman), Shahana (Nadira), Aamire Raza Husain (Rajah of Hilas), John Castle (Narrator)

Filmed on location in northwestern India, this production ran into the

Kim (London Films, 1984). Poster.

Kim (London Films, 1984). Peter O'Toole, Ravi Sheth.

usual problems attendant with shooting in unfamiliar territory. During the early stages of filming, landslides and floods in Manali caused some anxious moments. Two unit members were almost swept away in their car; fortunately, they made a safe escape. Locations utilized included Manali, Jodhpur and Agra. Shooting began in late September 1983 and took eight weeks, with interiors filmed at Elstree Studios outside London.

The Maharajah of Jodhpur proved most cooperative, loaning part of his palace for one scene in which specially cast statues of the Buddha were utilized. These statues so impressed the Maharajah that he purchased them for permanent display.

On more than one occasion, fif-teen-year-old Bombay-born Ravi Sheth, who portrayed Kim, had to do some fast talking when his beggar's garb proved too realistic. Chosen from among thousands of applicants, Sheth is the son of an American mother and Indian father.

The other lead actors made this a truly cosmopolitan cast: Irishman Peter O'Toole, Welshman John Rhys-Davies and Australian Bryan Brown, who followed in the footsteps of his countryman Errol Flynn in the role of Mahbub Ali.

A more faithful adaptation than the 1950 film, this production differs from its source in but a few details.

Hugely successful, *Kim* has been shown in a total of 60 countries, and is still being sold today.

Kim (London Films, 1984). Ravi Sheth, Bryan Brown.

The Light That Failed
(novel, 1890)

SYNOPSIS: Dick Heldar and Maisie live at a foster home, where they are beaten regularly by Mrs. Jennett. One day they buy an old revolver and some cartridges and go to the beach. While Maisie is holding the gun, it goes off accidentally near Dick's face, nearly blinding him. Dick tells Maisie of his love for her, only to learn that she is going away to school. He vows to her that he will become an artist, as that seems to be his sole talent.

The narrative jumps ahead several years. Dick is in the Sudan where he meets a correspondent named Torpenhow, who is covering the British Army's campaign. Dick is sketching and asks Torpenhow for work. The latter telegraphs his employer and Dick is hired for three months trial. During a battle, Dick sustains a severe head wound. After the campaign, Torpen-how returns to Britain, but Dick remains in Egypt. There he engages in "riotous living" in Port Said. One day he gets a telegram from Torpenhow which reads: "Come back quick. You have caught on. Come." Dick has his friends the Binats, who own the inn where he is staying, throw one last wild party for him.

After a month of privation in London, Heldar finds Torpenhow and takes a studio in the same building, which Torpenhow had already rented for him. Dick has become swell-headed about his work, realistic depictions of soldiers in the field, and Torpenhow tells him to pray to be delivered from arrogance.

In Dick's studio one day, Torpenhow discovers a cleaned-up version of an earlier work and finds that his friend is now working solely for money. Torpenhow puts his foot through the newer painting.

Dick encounters Maisie while he

is out walking and learns that she is also doing some painting, even though she still has her inheritance. They discuss their feelings for each other. Dick offers to help Maisie with her work; she is unaware of his success until he shows her some of his work in a gallery window. She then accepts his offer of help, telling him he may visit her on Sundays in her apartment which she shares with a red-haired girl.

Dick begins visiting Maisie regularly on Sundays, but they always quarrel about artistic techniques and he does not get along with her roommate. On one occasion, Dick takes Maisie back to their childhood home by the sea.

Torpenhow and the Nilghai, another correspondent, begin to worry that Dick will settle down and his work will be spoiled. Dick continues to see Maisie until he realizes that it is not yet time for them to be together.

Maisie gets an idea for a head from a poem and calls it "Melancolia." When Dick tells her she has not the skill, she goes off to Paris to study under his former teacher. Dick decides to do his own "Melancolia."

Back home, Dick discovers that Torpenhow has a woman in his room. His friend explains that he found her fainting on the street. After one look at her emaciated condition, Dick hires her as a model for his "Melancolia." She gives her name as Bessie Broke.

She is very grateful to Torpenhow and after a few weeks of modeling asks if she can stay with him. He reluctantly agrees, but says she can stay only until he is called on another assignment. Dick overhears their conversation and convinces Torpenhow to take a vacation. Shortly thereafter, the artist begins to be bothered by spots before his eyes, so he visits an oculist. The doctor tells him it is the old head wound which has damaged his optic nerve; if he takes care of himself, he will have a year left before going blind.

Distraught, Heldar can only wonder how much time he has to see. He begins to work feverishly on a better "Melancolia," driving Bessie hard. He begins drinking heavily, but finishes the painting to his satisfaction.

He shows it to Torpenhow, who now hardly notices Bessie, fuelling her anger against Dick. When they have gone, she smears turpentine over the picture and slashes it. Torpenhow sees the result first, but Dick goes blind overnight, before he can look at the work again; Torpenhow says nothing.

He and Dick's other friends rally to him in his hour of need. Torpenhow takes care of most of his daily needs. Not long after, war breaks out in the Sudan again and Dick's friends prepare to cover it.

Meanwhile, Maisie has been studying art in France without success. Unaware of Dick's affliction, she is angry that she has not heard from him in six weeks. Torpenhow secretly goes to Maisie and brings her back to London. Dick, full of self-pity, says he will not be a burden to anyone. He shows the "Melancolia" to Maisie and she pretends it is a masterpiece. She then runs out of the apartment and Dick's life.

On the eve of his departure, Torpenhow is told by Dick that he and Maisie are to be married.

Dick is out walking with his

landlord one evening when the latter spots Bessie and goes over to her at Dick's request. The landlord tells her of Dick's blindness. She agrees to go back to Heldar's apartment. There she straightens up and Dick hires her to take care of the place. He tells her he has money and that he can sell the "Melancolia" if the need arises. When she finds out when Dick became blind, Bessie tells him what she did to the picture. The artist laughs at first, then thinks. He has Bessie take him to the bank and then has her buy him a steamship ticket for Egypt. With his landlord's help, he makes out his will. He sells his furniture to the landlord and gives that money to Bessie, who takes him to the ship.

Arriving in Port Said, Heldar goes to the inn run by the Binats. Mr. Binat has died, but his widow still runs the place. She makes arrangements for his journey to the British camp. He rides into the camp atop a camel and calls for Torpenhow. Just as his friend reaches him, Dick Heldar is shot through the head.

The Light That Failed

Feature Film Corporation/Pathé Exchange, Inc.— Gold Rooster Plays; Released October 15, 1916; 5 reels; DIRECTOR: Edward José; SCENARIO: George B. Seitz; PHOTOGRAPHY: Ben Struckman

CAST: Robert Edeson (Dick Heldar), Jose Collins (Bessie, the Model), Lillian Tucker (Maisie), Claude Fleming (Torpenhow)

Variety, October 27, 1916:

Robert Edeson is the [star] of the Pathé Gold Rooster feature in five parts of Rudyard Kipling's novel, which might have been more kindly treated by the writer of the scenario. There are senseless departures from the story…. The bare tale is told, to be sure, with some attempt at completeness, and perhaps moving picture followers who have no acquaintance with the novel will find it interesting, but the fine lights and shadows of the original are absent and the producer has made no effort to reproduce them. He has turned out a straight away theatrical feature. An instance: Dick, the hero, visits the dive in Port Said in proper form, but instead of spending his evening drawing the face of Biset, the worn out profligate, and watching "a Zanzibar dance of the finest," he becomes involved in a brawl over a dancing girl, knocks out two other men in a very stagey encounter and then chastely declines to receive the grateful girl's seductive advances…. Another bit of crude substitution was the incident in which Dick, after his return to London, is set upon by highwaymen, who blackjack him and thus bring on his blindness. All preparation had been made for the hero's loss of sight and the incident could have had no other purpose than to put "action" into the screen. The Pathé people have elected to use the story version in which Dick dies…. But the details of the end have been altered. By the book Dick reaches the British camp at the front riding a camel, but as he is about to dismount a stray bullet strikes him down. In the film he dismounts at a distance and wanders through a hundred feet of "battle stuff," before he receives a bullet, and according to the screen version, during these developments Torpenhow is in London, of all things, apparently making love to Mazie [*sic*]. Why didn't they follow the book? Kipling writes better stories than the Pathé scenarist. Another detail shows the carelessness of the staging. The British troops occupy a deep trench in their battle against the

Desert tribesmen who are armed only with spears. Kipling had said bitter things about mutton-headed British commanders, but he never accused them of anything like that. Edeson does some capital acting. So does Jose Collins as Bessie, the woman of the streets who serves as Dick's model. The others played well. A picture producer who undertakes to screen anything as fine as *The Light That Failed*, must set a higher standard of art. This attempt falls short in finesse.

The Light That Failed

Paramount/Famous-Players; Released November 11, 1923; seven reels; DIRECTOR: George Melford; SCENARIO: F. McGrey Willis, Jack Cunningham, based on the novel by Rudyard Kipling

CAST: Jacqueline Logan (Bessie Broke), Percy Marmont (Dick Heldar), David Torrence (Torpenhow), Sigrid Holmquist (Maisie), Mabel van Buren, Luke Cosgrove, Peggy Schaffer, Winston Miller, Mary Jane Irving

The happy ending, wherein Dick Heldar is reunited with Maisie, was utilized for this production. The time period was also updated to the pre–World War I era, allegedly with Kipling's consent.

An actual Dervish drum which was carried at the Battle of Omdurman was used in the film. It was obtained in Port Said by a British veteran in 1911 and appeared in the scenes depicting that Egyptian city. All of the major performers, except Swedish actress Sigrid Holmquist, were stage actors. Most of the extras seen as soldiers were actual veterans, and came from a number of famed regiments from all over the United Kingdom.

Harrison's Reports, December 8, 1923:

> This picture ... provides further proof that an excellent book does not

The Light That Failed (Paramount, 1923). Jacqueline Logan, Percy Marmont.

necessarily make an excellent picture. For one thing, Sigrid Holmquist is a poor choice for the important role of Maisie; she is attractive enough physically, but lacks personal charm. In addition to this, the picture has a way of fully arousing one's interest in one scene or in a sequence of scenes only to lose it almost in the next; this "steady by jerks" sort of interest is felt all through the picture. Percy Marmont gives an appealing sympathy-arousing interpretation of the hero's role. Jacqueline Logan, as "Bessie Broke," the little waif of the London streets, does as good work, if not better, as she has yet shown herself capable of.

A little boy and girl, childhood sweethearts, are separated when the little girl is sent to France to attend school. Twenty years later they meet again in London. By this time, the boy is a famous artist. The boy and girl attachment ripens into the mature love of a man and a woman. Just before their wedding day, and just as he is finishing the picture he believes will be a masterpiece, he is stricken blind. He stops all communications with his fiancée, feeling that now he will be a burden to her. Later, she learns of his affliction and hurries to him; assuring him that her love has not changed, she receives his promise to return home with her.

The picture should appeal to the literary people, but hardly to the masses.

The Light That Failed

Paramount; Released December 22, 1939; 97 minutes; PRODUCED AND DIRECTED BY William Wellman; SCREENPLAY: Robert Carson, based on the novel by Rudyard Kipling; SECOND UNIT DIRECTOR: Joseph Youngerman; PHOTOGRAPHY: Theodor Sparkuhl; ART DIRECTORS: Hans Dreier, Robert Odell; SET DECORATOR: A.E. Freudeman; EDITOR: Thomas Scott; MUSIC: Victor Young; SOUND: Hugo Grenzbach, Walter Oberst; STUNT COORDINATOR: Yakima Canutt

CAST: Ronald Colman (Richard Heldar), Ida Lupino (Bessie Broke), Walter Huston (Torpenhow), Muriel Angelus (Maisie), Dudley Digges (The Nilghai), Ernest Cossart (Beeton), Ferike Boros (Madame Binat), Pedro deCordoba (M. Binat), Colin Tapley (Gardner), Ronald Sinclair (Dick as a Boy), Sarita Wooten (Maisie as a Girl), Halliwell Hobbes, Colin Kenny (Doctors), Francis McDonald (George), Fay Helm (Red-haired Girl), Charles Irwin (Soldier Model), Major Sam Harris (Wells), George Regas (Cassavetti), Wilfred Roberts (Barton), Connie Leon (Flower Woman), Cyril Ring (War Correspondent), Pat O'Malley (Bullock), Clara M. Blore (Mother), Barry Downing (Little Boy), George Chandler, George H. Melford (Voices), Barbara Denny (Waitress), Leslie Francis (Man With Bandaged Eyes), Harold Entwhistle (Old Man With Dark Glasses), Charles Irwin, Clyde Cook, James Aubrey, Charles Bennett, David Thursby (Soldiers).

The Light That Failed had been slated to star either Gary Cooper or Ray Milland, and was to be filmed in Technicolor. The studio heads settled on British actor Ronald Colman (1891–1958) and decided against the use of color before shooting started. Thomas Mitchell had been chosen for the role of Heldar's friend Torpenhow, but had to bow out shortly before filming began. He was replaced by Walter Huston (1884–1950), an expert at projecting integrity.

Colman had wanted Vivien Leigh to play Bessie, but was overruled by director William Wellman (1896–1975), who cast a very eager Ida Lupino (1918–1995). She ended up stealing the picture.

Wellman and Colman were birds of decidedly different feathers. Not for nothing was the director called "Wild

Bill"; a former World War I flyer, he had hit Hollywood like a hurricane, helming the first Best Picture Academy Award winner, *Wings*, in 1927. Following that success, he built his reputation on gritty gangster films like *The Public Enemy* (1931) and topical dramas such as *Wild Boys of the Road* (1933). A director who favored printing first takes, his clash with perfectionist Colman was inevitable. By his own account, Wellman said they settled their differences and became friends after he made it very clear to the actor that his physiognomy would be greatly altered if he continued to forget his lines as he did one day on the set of *The Light That Failed* .

The scenes set in the Sudan were filmed in a desert near Santa Fe, New Mexico. A number of black cowboys portrayed the tribesmen, and the members of the New Mexico National Guard stood in for the British Tommies.

The picture opens with the very young Dick Heldar and Maisie playing on a beach. Dick has a gun which he lets Maisie use; she accidentally fires it near his face, and he is blinded by the powder. Dick becomes upset when Maisie tells him she is going away to school. They vow to meet as adults and to become artists.

Years later, Dick is in the army as an artist, with his company in the Sudan. During a battle he sustains a blow to the head. Months afterwards, he is in Cairo when a telegram arrives from his friend Torpenhow telling him that his work has been recognized. He becomes famous for his realistic renditions of the Sudan campaign. Dick

The Light That Failed (Paramount, 1939). Muriel Angelus, Ronald Colman.

meets Maisie at a zoo one day and they rekindle their old friendship. His success has gone to his head, however, and he tells Maisie he can do a better job than she painting a character she calls "Melancholia," which is based on the poem "The City of Terrible Night." One day the pair goes to the beach where they played as children, and Dick proposes to Maisie. She tells him that she is going to Paris to study with his old instructor, because of his view of her talent. She sees him as a good friend, but no more.

Dick returns home and finds that his friend Torpenhow, who lives across the hall, has a young woman he has saved from starving in his apartment . Heldar offers the girl, Bessie Broke, a job as a model for £3 a week. He uses her for his version of "Melancholia." After a while Bessie makes a play for Torpenhow, who consults with his buddies Heldar and the Nilghai. They agree that the girl must go. Torpenhow tells Bessie to leave.

At Heldar's the next day, Bessie argues with the artist, blaming him for coming between her and Torpenhow. She vows to get even.

When his vision becomes blurry, Dick goes to an eye doctor. He is told that the optic nerve has begun deteriorating and that nothing can be done to save him from blindness. He begins drinking heavily. He decides to change the painting and makes Bessie laugh continuously until she can stand it no longer. She runs from the studio right into the arms of Torpenhow, who has just returned home.

Dick tells "Torp" of his impending blindness. When Torpenhow, a journalist, informs Bessie that he is going off on another assignment, the girl smears turpentine on Heldar's painting and slashes it. Torpenhow is the first to see what she has done; Dick has gone blind in the meantime. Torpenhow does not tell Dick what has happened, but sends for Maisie. She tells Dick she has come to stay, but Dick feels she is only doing so out of pity. When he shows her the painting, she says that it is a masterpiece. Dick then sends her away.

The artist runs into Bessie and invites her over, still unaware of what she has done. Dick offers her a housekeeping job, but tells her he may have to sell "Melancholia" one day to have enough money. Realizing that he does not know what she did to the painting, she confesses. Instead of being angry, Dick thanks her and has her help him get his affairs in order.

Returning to the Sudan, Heldar finds his old regiment with the help of a man he meets in Cairo. Meeting Torpenhow and the Nilghai, he asks to be put in with the lancers. His friends do so, and Heldar goes riding off straight at the enemy. He is shot in the first volley. The Nilghai and Torpenhow later find him, and the latter says: "Nilghai, God has been very good; he is dead." This final sequence differs from the novel where Dick is shot as he arrives in camp atop a camel, and Torpenhow says nothing as he holds his friend's body in his arms.

Much of the dialogue in this production is taken verbatim from the novel. The opening scene is also straight from the source, except for the omission of the Jennett character. There

The Light That Failed (Paramount, 1939). Ida Lupino.

are other minor differences between film and book, such as the omission of a few characters (some of whom apparently had their scenes deleted, as they are listed among the cast), but on the whole, this is an exceptionally faithful adaptation.

The New York Times, December 25, 1939 (Frank S. Nugent):

> The letter-perfect edition of ... The Light That Failed ... has a fine tweedy, tobaccoey stout-booted air to it; a directness of approach and clarity of thought ... the comforting impression that the characters ... will never concede that it's a woman's world they're living in. Mr. Colman has rarely handled a role with greater authority or charm ... a sincere, reticent and capitally directed version of a good old book....

Mandalay
(poem, 1890)

SYNOPSIS: This piece is comprised of the reminiscences and longing of a cockney soldier for a lady he knew:

> On the road to Mandalay
> Where the flyin'-fishes play,
> An' the dawn comes up like
> thunder outer China 'crost the Bay!

He tells how they met and how no number of British women can compare with her, nor can the English climate compare with that of Burma, "When the mist was on the rice-fields an' the sun was droppin' slow..." Nothing can take his mind from his days in Burma, "For the temple bells are callin', an' it's there that I would be; By the old Moulmein Pagoda, looking lazy at the sea..."

A Maid of Mandalay

Vitagraph; Released August 21, 1913; one reel; DIRECTOR: Maurice Costello; SCENARIO: James Young; Based on the poem Mandalay.

CAST: Clara Kimball Young (Ma May), Maurice Costello (Tommy Wilkins), William V. Ranous (Gunga Din), Mrs. Ranous (Ma May's Mother).

A Maid of Mandalay was filmed on location during a six-month world tour arranged by Vitagraph to keep their very popular leading actor Maurice Costello (1877–1950) away from competitors' offers. James Young (1878–1948), Clara's husband, wrote the screenplay. He was apparently something of a Kipling aficionado, for the name he gave the Burmese woman's father was Gunga Din! Young opens the action at the time when the soldier is stationed in Burma. He saves a native woman from a beating by her father and the two begin meeting secretly in a park. The soldier is recalled to Britain, but eventually returns to Burma, where he finds his love at their old meeting place. This last sequence is clearly a departure from the poem; it is supposition of what might have happened had the soldier had the opportunity to return to Burma.

Costello, a stage actor since 1894, had been in films at least four years at the time of this production. He had also been the winner of the first screen popularity contest ever held. His daughters Dolores and Helene would achieve fame of their own in the 20s, the former becoming the wife of John Barrymore for a time.

Clara Kimball Young (1890–1960) would soon achieve star status in My Official Wife (1914). She and Young were divorced in 1916. Shortly thereafter, some ill-advised business deals sent her career into a tailspin from which it never recovered. She appeared in several sound films, but always in supporting and lesser roles.

Moving Picture World, September 6, 1913:

> Illustrating Kipling's Mandalay song, this picture needs the music to give it life. We saw it accompanied by the usual drumming on the piano and it fell very flat; but it has this quality that it does illustrate the words and sentiment of the song, and the two together should go very well.... Clara Kimball Young is not very effective as the Burma girl who prays to the idol; but is more so than W.V. Ranous as her father. The backgrounds are often full of interest. It is clearly photographed.

The Man Who Would Be King
(short story, 1888)

SYNOPSIS: On board a train in India, Rudyard Kipling meets "a big blackbrowed gentleman" who asks him to alter his schedule so that he may give a message to the man's friend. Kipling agrees; the message is: "He has gone South for the week." He describes his friend as a big man with a red beard. Eight days later, Kipling finds the man where he's supposed to be and delivers the message.

The first man having admitted to impersonating a journalist gives Kipling cause to think some trouble may arise from his so doing. He gives descriptions of both men to the authorities.

Some time later, Kipling encounters the pair when leaving his office late one night. Aware of what he did, they ask for a half-hour of his time and a drink. They introduce themselves as Brother Peachey Carnehan and Brother Daniel Dravot, showing themselves to be Masons. Asking to see maps and books about Kafiristan, they explain to the reporter that "India isn't big enough for such as we." and that they are going to Kafiristan to become kings. Kipling warns them they will either be turned back at the frontier or cut to pieces as soon as they enter Afghanistan. Carnehan then shows him the "contrack" they have drawn up and signed.

The next morning, the journalist goes to bid farewell to the two former soldiers at an inn and meets a mad priest and his servant. He soon realizes that they are Carnehan and Dravot. Away from town he talks with them and discovers they have 20 Martini rifles hidden in their packs. For past services rendered, Kipling is promised half their kingdom.

Ten days later, he gets a report of a mad priest that proves the pair made it safely into Afghanistan.

Two years later, on a summer night, Kipling has just put the newspaper to bed "when there crept to my chair what was left of a man. He was bent into a circle, his head was sunk between his shoulders, and he moved his feet one over the other like a bear. I could hardly see whether he walked or crawled — this rag-wrapped, whining cripple who addressed me by name, crying that he was come back." The figure begs a drink and asks Kipling if he knows him. The reporter does not; the figure identifies himself as Peachey Carnehan.

Kipling asks Peachey to tell him everything. Carnehan entreats the reporter to look him in the eyes while he speaks. Kipling takes a look at his hand and notes a ragged red diamond-shaped on it. "No, don't look there. Look at *me*," says Peachey.

He describes the pair's journey into Afghanistan, how two men tried to rob them, but Dravot broke the neck of one and the other ran away. They thus acquired some much-needed mules.

Once in Kafirsitan, they encounter a force of 20 men fighting a group of ten, so they took two rifles and picked off most of the 20.

They travel through several valleys and villages, teaching the men how to fight and setting up judges in each. Carnehan stays at one village as ruler after helping its chief conquer his enemy. One day Dravot shows up at the head of an army and with a crown on his head. He gives Peachey a crown and tells him: "I am the son of Alexander [the Great] by Queen Semiramis and you're my younger brother and a God too!" Dravot tells Carnehan that fighting is out and the Craft (meaning Freemasonry) is the wave of the future. They proceed to run things accordingly after one Billy Fish (named for someone they once fought alongside) shows Peachey that he knows the secret handshakes of the Masons.

They hold a meeting one night with big bonfires at which Dravot tells the assemblage of Kafiris that he and Peachey "were Gods and sons of Alexander, and Past Grand-Masters in the Craft, and was come to make Kafiristan a country where every man

should eat in peace and drink in quiet and specially obey" them.

The following night, at a Lodge meeting, just as Dravot dons his Master's apron, an old priest becomes excited and, with the help of several other priests, overturns the stone on which Dravot was sitting. On the bottom of the stone is a mark which exactly matches that on the Briton's apron. The priest falls to the ground and kisses Danny's feet. At this, Dravot tells Carnehan, "Luck again, they say it's the Missing Mark that no one could understand the why of. We're more than safe now." He declares himself Grand-Master of all Freemasonry in Kafiristan and King of Kafiristan equally with Peachey. They raise Billy Fish and several priests a couple of degrees in Masonry.

For the next six months Peachey taught the people to plow and drilled the men. He also acquires more rifles and ammunition through trade and soon has a passable fighting force of several hundred men.

Realizing this, Dravot begins having grandiose thoughts. He now says he will acquire an empire, for the Kafiris are whites. He also desires a wife for the winter months. Carnehan advises against such a move and they argue.

Danny puts the idea before a council and gets no reply until Billy Fish tells him to ask the girls. Dravot loses his temper and Peachey tries to calm him by reminding him that these people are English and that's how it's done. Danny stalks from the council room.

Peachey asks Billy Fish the real reason for the problem and is informed that if a woman marries a god or demon, she will die.

That night, a flourish of trumpets and a woman's sobbing indicate that a girl has been chosen to marry Dravot. Fish tells Carnehan that if he can talk Dravot out of the marriage idea, he'll be doing them both a great service. At the same time, he swears his loyalty and that of his 20 men.

Peachey asks Danny one last time to drop the idea. The latter calls him foolish by not doing the same, then calls for his bride-to-be. She is brought forward, amidst much horn-blowing, dressed in silver and turquoise.

Dravot is satisfied with her and tells her to kiss him. She buries her face in his beard and he yells that he has been bitten. He puts his hand to his face and withdraws it covered with blood. Seeing this, the priests exclaim: "Neither God nor Devil but a man!" Billy Fish and two of his men drag Danny into their midst and a priest slashes at Peachey.

Badly outnumbered, the Britons and Fish and his men put up a fight, but are forced to flee down the valley. Only nine (the Britons, Fish, and six of his men) make it alive after the priests roll boulders down upon them and others fire at them. Dravot blames Carnehan for the mutiny. The latter persuades him to go to Fish's village, where they can be protected. They travel all day and night.

At noon the next day, upon reaching the top of a flat mountain, they find an army lined up in the middle waiting for them. A few begin firing and Dravot is hit in the calf. He becomes his old self again and orders Fish to take his men and Peachey out of there, that he will face the Kafiris alone. Fish and Peachey refuse to leave, but Fish's men run away.

The Kafiris advance and seize Dravot, who knocks down the first man to touch him. Carnehan fires his last round and Billy Fish has his throat cut. All the while, not a single sound is uttered by the Kafiris.

Dravot asks for Peachey's forgiveness, which he receives. He is then forced onto a rope bridge which crosses a deep ravine above a river. When he is halfway across, the ropes are cut and he plunges to his death. Carnehan is crucified between two pine trees with wooden pegs for his hands and feet. He manages to survive until the next day, when he is cut down. Taken to the temple and fed, he is then given Danny's head in a bag as a reminder not to return, and is sent on his way.

At this point Carnehan opens the bag and out rolls Dravot's withered head, the crown still on it. A bit delirious now, Peachey gets up to leave, asking only for whiskey and some money. At noon Kipling finds him begging and singing in the street, although there is no one around. The reporter puts him in his carriage and takes him to a missionary until he can be taken to an asylum. Two days later, upon inquiring of the former soldier at the mission, Kipling learns that he died of sunstroke the day before.

The Man Who Would Be King

Persky-Bright/Devon/Allied Artists/ Columbia; Released December 1975; 128 minutes; Filmed in Technicolor and Panavision; DIRECTOR: John Huston; PRODUCER: John Foreman; SCREENPLAY: John Huston, Gladys Hill, based on the short story by Rudyard Kipling;

PHOTOGRAPHY: Oswald Morris; EDITOR: Russell Lloyd; PRODUCTION DESIGNERS: Tony Inglis, Alexander Trauner; MUSIC COMPOSED AND CONDUCTED BY Maurice Jarre; ASSISTANT DIRECTOR: Bert Batt; PRODUCTION SUPERVISOR: Ted Lloyd; COSTUMES: Edith Head; SECOND UNIT DIRECTOR: Michael Moore; MAKE UP: George Frost; HAIRDRESSER: Pat McDermott; STUNT COORDINATOR: James Arnett; SPECIAL EFFECTS: Dick Parker; OPTICAL EFFECTS: Wally Weevers; MATTE ARTIST: Albert Whitlock; SET DRESSER: Peter James; Filmed on location in Morocco and at the Grande Montée, Chamonix, France; Completed at Pinewood Studios, London, England

CAST: Sean Connery (Daniel Dravot), Michael Caine (Peachey Carnehan), Christopher Plummer (Rudyard Kipling), Saeed Joffrey (Billy Fish), Jack May (District Commissioner), Karroum Ben Bouih (Kafu-Selim), Shakira Caine (Roxanne), Paul Antrim (Mulvaney), Mohammed Shamni (Babu), Doghmi Larbi (Ootah), Albert Moses (Ghulam), Graham Acres (Officer), The Blue Dancers of Goulamine (Dancers)

ACADEMY AWARD NOMINATIONS: Writing, Screenplay Adapted from Other Material; Best Editing; Best Art Direction/Set Decoration; Best Costume Design

In 1952, veteran screenwriter-director John Huston (1906–1987) got the idea to direct a film based on Kipling's 1888 short story *The Man Who Would Be King*. The story of two "gentlemen at large" who attempt to rule a mountainous region in northern Afghanistan had never been filmized. His original choices for the two adventurous former British soldiers were his good friend Humphrey Bogart and the one-time King of Hollywood, Clark Gable. Other projects kept interfering. When Bogart died of cancer in January 1957, Huston had no immediate replacement. The idea was again shelved. It continued gathering dust for well over three years, then Gable died of a heart attack in November 1960, just weeks after completing his work on Huston's *The Misfits* (1961). Again relegated to the back burner, *The Man Who Would Be King* lingered while the director completed other films. He continued to dabble with a treatment, working with Aeneas MacKenzie, Steve Grimes and Tony Veiller, before settling on one on which screenwriter Gladys Hill collaborated. Finding the original story too short for a feature film, they added material thoroughly in keeping with the author's mood, such as the fact of Carnehan, Dravot, and Kipling all being Masons.

By then it was 1973; still searching for actors for the starring roles, Huston had Paul Newman suggested to him. He had just directed Newman in *The Mackintosh Man* (1973). The director sent him the various scripts, along with some changes of his own. The actor responded favorably; his co-star in two previous films, Robert Redford, was named for the other lead role. Then Newman, truly concerned about the project, realized it could only be successful if two Britons played the leads, so he told Huston to get Sean Connery and Michael Caine. Seeing the wisdom in this thought, the director duly signed up the Scot and the Englishman. According to Michael Caine's autobiography *What's It All About?*, Huston secured his services by telling him that he was getting the role Bogart was to have played. (Caine is a great admirer of Bogart's.)

The cost of the production was estimated at $5,000,000; Huston had to convince his backers it would be worth that much. His producer, John Foreman, finally got Columbia Pictures to put up some of the money in return for the European distribution rights. Allied Artists also chipped in, in return for the distribution rights in North and South America. With the funding settled, the next task was to scout locations for shooting.

Kafiristan itself was out of the question, as it was closed to foreigners. This was just as well, as its topography made filming of any sort highly impractical. Turkey was then considered; Huston figured he would shoot the bulk of the scenes there, adding street and market scenes done in India and background shots in Afghanistan. However, a dispute between that country and the United States over the current poppy crop ruled it out.

In early 1975, the company visited Morocco, where writer Steve Grimes had earlier done some scouting. Finding this site most suitable, they worked out of Marrakesh, shooting scenes in the Atlas Mountains and actual Berber villages, also using the residents as extras. Huston himself found three ancient men among the locals and used them as the High Priest and his two assistants. Mountainous regions of France were also utilized. The holy city of Sikandergal was built just outside of Marrakesh. The set for the temple cost half a million dollars.

Caine and Connery having been engaged for the lead roles of fortune hunters Peachey Carnehan and Danny Dravot, Huston next searched for a blond blue-eyed actress to portray Roxanne, the Kafiristani princess. A blonde

being a rare commodity in Morocco, he settled for Caine's Indian wife, Shakira. Although she was no actress, she was a ravishing beauty and more than filled the bill. Canadian Christopher Plummer became the third actor to portray Rudyard Kipling on film. (Reginald Sheffield, played Kipling in 1939's *Gunga Din*. In a 1966 episode of the TV series *The Time Tunnel*, "Night of the Long Knives," Kipling was portrayed by David Watson, *sans* mustache and eyeglasses.) He appears in Kipling's initial occupation of reporter, encountering the pair before their fateful adventure (and the survivor, Peachey Carnehan, following it).

Caine and Connery work very well together and are completely convincing in their roles. As two former soldiers bent on establishing themselves as rulers of a foreign land, they represent a microcosm of the British government of the day, getting involved where they have no right. When Danny Dravot oversteps his bounds, he and those with him are inevitably brought down by their own greed. The two actors even improvised one scene, wherein the pair is rebuked by the Governor of the Province. They quickmarch in and out of his office, saluting energetically.

Although utilizing much of the author's dialogue verbatim, there are a number of differences in the events, due, in part, to the necessary fleshing out of the 40–page story to feature film length. The order of events is also slightly altered; the film opens with Peachey's return to Kipling's office after the adventure (which then becomes a flashback), whereas the story is told in

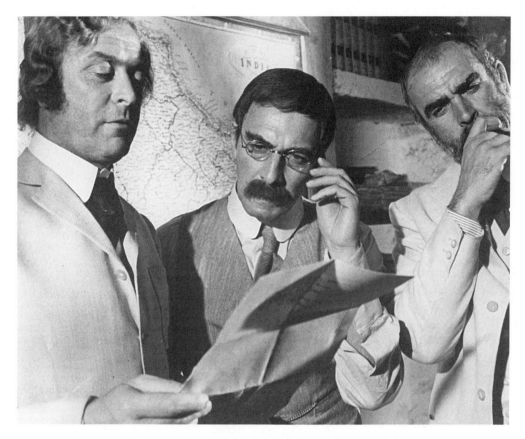

The Man Who Would Be King (Persky-Bright/Devon/Columbia, 1975). Michael Caine, Christopher Plummer, Sean Connery.

chronological order. The other major difference is in the appearances of the two major characters. In the story, Dravot is a large man with a red beard; in the film, he is played by black-haired Sean Connery with mutton-chop whiskers. Carnehan is a black-browed gentleman in the story and played by blonde Michael Caine; the director would have done better to switch the roles.

Peachey Carnehan lifts Kipling's watch at a railroad station; when he sees a Masonic pendant attached, he realizes that he must return the item,

since he also is a Mason. On the train, he cleverly passes the blame to an Indian passenger, whom he then throws from the moving train. He asks Kipling to give a message to his friend who will be on a certain train eight days hence: "Peachey has gone south for the week," replacing the pronoun "he" with his name. As Kipling detrains, he informs Carnehan that he missed his watch back at the station—a true Huston touch.

After giving the message to Dravot, Kipling learns that their next scheme is to impersonate the representative from

The Man Who Would Be King (Persky-Bright/Devon/Columbia, 1975). Sean Connery. (Courtesy Collectors Book Store.)

The Northern Star in order to blackmail a certain rajah. Since *he* is that representative, Kipling goes to the authorities and (unlike the story) he keeps the pair from being charged with any serious crime. The scene in Kipling's office faithfully follows the story, including some verbatim dialogue.

An inside joke is included in the sequence when Dravot and Carnehan begin their journey to Kafiristan. As they pass a British guardpost, Dravot throws his voice at the guard, who is named Mulvaney, one of Kipling's "Soldiers Three." He has him step double-time at his post, causing his officer to put him under arrest for drunkenness.

When the pair reaches Kafiristan, their entry is blocked by an abyss. As

they sit by a fire talking of old times, their laughter causes an avalanche which conveniently fills the gorge, giving them a path into the country.

At the first town they come to, the Britons find a Gurkha named Billy Fish, here the only survivor of an archaeological party which had been buried by an avalanche, rather than a village chief whom the Britons give the name. He becomes a handy interpreter as they deal with the natives. Upon being introduced to Ootah, the village chief, they explain that they tumbled from the sky. Asked if they are gods, Carnehan replies, "Not gods. Englishmen, which is the next best thing."

As they begin training the townsmen in the use of arms, Dravot says,

The Man Who Would Be King (Persky-Bright/Devon/Columbia, 1975). Sean Connery, Michael Caine. (Courtesy Collectors Book Store.)

"We're going to teach you soldiering, the world's noblest profession. When we're done with you, you'll be able to stand off and slaughter your enemies like civilized men." One poor "recruit" cannot seem to get the hang of things. A local utilized by Huston, he adds a touch of humor and *cinema verité* with his embarrassed grin and awkwardness.

As Ootah's men are about to begin their first engagement, they are interrupted by a half dozen holy men passing by. Combatants on both sides drop their arms and fall on their faces until the priests are gone. During the battle, Dravot is struck by an arrow in his bandolier, which does him no harm. He continues fighting awhile, then pulls it out. When the natives see this, they all grovel on the ground. The Britons learn that the Kafiris think that Dravot is the son of Alexander the Great, whom they have been awaiting for centuries. This is one of several episodes in the story which were depicted in greater detail in the film. Huston also keeps the pair together throughout the action, whereas in the story they separate for a time after entering Kafiristan. This proved to be a wise move, given the fact that Connery and Caine worked so very well together.

While receiving tribute afterwards, Danny spots a beautiful woman, whose name just happens to be Roxanne, the

The Man Who Would Be King (Persky-Bright/Devon/Columbia, 1975). Sean Connery. (Courtesy Collectors Book Store.)

same as that of Alexander the Great's wife (Semiramis in the story). Dravot is getting ideas. From here on, the film alters only the details of the story, adhering closely to the basic plot. A couple of examples are the aforementioned meeting with Roxanne; in the story, when Danny gets the marriage bug, a woman is chosen for him, rather than his picking his mate. Another change involves the discovery by the priests at Sikandergal of the Masonic symbol; in the story it is on his apron, while in the film, it is the pendant given Dravot by Kipling. In the story, it is merely stated that any woman who mates with a god will die; the script takes it a step further and says that when a woman mates with a god, she goes up in flames and nothing remains, not even ashes. When Carnehan visits Kipling again, a mere shell of a man, he merely shuffles off; his begging in the streets, being taken to an asylum by the reporter and his death are not mentioned.

With interiors shot at Pinewood Studios in London, *The Man Who Would Be King* is a handsome production filled with detail, from the bustling bazaar scenes to the newspaper office of the fictitious *The Northern Star* where Kipling plies his trade. It ranks with *The Light That Failed* (1939) as the most literal and with *Gunga Din* as the most entertaining film adapted from Kipling.

The world premiere was held in New York on December 17, 1975, with Caine in attendance. The next day, a royal premiere was graced by the presence of Princess Anne in London (Caine flew over for that, too). Connery was already at work on his next project, and so he missed both premieres. The picture grossed $6,500,000 in the United States, and was among the Top Ten films at the box office for three months.

The New York Times, December 18, 1975 (Vincent Canby):

> *The Man Who Would Be King* manages to be great fun in itself while being most faithful to Kipling. Although it is about as romantic and implausible an adventure as you're likely to see, it's not an anachronism....

The Naulahka
(novel, 1892)

SYNOPSIS: Nicholas Tarvin of Topaz, Colorado, is in love with Kate Sheriff. She rejects his marriage proposal because she feels a calling to help the women of India after hearing an Indian woman lecture about their plight. Kate had hoped to go as a doctor, but her parents refused to let her attend medical school, so she became a nurse instead. Tarvin also happens to be running for the state legislature against Kate's father. Believe it or not, it gets worse.

A railroad is planning a route through the area and Topaz has a rival in the town of Rustler. Tarvin, who happens to be something of a gemolo-gist, meets the wife of the president of the railroad, who happens to be fond of jewelry. Nick promises to bring her a fabulous Indian necklace known as the Naulahka if she sees to it that the railroad will run through Topaz. She agrees. Nick then has another discussion with Kate, in very bad dialogue for several pages, which fails to change her mind. She does agree not to marry anyone else, however. Tarvin sets off for India alone. For anyone still reading, I admire your courage.

When Nick detrains somewhere in India, he takes a ride on a bullock cart for four days. Arriving at his destination, he meets several white representatives of business firms awaiting payment for their goods. Pretending to be one of them, he learns that if he can get the rajah's women interested in an item, it's a definite plus.

By telegram he learns that he has won the election. He meets an American missionary couple, the Estes, and learns that Kate is on her way there. Mrs. Estes takes him to the palace and introduces him to the maharajah. Tarvin gains the rajah's favor, loses it on account of Sitahbai, the current maharanee, who is a gypsy and murderess, then regains it. He also meets the rajah's sickly son by the previous ranee.

Kate shows up to treat the boy. Seeing Nick, she asks him to leave. More bad dialogue ensues as Nick pleads his case.

Mrs. Estes takes Kate on a tour of the palace, including the mysterious section comprised of several levels wherein dwell many women. All of them are in varying degrees of distress.

Many refuse any help from Kate, others beg her to save their children. Kate realizes that the reality is quite different from the picture presented by the lecturer.

The queen mother sends a gift to Kate via her son — a gaudy and crudely sewn comforter. The son gives a speech indicating that Kate is to watch over him, for Sitahbai wants him dead, though this must be explained to her by Nick.

Kate visits the local dispensary. Among the crowd of women outside is one who takes her side, threatening any who would harm the white lady. The American finds conditions there intolerable. She also learns that her colleague, an Indian graduate of medical school, takes opium and dispenses it to patients. She immediately sends an order to Calcutta for drugs and medical supplies.

Meanwhile, Nick spends much time with the rajah getting into his good graces in hopes of seeing (and purloining) the Naulahka. He convinces the ruler that there is gold in the local river, and that if he is allowed to dam it, the precious metal could be easily extracted. The rajah is unsure of its whereabouts, but suggests it may be in a place called the Cow's Mouth, a deep hole in the ground some distance away. Nick sets out, arriving at the place at night. Dawn reveals a nearby dead city, which he explores. Returning to the Cow's Mouth, he begins his descent. Discovering a hole in the side of the wall, he enters, only to find a crocodile, which causes him to retreat. Resolved never to return, he rides back to the palace. There he gets the men needed to build a dam and sets to work.

Kate's work begins to receive recognition; women from all over the area come to the dispensary. She has an unpleasant meeting with Sitahbai and decides to avoid her apartment thereafter. The gypsy has also treated the queen mother shamefully, causing her to withdraw from palace society. She also meets with Kate and asks her to protect her son.

Soon thereafter, the rajah's son is betrothed to a three-year-old princess. At the celebration, the youngster wears the Naulahka. After the ceremonies, he collapses and is brought to Kate, who believes his symptoms are due to hemp poisoning. She and Nick immediately suspect Sitahbai. When Nick tells the rajah, the latter laughs off the accusation. On his way back from the palace, Nick is attacked by a great ape, which he kills with two shots from his revolver.

Sitahbai sends a eunuch to fetch Tarvin to an audience at a watch-tower near a dam. She admits to arranging all the attempts on his life and that she overheard the accusation he made to the rajah. The gypsy also tells Nick that she has a son whom she hopes to see ascend the throne, her reason for wanting the young rajah dead. She urges Tarvin to leave India; he refuses. Realizing his strength of character, Sitahbai uses her charms on the American. As she leans against him, Nick puts his arm about her waist and feels the Naulahka beneath her clothing. Sitahbai talks of ruling the region with him as her prime minister. Nick simply asks for the Naulahka. The gypsy hesitates, then asks for the boy's life in exchange. Nick reminds her that dawn is fast approaching; for her to be caught outside the palace means death. She surrenders the necklace. Tarvin kisses her as he puts her on her horse; she throws a knife at him, but misses.

As Nick rides back to the city, he is fired at by the eunuch, who likewise misses. His gun then jams, and Nick rides up to him and takes him back to Sitahbai's quarters.

At the Estes', Nick talks of marriage to Kate in extremely trite terms, and she replies in kind, again rejecting him. He warns her about Sitahbai, but she insists on remaining. Nick is now determined to stay also.

While at the Estes' home, the young rajah receives a basket of fruit from Sitahbai. As Kate makes some sherbet for him, his pet monkey steals a banana and dies after eating part of it. Kate disposes of the fruit, realizing it has been poisoned.

Later, at the dispensary, Kate is met by a number of angry people. The old woman who has been with her all along defends her again. A local holy man is stirring up the people inside. Kate goes in and stills him, then speaks. The priest prevails, however, and soon the dispensary is deserted, save for Kate and her friend. Together they go to the Estes' home, pick up the rajah's son, and take him to his mother. They tell the queen of the danger her son faces. After much bandying of words, it is determined that the older woman shall take care of the young rajah until the danger is past.

Meanwhile, Nick's horse is hamstrung and has to be shot. Nick disarms an assassin sent to shoot him. On a road, Tarvin encounters the young rajah and Sitahbai's son out for a ride. He grabs the gypsy's son to use as a hostage. Going to see Kate, he finds that she has finally cracked under all the stress. She finally agrees to return to the United States with Nick. He gives her the Naulahka and has her return it to Sitahbai while he holds the gypsy's son as hostage. Once Kate is safe, Nick goes to the rajah and tells him that there is no gold in the river. He agrees to blow up the dam, then leave India for good. This he does, marrying Kate first and returning to Topaz without the Naulahka.

And that, dear reader, is why no one has ever heard of Topaz, Colorado.

The Naulahka

Pathé; Released February 24, 1918; six reels; DIRECTOR: George Fitzmaurice; SCENARIO: George B. Seitz; PRODUCTION DESIGNER: William C. Menzies

CAST: Antonio Moreno (Nicholas Tarvin), Helene Chadwick (Kate Sheriff), J.H. Gilmour (President Mutrie), Warner Oland (Maharajah), Doraldina (Sitahbai), Mary Alden (Neglected Mother), Edna Hunter (Mrs. Mutrie)

The title of this work refers to a fabulous gem and is the Hindi word for nine "lakhs" of rupees (one lakh = 100,000 rupees). For some obscure reason, the authors transposed the "k" and the "h" when spelling the word.

This film was one of Latin actor Antonio Moreno's (1886–1967) more popular vehicles. The first of the "Latin lovers," the Madrid-born Moreno began in films with Rex-Universal in 1912 and went on to a long career. He appeared opposite such notable female stars as Pearl White, Pola Negri, Clara Bow and Greta Garbo.

Helene Chadwick (1897–1940) starred in a number of silent domestic dramas and was the first wife of director William Wellman.

Swedish actor Warner Oland (1880–1938) paid his dues playing Oriental heavies in the silent era, later gaining a measure of film immortality as the longest-lived "Charlie Chan" in the 30s. He was the only actor to portray both Chan and super-villain Fu Manchu on screen.

Doraldina enjoyed a brief vogue as an "exotic dancer" when the term meant just that. Hers was a popular act in New York, where she appeared at the Palace Theater with a program of Hawaiian dances.

The Moving Picture World, February 26, 1918 (Robert C. McElravy):

> Atmosphere is perhaps the strongest of several enjoyable features of *The Naulahka*, a Pathé play adapted from the original story by George Fitzmaurice. It has an abundance of plot material, so many threads of genuine interest in fact that it contains little of suspense. But it is a rich, colorful production and has a human quality that holds the attention firmly.
>
> Antonio Moreno and Helene Chadwick carry the love interest and are both well suited to their roles. Doraldina ... has the part of Sitahbai, the gypsy girl who has won the love of the Maharajah. Hers is a vampire role and she brings to its performance a wealth of native fascination and temperament.
>
> The general presentation is lavish in the way of settings and well-worded sub-titles with artistic embellishments. The story interest flows quite naturally.
>
> The adventures of the lovers in weird, mysterious India are packed with a continual threat of tragic consequences, and not the least enjoyable part of the story is that both survive and eventually return happily to their Colorado town.
>
> The story as a whole, while not intense in character, has an agreeable charm and leaves the observer with a sense of satisfaction at having seen it.

Soldiers Three
(collection of short stories, 1888)

SYNOPSES: Rudyard Kipling wrote a total of 17 stories featuring the characters of Privates Mulvaney, Learoyd and Ortheris. The seven synopsized here were the most collected in one volume. The others were scattered about in other short story collections. "The Three Musketeers," "The Taking of Lungtungpen" and "The Daughter of the Regiment" are included in *Plain Tales from the Hills* (1888). "The Incarnation of Krishna Mulvaney," "The Courting of Dinah Shadd" and "On Greenhow Hill" can be found in *Life's Handicap* (1891). "His Private Honour," "My Lord the Elephant" and "Love-o'-Women" appear in *Many Inventions* (1893). "Garm — A Hostage" is included in *Actions and Reactions* (1909).

"The God from the Machine" — Mulvaney tells Otheris a story of his youth, about a colonel's daughter who tried to elope with a no-good captain. She being an actress and Mulvaney a stagehand, he was able to spy on the couple. The night of the elopement the man goes on ahead to the station as the girl had to appear in a second play. Mulvaney thus has time to arrange things so that he manages to drive the girl to her father's home instead of the station. Then he goes to the captain and convinces him that his driver is drunk. After beating the driver, the captain returns to barracks and no elopement occurs.

"Private Learoyd's Story"—Learoyd is given charge of the colonel's dog. Mrs. DeSussa so admires the dog that she offers him money for it. Though the dog is not his to sell, Learoyd thinks quickly and says he will steal the dog for her. The deal is sealed. Instead of stealing the dog, he finds one of similar size and color and has Otheris add some details. He passes it off as the first dog and gets his money. He gives the dog to Mrs. DeSussa as she is leaving for a vacation.

"The Big Drunk Draf"—Mulvaney returns to India as a civilian, his period of service being up. He gets a job as a foreman of a coolie gang. The head man comes to him and tells him there is a large group of soldiers creating havoc in the area. Mulvaney takes six of his fastest men to meet the soldiers. He finds them at their camp, 50 of them, all drunk as lords. He tells the commanding officer, a young man, that he can set things right. With the help of some sober non-coms, he has the two leaders of the drunks spread-eagled with pegs on the ground as an example to the others. From then on, there is quiet in the camp.

"The Solid Muldoon"—Mulvaney almost becomes involved with another soldier's wife when he sees her being annoyed by a corporal. When he goes after the man, he finds that he cannot touch him because he is the spirit of a former regiment member whose wife died of cholera years before. The woman's husband then tangles with him, but Mulvaney beats him up. Mulvaney swears not to be bothering any more soldiers' wives.

"With the Main Guard"—The trio reminisces about a particular battle of the Second Afghan War, where they fought alongside the Black Tyrone, a disreputable regiment. A very young officer causes some trouble, but they handle it. Instead of merely dislodging an enemy unit, they wipe it out.

"In the Matter of a Private"—this story does not concern the "Soldiers Three."

"Black Jack"—After being punished unjustly by a sergeant, Mulvaney is reminded of an incident which involved him some years earlier. A sergeant named O'Hara was very hard on his men, so some of them plotted his death. Mulvaney was lying drunk in bed as they plotted nearby. Thinking him asleep, the leader planned to use Mulvaney's gun to do the deed, thus implicating him. After they left, Mulvaney altered the firing mechanism on the gun so that the bullet flew out backwards and wounded the shooter. O'Hara told Mulvaney that he was surprised that his rifle would be left on the rack in such condition. Mulvaney warns the sergeant that next time he might not be so lucky and he was not, for he was shot by a soldier with whose wife he had been involved.

Soldiers Three

MGM; Released March 1951; 87 minutes; DIRECTOR: Tay Garnett; PRODUCER: Pandro S. Berman; SCREENPLAY: Tom Reed, Malcolm Stuart Boylan, Marguerite Roberts; PHOTOGRAPHY: William C.

Mellor; MUSIC: Adolph Deutsch; ART DIRECTORS: Cedric Gibbons, Malcolm Brown; EDITOR: Robert J. Kern; GRETA GYNT'S COSTUMES BY Walter Plunkett; SET DECORATOR: Edwin B. Willis; ASSOCIATE SET DECORATOR: Fred MacLean; MAKE UP: William Tuttle; SOUND SUPERVISOR: Douglas Shearer; SPECIAL EFFECTS: A. Arnold Gillespie, Warren Newcombe

CAST: Stewart Granger (Private Archibald Ackroyd), Robert Newton (Private Jock Sykes), David Niven (Capt. Pindenny), Cyril Cusack (Private Dennis Malloy), Walter Pidgeon (Col. Brunswick), Robert Coote (Major Mercer), Greta Gynt (Crenshaw), Frank Allenby (Col. Groat), Dan O'Herlihy (Sgt. Murphy), Michael Ansara (Manik Rao), Richard Hale (Govind-Lal), Walter Kingsford (Fairfax), Patrick Whyte (Major Harrow), Movita Castenada (Proprietress), Harry Lang (Merchant), Cyril McLaglen (Scot), Harry Martin, Pat O'Moore, Dave Dunbar (Cavalrymen), Stuart Hall (Lieutenant), Clive Morgan, Pat Aherne (Soldiers)

This misbegotten effort was obviously an attempt to make another *Gunga Din*, but it failed miserably despite high production values and a sterling cast. As in the earlier film, the three leads were given less unusual names, this time Ackroyd, Malloy and Sykes. It even utilized the services of the same producer and leftover background footage from *Kim*. Also like

Soldiers Three (MGM, 1951). Cyril Cusack, Stewart Granger, Robert Newton. (Courtesy Collectors Book Store.)

Soldiers Three (MGM, 1951). Cyril Cusack, Robert Newton, Stewart Granger, David Niven. (Courtesy Collectors Book Store.)

Kim, the project was initially announced in the late 30s as a vehicle for Clark Gable, Spencer Tracy and Wallace Beery. At least the studio had the honesty to state that this production was "Suggested by the Rudyard Kipling stories," even though his name was included in the title. Elements from "The Big Drunk Draf" and "With the Main Guard" can be found if one looks closely.

An oversight running the length of the film was Robert Newton's character of Jock Sykes being called "Bill," perhaps a tribute to his chilling performance as Bill Sykes two years earlier in David Lean's superb rendition of Charles Dickens' *Oliver Twist*.

The sole purpose of the trio in this film is getting drunk. Newton, who was known to bend the elbow on a number of occasions, seemed to actually be in that state throughout the proceedings. He continually repeated the other actors' lines and had a glazed expression in all his scenes.

Once it appears, the plot concerns the colonel of the Rutlandshire Battalion (who tells the story in flashback) on the eve of his retirement. He is having trouble with some local tribesmen; a new colonel is sent to take over, and orders 50 men to an abandoned fort with ammunition wagons. Once there, the fort is penetrated by some of the enemy, who let in the remainder of their forces. In the ensuing battle, surviving British troops are locked in the powder house. Ackroyd deserts to be with his two friends and ends up saving the day for the British. The battle scenes are well-staged and the best part of the picture.

Viewing this movie is recommended only for diehard fans of the leads, not for Kipling aficionados.

The New York Times, March 30, 1951 (Bosley Crowther):

> The whole quality and character of the stories ... have been reduced to sheer slapstick and bombast.... Mulvaney, Learoyd and Ortheris ... are turned out as three clownish fellows who do little but drink and brawl without shrewdness or wit....

Toomai of the Elephants
(short story, from The Jungle Book, 1894)

SYNOPSIS: Ten-year-old Little Toomai, son of Big Toomai, comes to the attention of Petersen Sahib, chief elephant catcher for the Indian Government, when he assists a hunter during a *keddah* (elephant roundup). Petersen speaks to him and is impressed when the boy has his elephant, Kala Nag, lift him in his trunk so that he is almost eye-level with the agent. Petersen asks the boy, "And why didst thou teach thy elephant *that* trick? Was it to help thee steal green corn from the roofs of the houses when the ears are put out to dry?" "Not green corn, Protector of the Poor — melons!" replies Toomai. This causes much merriment among the hunters and *mahouts*. Petersen gives the boy a silver coin and tells him that one day he may be a hunter. He also tells him that *keddahs* are no places for little boys. Toomai asks if that means he is never to become a hunter. The agent responds that when Toomai has seen the elephants dance, he may join all the *keddahs*. The men all laugh again as this is a great joke among them, for no one has ever seen the elephants dance.

Toomai gives the coin to his mother and asks her what is meant by the elephants' dance. His father says it means that he will never be a hunter.

That night, Kala Nag breaks his picket and heads for the forest. Toomai awakes and calls to the beast, who turns back and lifts him onto his back. Together they travel deep into the forest. Finally they reach a spot where many elephants are gathering within a circle of tree trunks. Toomai lies flat on Kala Nag's back to be safe. Kala Nag walks into the center of the circle and begins rhythmically lifting one foot after the other. The other pachyderms follow suit until the very ground shakes with the sound of their stomping feet. At dawn's first light, the animals cease their "dance" and leave the area.

Returning to camp, Toomai tells Petersen that he has seen the elephants dance, and slides off Kala Nag's back in a faint.

After being given some quinine and brandy in milk, Toomai tells Petersen and the hunters what he has witnessed. He tells them to send someone to look at the spot which had been enlarged by the huge animals. They will also see many tracks about the area. He goes to sleep then and Petersen and chief hunter Machua Appa follow Kala Nag's trail to the spot where the elephants had danced. Machua Appa marvels at the sight, for he has been involved with elephants for 45 years and never known any man to see what Little Toomai saw.

That night a feast is held in camp. Toomai is feted and marked on the forehead with the blood of a freshly killed jungle-cock as proof that he is now a forester. Machua Appa holds the boy above his head and declares that henceforth Little Toomai shall be called Toomai of the Elephants, like his grandfather was, for he has seen the elephants dance and is favored by the Elephant-Folk. He exhorts all to honor the boy; at this, all the elephants raise their trunks and trumpet in salute to Toomai.

Elephant Boy

London Films/United Artists; Released April 23, 1937; 80 minutes; Based on *Toomai of the Elephants* from *The Jungle Books* by Rudyard Kipling; DIRECTORS: Robert Flaherty, Vincent Korda; PRODUCER: Alexander Korda; SCREENPLAY: John Collier; PHOTOGRAPHY: Osmond Borradaile; MUSIC: John Greenwood; SCREENPLAY COLLABORATION: Akos Tolnay, Marcia DeSilva; ASSISTANT DIRECTOR: David Flaherty; SUPERVISING EDITOR: William Hornbeck; MUSICAL DIRECTION: Muir Mathieson; EDITOR: Charles Crichton; SOUND RECORDIST: H.G. Cape; PRODUCTION ASSISTANT: Alex de Toth

CAST: Sabu (Toomai), W.E. Holloway (Father), Walter Hudd (Petersen), Allen Jeayes (Machua Appa), Bruce Gordon (Rham Lahl), D. J. Williams (Hunter), [Wilfrid] Hyde-White (Commissioner)

In 1934, Alexander Korda, (1893–1956) head of Britain's most successful film studio, London Films, was approached by famed documentary filmmaker Robert Flaherty (1884–1951). The Canadian-born Flaherty had an idea for a film; he was also desperately in need of money after the box office failure of his *Man of Aran* (1934).

He had co-written a story with his wife about a Mexican boy and a fighting bull. It was based on an incident witnessed by the pair in Mexico in 1928. Korda liked the idea, but had been reading Kipling, and seeing the similarity between Flaherty's story and one of the *Jungle Book* tales, "Toomai of the Elephants," he proposed that the director change his characters to fit the Kipling tale. An agreement was made, the rights were purchased for £5000, and soon Flaherty was off to India to search for a suitable site on which to make his picture.

Settling in Mysore, in southern India, Flaherty and his crew began filming, still lacking a boy to portray Toomai. They tested dozens unsatisfactorily. Then cameraman Osmond Borradaile discovered an 11-year-old apprentice *mahout* at the Maharajah of Mysore's stables. After viewing his test, all the other boys were dismissed. Young Selar Shaik had the job. Alexander Korda changed his name to "Sabu" and he went on to a long career in Britain and the United States, becoming India's only international film star.

Flaherty spent several months in his painstaking manner just shooting background footage. Even when reinforced by Korda's brother Zoltan and later by Hollywood director Monta Bell, he was still unable to satisfy his boss, so all three crews were recalled to Britain in June 1936.

At Denham, Korda's newly completed film complex, noted author John Collier was hired to create a workable storyline for Flaherty's footage. The result was an uncomplicated picture which adhered very closely to its source material. The differences are really

Top: *Elephant Boy* (London Films, 1937). Sabu. Bottom: *Elephant Boy* (London Films, 1937). Allen Jeayes, Sabu, Walter Hudd. (Courtesy Collectors Book Store.)

Elephant Boy (London Films, 1937). Sabu. (Courtesy Collectors Book Store.)

minor, save for the prologue delivered by Toomai, which was added to showcase Sabu's proficiency in English. The variations include a *mahout* who abuses Kala Nag and suffers for it, and Toomai's accompanying Petersen to show him the wild elephant herd rather than remaining asleep in camp. Another difference is that in the film Toomai is motherless, and his father is killed by a tiger. The initial encounter between Toomai and Petersen is almost verbatim from the story.

The film's most powerful scene resulted from a condition known as "musth," a form of temporary madness which strikes elephants. Sabu's elephant suffered from it; Flaherty filmed it and inserted the footage into the story.

The Kipling Society of England was among many who lauded this motion picture. It won the prize for Best Direction at the 1937 Venice Film Festival (the Cannes Film Festival of its day), which was shared by Flaherty and Zoltan Korda, and had a respectable box office return, despite its final cost of $450,000.

The New York Times, April 6 , 1937 (Frank S. Nugent):

> Sabu ... is a sunny-faced, manly little youngster, whose naturalness beneath the camera's scrutiny should bring blushes to the faces of the precocious wonder-children of Hollywood. He's a much better actor than the British players Mr. Flaherty tried to disguise behind frizzed beards and Indian names.... Having a simple story at its

Elephant Boy (London Films, 1937). Sabu, Walter Hudd. (Courtesy Collectors Book Store.)

heart, it has had the wisdom and good taste to tell it simply and without recourse to synthetic sensationalism.

(See also *The Jungle Book*, p. 30)

The Vampire
(poem, 1897)

SYNOPSIS: This hastily-written work, only six short stanzas in length, tells the tale of a man referred to only as a fool ("A fool there was and he made his prayer...") who becomes infatuated with a rather wretched-sounding woman ("a rag and a bone and a hank of hair") and is financially and emotionally destroyed by her.

The Vampire

Selig Pictures; Released November 12, 1910; 1000 feet; DIRECTOR: unknown CAST: Charles Clary

The first filmization of a Kipling work was *The Vampire*, the sole non-copyrighted work from Kipling's canon. Produced by the Selig Polyscope Company, it starred Charles Clary (1873–1931), an Illinois-born stage veteran who had joined Selig earlier that year.

This poem was utilized as text accompaniment for the catalogue for the salon painting of Rudyard's cousin, the artist Philip Burne-Jones. The work depicts a young man sprawled over a settee while a dark-haired, dark-eyed woman in a white robe leans over him. The model for the woman was allegedly the famous stage actress Mrs. Patrick Campbell.

Besides the lack of copyright, the poem is really very vague in its character and plot delineation, not to mention brief, leaving the door open for an imaginative scenarist to make of it what he would.

The Nickelodeon November 15, 1910:

> [T]he Vampire's vogue is on the wane. We have had her in poetry, in painting, in drama, in the dance, and now in the photoplay. Here she has been surrounded by a plot that is too tawdry and stagey for any use, but the vampire lady herself is interesting, being played by an actress who looked the part and acted with rare effectiveness. The producers have spent no little effort in rigging up unusual settings and stage effects, most of which were not worth the trouble.

The New York Dramatic Mirror, November 16, 1910:

> The subject is frankly morbid and disagreeable. From the title one cannot expect anything else, nor does he get it. The vampire was a beautiful woman who delighted in ruining men and in discarding them when she could get nothing more from them. One of her lovers was slain in a duel. His daughter married a foolish young man who also fell a victim to the heartless creature. What her subsequent career was the film does not relate. During the course of her devastation she met only one man who could resist her charm, and he finally married the other woman. The narrative is adequately developed in

mounting and in acting. The vampire is sufficiently beautiful to lend probability to it, although it is avowedly a fanciful collection of events. The use of the duel is especially out of color for duels are obsolete in America.

The Moving Picture World, November 26, 1910:

> Perhaps the attempt is successful in that it will be understood by those familiar with the picture and the poem. But what about those who are unfamiliar with them? Several near the writer were heard to ask what it all meant, and the possibility is strong that many others are in much the same position. It is artistic, it is beautiful in the literary quality it possesses, but it is scarcely plain enough to be understood by the average person in an audience.... [T]he producer failed to convey the sentiment of the poem, however well it was staged and acted.

The Vampire of the Desert

Vitagraph; Released May 16, 1913; 2 reels; Based on the poem *The Vampire; DIRECTOR:* unknown

CAST: Helen Gardner, Flora Finch, Tefft Johnson, Harry Morey, Leah Baird

Moving Picture World, May 31, 1913:

> This two-reel special is well staged and there are good people in the cast.... The picture is described as an allegory; certainly it is too strong on the "highbrow" stuff to serve as entertainment. The first reel is not coherent; the second reel is more understandable, but establishes no particular interest.

The Fool

Big Ben-Union/Pathé (Great Britain); Released July 12, 1913; 3 reels; *WRITER-DIRECTOR:* George Pearson; Based on the poem *The Vampire*

CAST: Godfrey Tearle (Sterndale), Mary Malone (Mrs. Brockwood), James Carew (Arthur Warde), Rex Davis

This was the first film produced under the British branch of Pathé Fréres new banner, Big Ben. It was also director Pearson's first commercial effort, after a year of making educational films. It was shot in a converted basement in Great Portland Street, London. An unknown critic described the film as a "tensely drawn tale of gambling and duplicity...." According to the synopsis in *Bioscope* (July 10, 1913), all ends happily as the fool, Sterndale, is redeemed by Mrs. Brockwood after committing "social suicide." The lady secures her own salvation after being "freed of a villainous husband" by doing social work.

Pearson (1875–1973) later founded his own company and was a key figure in popularizing British films in America. He was the first to suggest the importance of having a national film academy in Britain, which was finally formed in 1947. He was also among the first to receive a Fellowship in the new organization for outstanding creative work in filmmaking.

Godfrey Tearle (1884–1957) was the half-brother of the stage and film actor Conway Tearle. He appeared on stage at age nine and became a fixture on the London stage. His film career began in 1908 and continued well into the sound era, where he was in demand as a character actor.

James Carew (1846–1938) was the husband of legendary stage actress Ellen Terry.

A Fool There Was

William Fox Vaudeville Company; Released January 12, 1915; 6 reels; DIRECTOR: Frank Powell; PRODUCER: William Fox; Based on Porter Emerson Browne's play, which was based on Kipling's poem *The Vampire*; SCENARIO: Roy L. McCardell, Frank Powell; PHOTOGRAPHY: Gene Santoreilli and George Schneiderman

CAST: Theda Bara (The Vampire), Edward José (The Fool), Mabel Frenyear (The Fool's Wife), May Allison (The Wife's Sister), Runa Hodges (The Child), Clifford Bruce (A Friend), Victor Benoit (The Man), Frank Powell (The Doctor), Minna Gale (The Doctor's Fianceé)

One of Theda Bara's few surviving films, *A Fool There Was* caused a sensation in its day. The term "vamp" became a staple of American vocabulary, and the Vampire's command, "Kiss me, my fool!," became almost as popular.

This production was based on a play which was inspired by Kipling's, "The Vampire." Entitled *A Fool There Was* (the opening line of the poem), Porter Emerson Browne's dramatization of the Kipling piece was a hit as soon as it opened in New York in 1909 (See Rudyard Kipling Stage Adaptations.)

William Fox bought the film rights to the play and slowly brought together a cast. Belgian actor Edward José (1880?–1930) was selected for the male lead. He had worked with the director, Frank Powell, at Pathé before joining Fox. He had also done some directing (back at Pathé, he would direct the first filmization of Kipling's *The Light That Failed* in 1916). Of the other cast members, only May Allison, as the Fool's sister-in-law, had any future success in films. Before Bara was selected for the lead, Valeska Suratt, Madeline Traverse and Virginia

Pearson, who had played the role on Broadway, were all considered and rejected. It was director Powell who suggested the Cincinnati-born Bara (née Theodosia Goodman), after seeing her in a small part in *The Stain* (1914). She was signed to a five-year contract, with renewal options, by Fox, starting at $100 per week. (She received a raise to $150 when she discovered that she needed 17 outfits for the picture. Her contract stipulated that she supply her own contemporary clothes.)

The film was swiftly made and just as swiftly edited for release in January 1915. William Fox had already planned a publicity campaign. A now-famous interview had the unknown actress appearing in veils and furs in a room reeking of incense, reciting a phony biography — then rushing to the window gasping for air once the reporters were gone. At New York's Strand Theater, an actor recited the Kipling poem prior to each screening. The picture was a smash hit, and Theda Bara (1885–1955) skyrocketed into stardom overnight. Five years and 38 films later, her career was over. After a stab at stage work, she appeared in two minor films in the mid-20s before retiring for good.

A Fool There Was opens with the first verse of the poem and introductory shots of the Fool and the Woman, as the vamp was called. The Fool's family life is depicted as all sweetness and light. In contrast, the Vamp is shown browbeating her male friends with

A Fool There Was (Fox, 1915). Theda Bara, Edward Jose.

great relish. Given an official appointment overseas, the Fool sails on a cruise ship. Reading of his appointment, the Vamp books passage on the same boat. Just after the Fool leaves his family, a storm arises. Seeing it through the window, the wife wonders, "Storm and darkness. Is it an omen?" Either she's prescient or she read the entire script.

As the Woman arrives at the pier, a derelict confronts her; he is one of her former victims. She calls a policeman to take him away and boards the ship. She is followed by her current suitor, who is likewise rebuffed; he commits suicide right there on the deck, but at least has the consideration to do it off-screen.

Two months later (several months are skipped throughout the picture, much to this viewer's delight) the Fool is in the Woman's clutches. From Italy, he sends a cablegram to his wife, informing her of the situation.

Some months afterward, back in the States, the wife and child are riding in an open car when they encounter the husband and the Woman, also in an open car. The husband hides his face as the heartbroken wife passes. Later, the Woman chides him for not nodding and smiling, as she did.

Thinking of divorce, the wife's sister backs her, but the Friend urges her to stand by her man.

Things go from bad to worse for the Fool. He becomes an alcoholic; soon both his secretary and the Woman leave him. His wife visits him; he is by now a total wreck and very aged-looking. Just then the Woman returns and reclaims him. The wife makes one more attempt to win back her husband, bringing their little daughter along with

her. The Woman appears again, and the Fool chooses her over his family.

Soon after, the Fool has a fit and destroys some furnishings. This results in a fatal stroke. In the final shot, the Woman laughs as she strews rose petals over his corpse, a detail retained from Browne's play.

Filmed almost without style, *A Fool There Was* made its mark due to the depiction of the female lead, played with gusto by newcomer Bara. At a time when women still could not vote, seeing one of their number taking charge in any given situation was a real novelty. Who knows? Maybe this film was instrumental in the eventual enfranchisement of women.

Since this is based on one of the least of Kipling's works, this picture can be recommended only to those interested in seeing Theda Bara in action.

A Fool There Was

Fox; Released September 10, 1922; 10 reels; DIRECTOR: Emmet Flynn; PRODUCER: William Fox; SCENARIO: Bernard McConville, from the play by Porter Emerson Browne; PHOTOGRAPHY: Lucien Andriot

CAST: Estelle Taylor (Gilda Fontaine), Lewis Stone (John Schuyler), Irene Rich (Mrs. Schuyler), Marjorie Daw (Nell Winthrop), Mahlon Hamilton (Tom Morgan), Muriel Dana (Muriel Schuyler), Wallace MacDonald (Avery Parmelee), William V. Mong (Boggs), Harry Lonsdale (Parks)

This ill-advised remake was a failure all around. It was savaged by the critics and avoided by audiences. This time the Vamp has a name, Gilda Fontaine.

Harrison's Reports, July 22, 1922:

A more disgusting theme has not formed the foundation of a motion

A Fool There Was (Fox, 1922). Estelle Taylor. (Courtesy BFI Stills, Posters and Designs.)

picture lately.... The thought of a man, who seems to be about 55 years old, becoming infatuated with a heartless vampire and abandoning a loving wife, two adorable little children, friends, wealth and everything that made his life happy, and following the vampire is demoralizing.... [T]he action is full of dramatic, as well as technical errors. The suicide of the young man at the beginning, for instance, is altogether out of proportion to the effect sought. The showing of the vampire getting into the same boat as the hero gives away the conclusion—any one would know that the hero is to become infatuated with the vampire. The return of the pair from abroad is done suddenly, and without sufficient preparation. It is also obvious that the wife's leaving for a short time her husband after their reconciliation is done for the purpose of giving to the vampire the opportunity of becharming him again. ...Aside from the acting of beautiful Estelle Taylor and of Lewis Stone, and the good photography, there is hardly anything else to recommend it.

Wee Willie Winkie
(short story, 1888)

SYNOPSIS: Wee Willie Winkie is a blond, freckled-faced six-year-old, the son of Col. WIlliams of the 195th. He makes a friend of a subaltern named Brandis, whom he calls "Coppy" because of his red hair.

One day Winkie accidentally burns a wagon full of hay and is confined to quarters. From a window he sees Miss Allardyce, Coppy's fiancée, going out for a ride. He asks where she is going and she says, "Across the river." This river, which is dry at this time of year, is, in the boy's mind, the boundary keeping Goblins and Bad Men at bay. Fearing for Miss Allardyce's safety, he breaks arrest and rides after her.

From a distance he sees her horse fall. She sustains a severely twisted ankle and cannot stand. When he reaches her, she tells him to go for help. Instead, he sends his mount back to the post, for he has been taught that a man must always look after a girl.

Suddenly some Afghan men appear; Winkie tells them to go to the outpost for help and they will be paid. They merely laugh at him. The men decide to hold the pair for ransom. Din Mahommed, however, is for returning them then, for the boy is highly regarded and the British would wreak terrible vengeance if he were to be harmed.

The boy's horse returns to the post and a search party sets out to find him. The Afghanis are still debating what to do when their lookout signals that the British are approaching. The Afghanis scatter.

The men of the 195th carry Winkie back to the post. Miss Allardyce puts in a good word for the boy with his father, so that he is not punished for having broken his arrest. Winkie explains his actions to Coppy, who calls him a hero. The lad replies that he must not call him "Wee Willie Winkie" any more. "I'm Percival William Wlliams."

And in this manner did Wee Willie Winkie enter into his manhood.

Wee Willie Winkie

20th Century-Fox; Released July 30, 1937 (with tinted sequences); 99 minutes; DIRECTOR: John Ford; PRODUCER: Darryl F. Zanuck; ASSOCIATE PRODUCER: Gene Markey; SCREENPLAY: Ernest Pascal, Julian Josephson, from the story by Rudyard Kipling; PHOTOGRAPHY: Arthur Miller; SET DECORATOR: Thomas Little; MUSIC: Alfred Newman; EDITOR: Walter Thompson; COSTUMES: Gwen Wakeling; ASSISTANT DIRECTOR: Ed O'Fearna

CAST: Shirley Temple (Priscilla Williams), Victor McLaglen (Sgt. MacDuff), C. Aubrey Smith (Col. Williams), June Lang (Joyce Williams), Michael Whalen (Lt. "Coppy" Brandes), Cesar Romero (Khoda Khan), Constance Collier (Mrs. Allardyce), Douglas Scott (Mott), Willie Fung (Mohammed Dihn), Gavin Muir (Capt. Bibberbeigh), Brandon Hurst (Bagby), Lionel Pape (Major Allardyce), Clyde Cook (Pipe Major Sneath), Lauri Beatty (Elsie Allardyce), Lionel Braham (Major General Hammond), Mary Forbes (Mrs. McMonachie), Cyril McLaglen (Corporal Tummel), Pat Somerset (Officer), Hector Sarno (Conductor), Scotty Mattraw (Merchant), Jack Pennick (Soldier), Noble Johnson (Sikh Policeman)

The major difference between this adaptation and its source was casting a girl in the role of Winkie. The girl being Shirley Temple (b. 1928), and she being the biggest money-making star in Hollywood at the time, no one quibbled. She has a mother, but no father in the film; the colonel-father of the story becomes the grandfather here, possibly another bow to casting. Venerable British character actor C. Aubrey Smith (1863–1948) played the role in his patented gruff but loving manner. Sgt. MacDuff, a character added by the screenwriters, was played with his usual soft-hearted swagger by army and film veteran Victor McLaglen. *Wee Willie Winkie* being only 12 pages long, characters and events had to be fleshed out to make a feature film.

Priscilla Williams and her mother, a widow, go to India to stay with her father-in-law, the colonel of a frontier regiment. At the depot, a ruckus occurs when some smuggled rifles fall from a wagon and are discovered by the police. The leader of the hillmen is captured and taken to the fort. Priscilla picks up the necklace he had lost, later taking it to him at the jail. The chieftain blesses her.

Priscilla tries to fit in at the post, and does for a while, befriending Sgt.

Wee Willie Winkie (20th Century–Fox, 1937). Victori McLaglen, Shirley Temple.

Wee Willie Winkie (20th Century–Fox, 1937). Cesar Romero, Shirley Temple.

MacDuff, who takes her under his wing. She is given a uniform and a toy gun and allowed to drill with the privates. MacDuff, feeling she needs a more soldierly name, christens her "Wee Willie Winkie," after a character in a Scottish song. Meanwhile, her mother and "Coppy" have taken a shine to each other. Miss Allardyce is relegated to a minor part in the film, always whining about losing Lt. Brandes to Mrs. Williams. As in the story, Winkie dubs Lt. Brandes "Coppy" for the color of his hair.

One night the hillmen raid the arsenal and free their leader, Khoda Khan, from the jail. Lt. Brandes was off with Mrs. Williams when he had sentry duty; he is arrested for deserting his post. The hillmen cut all telegraph and phone wires. A patrol is sent out to repair them and is ambushed; Sgt. MacDuff dies of his wounds at the fort.

Mohammed Dihn, a sepoy, is really a spy for Khoda Khan. After Winkie has a talk with the colonel about the present situation, she decides to go see Khoda Khan and talk him into stopping the imminent war. She runs into Dihn, who offers to lead her to Khan. Once at Khan's hideout, he feels the British will follow and the hillmen will be able to wipe them out. The British do follow, but keep their

Wee Willie Winkie (20th Century–Fox, 1937). Poster.

distance, sending a note to Khan to deliver the girl or be attacked. Khan refuses and the colonel decides to parley with him. Winkie joins them and somehow manages to bring about an understanding and avert a war. Lt. Brandes apparently ends up with Winkie's mother and becomes her stepfather.

Wee Willie Winkie is basically a Temple vehicle, but John Ford does not let the fact interfere too much with his style. The requisite humorous scenes with McLaglen are here, and close attention is paid to British military ritual. A little more respect is accorded the hillmen, as they are not afraid of encountering the British, as the Afghanis in the story are.

Instead of being so mischievous as to cause his arrest, this distaff Winkie is merely forbidden from joining in any more soldierly activities. It is doubtful that audiences would have stood for Shirley Temple causing a fire, even accidentally.

It is hard to say who comes out ahead in this Temple-Kipling mix, but as a film it is worth watching.

The New York Times July 24, 1937 (Frank S. Nugent):

> [I]t is a pleasing enough little fiction sure to delight every Temple addict.... The photography, in warm sepia and restful blue tones, is a pleasant change from the ordinary black-and-white stock.

Without Benefit of Clergy
(short story, 1890)

SYNOPSIS: John Holden, a British government employee, is living secretly with a 16-year-old Indian girl, Ameera, who is expecting their child. Holden is ordered on special duty for two weeks. He gives a pre-written telegram to the watchman of the house as he departs. It is to be sent when the child arrives. He does not receive the telegram while on duty and returns to find that he has a son.

Leaving his wife to rest, he goes outside, where the watchman hands him an old saber with which to sacrifice two goats for the child's safety. Holden slays the goats and the watchman claims the meat.

A while later, Ameera tells her husband that she has prayed to both the Prophet and the Virgin Mary, and that if necessary, she shall die in place of either her child or her husband.

Still in its infancy, their child dies suddenly from autumn fever. The parents are grief-stricken; Ameera has to be restrained from throwing herself down a well.

The following summer, a cholera epidemic strikes the region. The English all send their wives to the hills. Holden begs his wife to go, too, but she refuses. One day the watchman brings news to Holden that his wife has the cholera. Holden races to her side. He listens as she tells him to keep nothing of hers and to always remember her. Her last words are: "I bear witness that there is no God but—thee, beloved."

Holden mourns for her while his mother-in-law removes all the furniture. When the body-washers arrive, he finally leaves. At his office, his butler, Ahmed Khan, tries to get him to eat in order to ease his grief.

Three days later the devastated widower returns to the empty house. There he meets the landlord, Durga Dass, who asks Holden if he still wishes to let the place. Assured that the place will be let again if he doesn't renew, he says he will continue to rent it. But Dass says he would rather raze the house and sell the lumber, allowing the city to build a road through the property "so that no man shall say where the house stood."

Without Benefit of Clergy

Robert Brunton Productions/ Pathé; Released July 1921; 5,200 feet; DIRECTOR: James Young; SCENARIO: Randolph Lewis
CAST: Virginia Brown Faire (Ameera), Thomas Holding (John Holden), Evelyn Selbie (Ameera's Mother), Otto Lederer (Afghan Money Lender), Boris Karloff (Ahmed Khan), Nigel DeBrulier (Pir Khan), Herbert Prior (Hugh Sanders), Ruth Sinclair (Alice Sanders), E.G. Miller (Michael Devenish), Philippe DeLacey (Tota at Five).

Without Benefit of Clergy was the only adaptation of a Kipling work in which the author took an active part, furnishing the set designs and collaborating on the script. The authenticity of the sets received the endorsement of one Harry Corson Clarke, a famed globetrotter of the day.

The female lead was given to 17-year-old Virginia Brown Faire (1904–1980), a beauty contest winner who had appeared in some East Coast productions before being signed by Universal.

All that exists of this picture is a six-minute clip which includes the story's highlights. It appears to be a very faithful adaptation save for the beginning, which depicts a possible prologue to the action as told in the short story. We see Ameera's mother being told by a money-lender that he knows a man who will pay a handsome dowry for her daughter. Ameera is taken by the money-lender to the man, but is shocked to find a very old man to be her prospective husband. She runs from the house, but is caught by the money-lender. Just then Thomas Holden is passing by with his butler, Ahmed Khan. He intercedes, allowing the girl to go free, while casting a favorable eye upon her. He later pays the mother a very tidy sum for Ameera, and the two begin living together. From that point on, the film is a true rendition of the source material, with some of the intertitles being taken verbatim from it. The characters of the Sanders, Pir Khan and Michael Devenish are not seen in the clip. One critic complained of a surfeit of intertitles; even in this clip they are numerous.

Harrison's Reports, June 25, 1921:

Mr. James Young has certainly made an artistic picture out of Rudyard Kipling's story "Without Benefit of Clergy." It not only holds the interest, but also appeals to the emotions of pathos. The convincing acting of the characters, particularly that of Virginia Brown Faire and Thomas Holding, makes the spectator take an active part, and feel their joys and sorrows as intensely as they themselves feel them. Little five-year-old Philippe De Lacey, who assumes the role of the hero and heroine's only child, with his sweetness as well as naturalness endears himself to the spectator.

The story is a tragedy, and treats of a British Government employ, living in India, who falls in love with a native

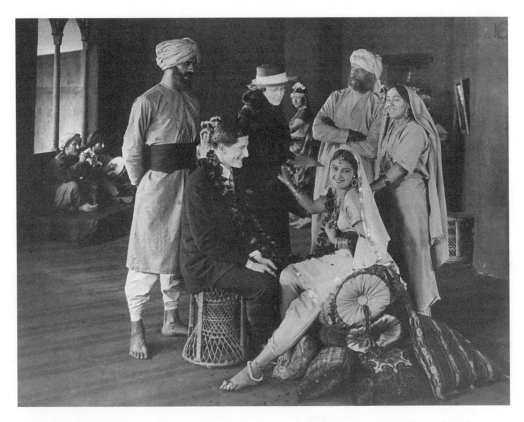

Without Benefit of Clergy (Robert Brunton, 1911). Boris Karloff, Thomas Holding, Virginia Brown Faire.

woman. They have a child. The woman loves her husband and her child devotedly, and the husband reciprocates that sentiment. The child becomes ill and dies, and father and mother become heart-broken. A cholera epidemic strikes the territory, as a result of which people fall dead right and left. The wife dies; so the hero, heart-broken and unconsolable, leaves the country to seek solace in other parts, far away from the place of his sad memories.

The scenes showing the Hindus dropping dead in the streets as a result of the cholera epidemic is not very pleasant, but necessary to the play....

Moving Picture World, July 2, 1921:

Having set out to produce a screen version of a Rudyard Kipling story, the Pathé Company went about it with great care. The story was selected by Kipling himself ... and the distinguished author put his stamp of approval on the scenario and made drawings of the sets and properties so that the local color should be correct. These instructions have been faithfully carried out by the director. The atmosphere of India is always present in the picture. The story ... has strong human interest but lacks the variety of incident and unexpected turn of plot to give it physical action. There are long stretches of pretty domestic scenes that could be curtailed to advantage....

Virginia Brown Faire is an excellent selection physically for Ameera, the native girl, and is earnest and appealing, but there are depths of feeling in the character that she does not reach. The same criticism applies to Thomas Holding as the engineer. The part has all of Kipling's close study of emotion and range of sensibility, and calls for its adequate expression. Mr. Holding is always sincere but never fully equal to his task. Evelyn Selbie, Otto Lederer, Boris Karloff and Nigel DeBrulier are entirely satisfactory in East Indian roles....

H. Rider Haggard Filmography

Allan Quatermain
(novel, 1887)

SYNOPSIS: The introduction is an entry from Allan Quatermain's diary, dated two years earlier. His son Harry has died of smallpox. Now age 63, the hunter and guide is living in England. Henry Curtis and Capt. Good visit him and propose an African expedition to relieve their boredom. Quatermain proposes going to the Isle of Lanu, about 300 miles north of Zanzibar, for no white outsider has ever been there and there is a legend about a lost white race which dwells there.

Stopping at the British Consulate on Lanu, they learn of a man who had been at the home of a Scottish missionary upriver. He had been to a place where he found white people living in stone houses. Quatermain tries to hire some Wakoati men without success. One of them turns out to be his old Zulu friend Umslopogaas, who persuades the others to join the white men.

Three days later, on the river, they are spotted by a Masai warrior. They go ashore for dinner and find signs of a Masai encampment. Though they sleep in their canoes upon the water, they are attacked anyhow, losing one bearer.

They manage to keep the canoes from running ashore where the Masai awaited. They reach the home of the Scottish missionary without further incident. MacKenzie, the missionary, takes them in and they are served dinner by a French fugitive from justice named Alphonse. The latter provides the comic relief, boasting of his prowess as the descendant of mighty soldiers.

Quatermain inquires about the man who had stopped there. MacKenzie shows him an unusual sword which the man said he had acquired from the white tribe. Unfortunately, the man was killed by a lion on the grounds one night.

Allan befriends MacKenzie's young daughter Flossie. When she sets out to find a rare lily to give him and fails to return, everyone becomes apprehensive. Umslopogaas is certain there will be a battle.

That night, the head of one of Flossie's guides is thrown onto the veranda. A spy sent out by the missionary reports that there are 250 Masai approaching and they have Flossie and her nurse. The Masai send a messenger with the proposal that a white man be exchanged for Flossie. MacKenzie is told that his daughter will be killed if he refuses the terms. Quatermain volunteers to go, with a view toward suicide first. MacKenzie vetoes this idea. The messenger is told he will have an answer at dawn.

Umslopogaas devises a battle plan: though it is 30 against 250, an unexpected night attack should succeed. The Zulu slays the sentry, and the others begin to fire into the sleeping warriors. As Flossie makes her escape, she is chased by two Masai. Quatermain shoots one and the girl kills the other with the derringer she always carries.

The tide of battle begins to turn in the enemy's favor until one Masai's spear fails to wound Umslopogaas. Crying that the Zulu is bewitched, the man panics his fellows, who turn and flee. The battle won, the whites discover Alphonse hiding in a tree.

A week later, the British party leaves, taking Alphonse with them. MacKenzie is persuaded to move before the Masai can retaliate; he chooses to go to England.

Two months later, the British lose all their donkeys to tsetse fly bites. While navigating a deep lake in a crater, the party is swept away by a vortex through a long tunnel. At one point the heat becomes so intense that the water boils and the men are forced to remove their clothing. They come upon a column-like jet of white flame about a half-mile ahead: "[I]t struck the roof and spread out some 40 feet in diameter, falling back in curved sheets of fire shaped like the petals of a full-blown rose." Quatermain manages to steer the canoe past this phenomenon after the others have all passed out. He also passes out; when he awakes, the water is cold again. He awakens his compan-

ions with water. They drink and dress and find that they are outside again, floating down between two cliffs. Drifting onto a pebbled shore, they hear their voices echo off the cliffs. As they dine on cold meat, hundreds of huge crabs appear, attracted by the smell. After fighting off the determined creatures, the party resumes its journey.

Eventually they drift onto a large lake, where after an hour they perceive a sailing boat headed their way. When they are within hailing distance, they spot a white couple aboard the craft. The British try several different languages in hopes of a response, all to no avail. After donning their finest outfits, they turn their canoe towards shore. Suddenly a number of boats appears, one of which carries an old man with a sword. Attempting to impress these people, the outsiders fire upon a nearby family of hippos. One is only wounded and wrecks the first boat which they had encountered. Allan kills the hippo before it can harm the woman, as her male companion swims toward shore.

The outsiders are led into the harbor, where they behold a city of red granite in which one building of white granite stands out. They are fed and taken to the palace.

In the center of the hall is a piece of black marble shaped like a chair. They later learn that the rulers of Zu-Vendis, as the country is known, swear upon the chair to safeguard the empire and uphold its traditions. They meet the country's rulers, twin sisters named Nyleptha and Sorais. The former is fair, the latter is dark. As they pass the outsiders, the eyes of Curtis and Nyleptha meet, causing the latter to blush.

The day's events are related to the queens. Agon, the High Priest, is outraged by the killing of the hippos, for that animal is sacred. That particular family was tame and fed daily by the priests. Agon wants the outsiders burned alive. Nyleptha pleads for the strangers' lives, turning to a man named Nasta, who has hopes of marrying her. But he saw the look which passed between her and Curtis and does not take her side.

Quatermain explains to the queens how his party arrived in Zu-Vendis and discovers various facts about the country. Gold is plentiful and silver scarce, so the latter is legal tender. The capital city is called Milosis.

The next day, the strangers are taken to the temple via chariot. As Agon begins a chant, Nyleptha signals Quatermain with her eye to move away from the center of the floor. As the chant ends, the floor opens suddenly, revealing a fiery furnace below. The British draw their revolvers. The priests draw swords and attack them; Quatermain shoots one, who falls into the furnace. The others suddenly halt. Sorais issues a command and the strangers and queens are surrounded by a circle of soldiers.

The strangers are given a reprieve until they can learn the language, so as to explain their presence.

They are initially tutored by old men, of whom they grow tired. They are given young female tutors. All is well until Allan playfully throws a pillow at one of them just as Nyleptha enters. She orders the woman slain, but Curtis intercedes, and the girls are sent away and replaced by the previous teachers.

Curtis confesses his love for Nyleptha to Allan, who arranges a secret meeting for the pair in the Great Hall. They pledge their love for each other.

Nasta then proposes to Nyleptha and is backed by Agon, who states the political advantage of such a union. Nyleptha gives no answer. Nasta begs leave to return to his country up north and invites the queen to visit along with the strangers. She agrees, saying she will bring two men for every one of Nasta's. In short, there will be war.

Meanwhile, Good has fallen for Sorais, even to serenading her one night. But she also loves Curtis. During an audience with the latter, he tells her he is engaged to her sister. She dismisses him. Nyleptha learns of this, but is too busy preparing for war with Nasta to do anything about it immediately.

Sorais attempts to kill Nyleptha one night, but is prevented by Good. Umslopogaas had followed both and reports the event to Quatermain.

Sorais publicly confronts Nyleptha regarding her wish to marry Curtis. Nyleptha's answer is to put a gold torque around Curtis' neck, thus marrying him. Sorais becomes enraged after her sister tells of her assassination attempt, and declares war. She departs, taking her followers with her and kidnapping Alphonse on the way.

The royal couple is officially married by the High Priest, and yet again by Allan Quatermain, according to the rites of the Anglican Church.

Sorais is able to muster 100,000 troops against Nyleptha's 60,000, but the latter picks the battle site. Quatermain, Good and Curtis lead her army forward to the site. Both sides maneuver on the first day. The battle begins on the second day. Allan saves Good's life, but sustains a serious wound. After several hours' fighting, Sorais' troops fall back. A lone horseman suddenly rides into the camp of Nyleptha's forces; it is Alphonse, who has managed to escape his captors. He informs Quatermain and the others of a plan to have Nyleptha murdered by Nasta and Agon at dawn.

Allan and Umslopogaas immediately set out for Milosis, which is 100 miles away. With 20 miles to go, Allan's horse gives out; Umslopogaas gives him his and runs the rest of the way. At Milosis they get to the inner gate, which is opened by a faithful guard who had been seized and bound earlier, but who had managed to get free. He tells the pair that the rest of the guard have disappeared; he fears betrayal. They find Nyleptha alive and have her send two of her maids to bring faithful men from the city. As they flee, they find the doors to the temple have been removed, making access easy for the enemy. They build up a wall with marble blocks. Umslopogaas offers to defend the spot. He sleeps there and is joined by the guard next morning as the enemy rushes them. The Zulu kills Agon, but the guard is killed just as aid arrives. Nasta rushes the Zulu and deals him a mortal blow with his sword. Umslopogaas manages to pick up Nasta and hurls him to the rocks below. Then he struggles through the palace until he reaches the sacred stone. Calling for one more good stroke, he swings his ax at the stone so that "the massive marble split with a rending sound into a score

of pieces." This, it turns out, fulfills a prophecy; he and Allan are given great honors. The latter passes out and remains unconscious for two weeks. He awakens to see Good, who tells him of their victory and the capture of Sorais.

Umslopogaas' body is placed in a special coffin at the top of the stairs he defended so valiantly, facing Zululand, as he wished.

Sorais is brought before Nyleptha, who must condemn her to death. Curtis, however, asks for her life as a boon, and his wish is granted. Good says he will take her as his wife if she will have him. Sorais makes a speech about her feelings, then jabs the small spear she had been carrying into her side and expires.

One month later Curtis is formally made king. Quatermain is too ill to attend the ceremony. Some time later, he makes the final entry in his memoirs (i.e., the manuscript). He dies the next day. The narrative is completed by Curtis, who tells of the discovery of a passage out of Zu-Vendis. Alphonse departs with the manuscript, in the hopes of getting it published. Capt. Good develops a navy; Nyleptha gives birth to a son. The final note is by George Curtis, Henry's brother. He has received the manuscript by post from France, but he is unable to locate Alphonse.

Allan Quatermain

African Film Productions (South Africa); Released August 1, 1919; DIRECTOR: H. Lisle Lucoque; PHOTOGRAPHY: W. Bowden

CAST: Hal Lawrence (Allan Quatermain), Mabel May (Nyleptha), Elise

Hamilton (Sorais), Halford Hamlin (Sir Henry Curtis), Ray Brown (Capt. John Good, R.N.), Umpikayiboni (Umslopogaas), A.O. Glisson (Reverend Mr. MacKenzie), Florence Roberts (Mrs. MacKenzie), George Taylor (Prince Nasta), Abie Barker (Alphonse), Violet Woolls-Sampson (Flossie), Edward Vincent (Agon)

Yet another lost silent film, this was the second of three films directed in South Africa by Briton Horace Lisle Lucoque (?–1925).

King Solomon's Treasure

Gold Key Television/Canafex-Towers (Canada); 1978 (not released theatrically); 88 minutes; Based on *Allan Quatermain*; DIRECTOR: Alvin Rakoff; EXECUTIVE PRODUCER: Harry Alan Towers; PRODUCER: Susan A. Lewis; PRODUCTION MANAGERS: John Comfort, Mychle Boudrias; ASSISTANT DIRECTOR: Mireille Goulet; PHOTOGRAPHY: Paul van der Linden; SCREENPLAY: Colin Turner, Allan Pryor; CAMERA OPERATORS: Alan C. Smith, Yves Dupeau; EDITOR: Stan Cole; ART DIRECTORS: Vianney Gauthier, James Wetherup; MUSIC: Lewis W. Lehman; MAKEUP: Marie-Angle Protat; SOUND EDITORS: Patrick Drummond, Ellen Adams, Gary Oppenheimer SOUND RECORDING: Jean Rival; Filmed on location in Swaziland and Montreal.

CAST: David McCallum (Sir Henry Curtis), John Colicos (Allan Quatermain), Britt Ekland (Queen Nyleptha), Patrick Macnee (Capt. Good, R.N.), Ken Gumpu (Umslopogaas), Wilfrid Hyde-White (Oldest Club Member), John Quentin (Stetopatris), Veronique Beliveau (Neva), Sam Williams (Matawani), Hugh Rowse (Rev. McKenzie), Fiona Fraser (Mrs. McKenzie), Camilla Hutton (Flossie McKenzie)

A press release capsulized the plot of this film thus: "Three explorers cross the uncharted African bush to discover the lost city of the Phoenicians and their fabled treasure."

Despite the use of African locations, this production falls far short of being a decent Haggard adaptation. Made at a time when the Canadian film industry was in desperate straits, it included unconvincing dinosaur models and changed Zu-Vendis into Phoenicia. It did include the Scottish missionary family, however, proving that someone involved had read the source material.

Allan Quatermain and the Lost City of Gold

Cannon Group; Released January 1987; 110 minutes; Based on *Allan Quatermain*; DIRECTOR: Gary Nelson; PRODUCERS: Yoram Globus, Menahem Golan; EXECUTIVE PRODUCER: Avi Lerner; SCREENPLAY: Gene Quintano; PHOTOGRAPHY: Alex Phillips; MUSIC: Michael Linn; PRODUCTION DESIGNER: Trevor Williams; EDITORS: Gary Griffen, Alain Jacubowicz, David Loewenthal; SET DECORATOR: Portia Iversen; COSTUMES: Marianne Fassler; FIRST ASSISTANT DIRECTOR: Nicholas Batchelor; SECOND ASSISTANT DIRECTOR: Douglas G. Gardner; ASSOCIATE EDITOR: Kobi Dagan; STUNT COORDINATOR: Don Pike

CAST: Richard Chamberlain (Allan Quatermain), Sharon Stone (Jesse Huston), James Earl Jones (Umslopogaas), Henry Silva (Agon), Martin Rabbett (Robeson Quatermain), Robert Donner (Swarma), Doghmi Larbi (Nasta), Aileen Marson (Queen Nyleptha), Cassandra Peterson (Sorais), Rory Kilalea (Dumont), Alex Heyns (Dutchman), Themsi Times (Nurse), Philip Boucher (Bartender), Stuart Goakes (Trader), Fidelis Cheza (Eshowe Warrior Chief), Nick Lesley (Toothless Arab), George Chiota (George)

In terms of fidelity to its source material, this film is superior to its companion, *King Solomon's Mines* [q.v.], which was shot at the same African locations. The first half of this picture bears little resemblance to the book, save for a few details, but once the protagonists reach the lost city, it follows its source much more closely than the aforementioned 1985 release.

At the start, Quatermain is set to go to the U.S., where he and Jesse are to be married. A man chased by hooded natives makes it to Quatermain's house babbling of a golden city. He is murdered that night, but not before his story has whetted Allan's appetite for adventure, for the hunter's brother and best friends had gone looking for that city.

While trying to recruit men for a safari, Allan runs into his old Zulu friend Umslopogaas, who supplies him with five men. From this point on, the film basically becomes faithful to its source, save for the omission of the Scottish missionary and his family, and replacing Alphonse with an Indian as comic relief. The party encounters hostile natives along a river and travels through a rock tunnel which becomes heated from a pillar of flame. Instead of crabs, they are attacked by snake-like creatures. Along the way, the bodies of Quatermain's friends, here called Hudson and Tremont, are found at different points. This is the first major difference with the novel after Umslopogaas' entrance, for Curtis and Good survive the entire adventure.

While the lost city is not as impressive as many movie sets, its inhabitants are more politically correct, being a mix of blacks and whites, instead of white only as in the book. Instead of the hippopotamus, the lion is

Allan Quartermain and the Lost City of Gold (Cannon, 1987). Richard Chamberlain, Sharon Stone. (Courtesy Collectors Book Store.)

the sacred animal, and Allan is forced to shoot one in self-defense, incurring the wrath of the High Priest, Agon. Allan does find his younger brother, another variant with the source.

Lord Nasta is portrayed as a savage war lord and, instead of a chair, an altar is the symbol of the people's religion. Asked to show his power, Quatermain has Umslopogaas split the altar with his battle axe.

The High Priest here has an obsession with gold, which he melts and pours on people to make golden statues. Naturally, he suffers the same fate at the end of the battle, a great variance with the novel.

Agon and Sorais team up against Nyleptha, as in the novel, but the

Allan Quatermain and the Lost City of Gold (Cannon, 1987). James Earl Jones, Martin Rabbett, Richard Chamberlain, Sharon Stone. (Courtesy Collectors Book Store.)

battle is fought at night and in the city, rather than during the day on a distant plain. Here neither Allan nor Umslopogaas dies after their triumph, but Nasta, Sorais and Agon all meet their deaths, as in the source.

Over all, *Allan Quatermain and the Lost City of Gold* ranks as a worthwhile effort, nearly matching the mood of the source work, although Richard Chamberlain's Quatermain is too exuberant.

The picture grossed almost $4 million domestically.

Variety, February 2, 1987:

Gene Quintano's embarrassing screenplay jettisons Haggard's enduring fantasy and myth-making in favor of a back-of-the-envelope plotline ... story completely runs out of gas once the heroes arrive at their destination.

Beatrice
(novel, 1890)

SYNOPSIS: Beatrice Granger, a schoolteacher and the loveliest woman in Wales, meets Geoffrey Bingham one evening while she is canoeing and he is hunting curlew. She is lost and Bingham takes her home — a five-mile canoe trip. During the trip they get to know each other a little. They are caught in a squall and their paddle breaks. When Geoffrey asks Beatrice to pray, she tells him she is not a Christian. The canoe is tossed onto a large flat rock and Bingham is knocked unconscious. As he goes under, Beatrice grabs his hair and pulls him up, calling for help from the nearby lighthouse. As she begins to slip, old Edward arrives and saves them both. They are taken inside; Bingham comes around first, and finds his wife standing over him. Their daughter heard that her daddy was drowned, so she came to check on him. As she leaves, assured that her husband is all right, she is approached by a man in a cloak, who asks after Beatrice. Mrs. Bingham tells him that she is dead.

After hours of attempting to revive Beatrice, the doctor is successful. The man in the cloak hears about this and goes to see if it is true. He meets Elizabeth, Beatrice's sister, and she confirms the fact. The man, a wealthy squire named Owen Davies, is relieved, for he is in love with Beatrice. Elizabeth, however, is in love with him.

There is a flashback to the first meeting of Beatrice and Squire Davies. She is an adolescent and he the new owner of Bryngelly Castle. Davies falls for her after a while, but she despises him. Since there is no local library, Davies acquires books so Beatrice can satisfy her thirst for knowledge.

Bingham goes to see Beatrice; she awakens as he enters her room. She tells him of a dream she had, which indicated that their lives are now bound together, a thought which he had already had.

There is no love between Bingham and his wife, Lady Honoria. When she takes a three-week vacation, Geoffrey and his little daughter take rooms at the Vicarage, Beatrice's home; her father is the local vicar.

Davies proposes to Beatrice, but is rejected. He gets her to agree to let him ask again after one year. Elizabeth, who had been spying on them, talks to Davies after Beatrice leaves. She tries to make him believe that he has a rival in Bingham, hoping that the squire will throw over Beatrice for her.

When Beatrice tells Bingham about Davies' proposal, he is surprised, having thought the two were already engaged. Beatrice later helps Geoffrey solve a tough legal problem and he begins to move up in his profession.

Beatrice realizes she is in love with Geoffrey Bingham after a violent occurrence at an auction; a man was killed and she was wrongly led to believe it was Geoffrey. Each dreams of the other that night; the next day, Bingham asks Beatrice about a certain poem, one which she had recited to herself the night before. The lawyer realizes his love for the schoolteacher. Bingham departs for home; they agree to write each other. Geoffrey asks what to do with their situation, and Beatrice replies that dying is the only way to forget their feelings for each other.

Back home, things grow worse between Geoffrey and Honoria. She does not love their daughter, preferring material pleasures.

Bingham becomes a sought-after attorney, then his uncle dies, leaving him £20,000. Out of contempt he showers his wife with expensive gifts, and they return to their old, more fashionable residence. When asked to stand for a seat in Parliament, Geoffrey asks Beatrice's advice, and she encourages him; he wins a seat in the House of Commons.

When Mr. Granger is unable to collect enough tithes to keep going, his daughter Elizabeth convinces him to go to Bingham for a loan. He does so successfully. Geoffrey then goes to Bryngelly for a short visit. After speaking with Mr. Granger, Elizabeth and Mr. Davies, Geoffrey takes it upon himself to advise Beatrice to marry Davies. She becomes angry at first, then kisses the lawyer, admitting her love for him.

That night, during a storm, Beatrice walks in her sleep and ends up in Bingham's room. A door crashing awakens her, but she passes out. Elizabeth and her father are also awakened. Seeing Beatrice gone, her sister suspects the worst, and sees Geoffrey carrying Beatrice back to her room.

Geoffrey and Beatrice meet on the beach the next morning and promise to never again see each other. Elizabeth plays her hand and sends an anonymous letter to Lady Honoria about the sleepwalking incident, misconstruing the incident. She adds that Bingham's wife should check with Elizabeth Granger about the occurrence. Lady Honoria does so and Elizabeth replies with an implication of what happened that night. Lady Honoria confronts Geoffrey about this and says she will keep their daughter if it comes to divorce as she knows Geoffrey cannot bear to lose his daughter. She then writes to Beatrice, threatening her with legal action against Geoffrey if she does not break off all communication with him. Bingham also writes to Beatrice, asking her to come to him and face the consequences together. Her reply: "No, dear Geoffrey, things must take their course."

Owen Davies proposes to Beatrice once more in the presence of her family. Elizabeth denounces her as Bingham's mistress. Beatrice denies it, saying that she was sleepwalking. Davies threatens to ruin Bingham unless Beatrice marries him. She asks for one week in which to decide and makes all present swear not to discuss the matter during that time. Taking a ride in her canoe, she thinks out the situation and decides not to involve Geoffrey. She picks suicide as her only course. Deciding to see Geoffrey one last time, she goes to London to hear him speak in the House of Commons. A stranger, who happens to be a friend of Bingham's, helps her get a seat. He tells Geoffrey about her after the session. The two pass close by her outside later. A minute later, the friend turns and sees her; just then, Geoffrey has a strange feeling, but the woman is gone. Thinking it may be Beatrice, he goes to a railroad station hoping to find her, but he picks the wrong station. She returns home from another one.

Upon her return home, Beatrice posts a letter to Geoffrey. She goes about her usual routine that day. The only disruption is a visit to a dying girl whom she knew and who dies in her arms. That evening she goes out in her canoe and drowns herself.

While in the House of Commons the next morning, Geoffrey gets a dread feeling and feels a cold wind. He then gets Beatrice's letter, which explains everything, including her suicide.

Bingham goes to Bryngelly. Finding Beatrice absent, Geoffrey searches along the ashore and finds her canoe with one shoe in it. Returning to the Vicarage, he encounters Mr. Granger and Elizabeth, who have just returned from a short trip. He confronts them about the accusations made against

Beatrice, then informs them of her death. Davies appears and Bingham threatens to kill him if he mentions the affair.

Returning to London, Geoffrey finds his daughter ill and untended. He looks after her, then fires the nanny for negligence. His wife is attending a fancy ball. News arrives that he is heir to £8,000 a year and has been nominated for attorney general. Lady Honoria also hears the news at the ball. Shortly afterwards, she burns to death when her dress catches fire from an overturned candle.

Beatrice
(U.S.: *The Stronger Passion*)

Caesar Film/Unione Cinematografica Italiana (Italy); Released May 5, 1922; 8 reels; U.S. Distribution by Lee-Bradford Corp.; DIRECTOR: Herbert Brenon; SCENARIO: Herbert Brenon, from the novel by Henry Rider Haggard; ART DIRECTOR: Alfredo Manzi; PHOTOGRAPHY: Giuseppe Filippa

CAST: Marie Doro (Beatrice), Sandro Salvini (Geoffrey Bingham), Marcella Sabbatini (Elizabeth), Mina D'Orvella (Lady Honoria), Mimi (Bingham's Daughter), Francesca Bertini, Angelo Gallini, Silvana, Livio Pavanelli, Amleto Novelli

In 1919, top Hollywood director Herbert Brenon (1880–1958) was invited to make films in Italy by Giuseppe Barattolo, the owner-producer of Caesar Film. This move was part of a large-scale scheme to produce "international" films using American technicians and actors working with established Italian stars. Brenon had been making films in England, but a breach of contract suit forced him to leave.

Shot almost entirely in Taormina,

Sicily, *Beatrice*, as scripted by Brenon, tells of a parson's daughter named Beatrice, who loves a married man. When the man's wife dies in a theater fire, he seeks out Beatrice, only to find a farewell note; she has gone and drowned herself. This very brief synopsis leaves one wondering how much of the detail is retained in the film. The only difference here is having Lady Honoria die in a theater rather than at a ball.

Canadian-born Marie Doro (1882–1956) was an established Broadway actress who gained fame as the title character in *Oliver Twist*, a role she also essayed in the Lasky company's 1916 film version. She later made films in France and England and retired from acting in 1922.

La Vita Cinematografica, April 7, 1922 (Dionisio):

> When *The Mysterious Princess* was first performed in Italy by Herbert Brenon and Miss Marie Doro, we did not conceal our astonishment at the poor artistic direction and staging technique, as shown by this American *metieur-en-scene*, and by the meaningless artistic personality of this American actress.... *Beatrice*, the movie, only reiterates it. Herbert Brenon is not worth one of our cheaper directors, Miss Marie Doro is not worth one of our mediocre actresses. The author of the drama, Rider Hagar [*sic*], is no way above the Italian screenwriters.
>
> Are these, therefore, the foreign lights which were to dispel the shadows of the national cinema decay?
>
> Let the famous director and actress go back home; they did not teach anything in either art, or technique or even skill. Brenon's art is not overly creative, the staging is poor and the technique is common. The actress

is striking neither for look nor for diction: she is simply pitiful. Her impishness is as disappointing as a ghost's could be. We can only regret the money wasted, if it is indeed true so much was spent, and finally acknowledge once more the enlightened and amazing artistic insight and administrative openhandedness of the U.C.I. officials....

The Bioscope May 12, 1921:

As adapted to the screen, *Beatrice* is a somewhat conventional story of ill-fated love, and such dramatic incidents as the film contains have no very vital bearing on the main theme ... contains much of Mr. Brenon's best work.... [A] continuous series of very lovely pictures is reproduced with perfect taste and supreme technical skill.

Cleopatra
(novel, 1889)

SYNOPSIS: This work was written on papyrus rolls discovered in a tomb near Abydos, Egypt. It tells the history of Harmachis, trained for the priesthood but a future Pharaoh according to a prophecy. The same prophecy says he will become Pharaoh by driving the Ptolemies from the land, so the current Pharaoh sends men to slay him. He is switched with his foster brother and thereby spared. On his seventeenth birthday he is told by his father, the High Priest, that he is his real son and destined to be Pharaoh.

By this time Egypt is ruled by Cleopatra, who was born on the same day as Harmachis. The latter learns her history from his uncle in Memphis and again told he is to deliver Egypt. Harmachis communes with the goddess Isis, who asks him to restore her worship. He vows to overthrow Cleopatra. His father warns him of danger in the form of a woman.

As Cleopatra rides through the city in a golden chariot, Harmachis grapples with a Nubian guard who had knocked down a defenseless woman. Cleopatra asks his name and has the Nubian punished.

At the home of his uncle, Sepa, Harmachis meets a cousin, Charmion, who is a handmaiden to Cleopatra. She is working undercover until Harmachis can slay Cleopatra.

Cleopatra grants Harmachis an audience, then makes him court astrologer after he performs some magic and interprets a dream of hers. Visiting Harmachis later, Cleopatra learns of their same birth dates and asks the astrologer to be her friend, as she has none. Harmachis meets with the other conspirators and plans are laid.

On the appointed night, Harmachis is seduced by Cleopatra and given drugged wine, for one of the rebels betrayed him. The queen could have killed Harmachis, but does not. The rebels are all dealt with save Charmion, for her treachery is not known. Harmachis is confined to his quarters for 11 days. When free, he is in love with the queen.

A Roman envoy comes to the Egyptian court and bids Cleopatra go to Mark Antony in Cilicia to answer charges against her. Needing gold to fight, Cleopatra asks for time and then asks Harmachis about a fabled treasure. Harmachis leads her to it—a number of emeralds and pearls buried inside the mummy of a 3,000-year-old Pharaoh. The Pharaoh's spirit, in the form of a giant white bat, kills a eunuch, but flies off without harming either of the grave robbers.

On their way to Alexandria, the two spend four nights together on a boat. Cleopatra promises to wed Harmachis and make him Royal Consort. When the envoy comes for an answer, Cleopatra offers him peace rather than war, and does not name Harmachis as her consort.

She and the astrologer argue, and the queen orders Harmachis arrested. Maddened, he struggles valiantly with the guards before he is wounded and overcome. He lies near death for two days but recovers. He accompanies Cleopatra on her visit to Antony.

Antony and Cleopatra pledge their love for each other and the Roman is offered co-rule of Egypt.

With Harmachis ruined, Charmion reveals her treachery and tells the astrologer to kill her, but he cannot. She disguises him as a merchant so he can flee the country. His ship is wrecked and Harmachis abides with some Greek fishermen for a time. When he returns home, he finds his father old and blind. His father curses him for his failure but offers him a chance for atonement before dying in Harmachis' arms. Isis appears to him and tells him he must take revenge on Cleopatra.

Atoua, his old nurse, comes to the temple and is told of the High Priest's death. She hides Harmachis until after the funeral. They leave for Thebes, where Harmachis dwells in a tomb, meditating and praying for eight years. Word of a holy man with healing pow-

ers spreads abroad, so Atoua teaches Harmachis how to mix remedies. People come to him with their sick; he takes the name Olympus, as Harmachis is believed dead.

He learns that Cleopatra has been deserted by Antony, who has returned to Rome and taken a new wife. He sends Atoua to Alexandria to see if Charmion is still loyal. Finding her faithful yet, Atoua tells Charmion that Harmachis lives.

Meanwhile, Cleopatra has been sending letters to Olympus asking how she may win back Antony's love. His answers prove true; the two are reunited, so Cleopatra sends for him, but as it is not yet time, he refuses. He continues to counsel the rulers from Thebes.

Olympus has a vision of his father in which he sees the fleet of Antony and Cleopatra battling a Roman one at Actium; the queen suddenly flees and Antony is defeated.

Olympus hears from his father in a dream that the time of vengeance is now at hand. When summoned by Cleopatra, he goes.

First he meets with Charmion, who repeats her love for him, although he is older and limps. The queen again needs Olympus' help to win back Antony, who had followed her when she fled the battle at Actium, deserting his army. He now lies alone and feverish. Olympus and Charmion convince him to go to Cleopatra after giving him a restorative potion.

At a feast given for Antony, Olympus puts poison on a rose wreath worn by the Roman. Cleopatra tells him to dip the flowers in his wine before drinking it. However, she stops him before he can, and makes a man whom she suspects of poisoning the wreath drink the wine. The man dies and thus Cleopatra proves her love for Antony.

Olympus and Charmion conspire with Antony's general, convincing him to surrender to Rome so that Antony and Cleopatra are lost. Cleopatra obtains a poison from Olympus with which to take her own life. News arrives that Antony's forces have driven back the Romans. Antony rallies his men and prepares for battle on the next day. His men fail him, though, fleeing before the enemy. Antony blames Cleopatra for this, but she sends word denying she had a hand in the affair. Antony attempts suicide, but is healed by Olympus. He is taken to Cleopatra, who declares her love for him. Olympus then reveals his true identity to Antony, who dies. When Cleopatra is told that she is to be taken to Rome in chains, she is distraught and asks Olympus to prepare poison for her. As she drinks it, Olympus tells her he is really Harmachis. As the queen dies, the bat from the Pharaoh's tomb appears, along with the spirits of all whom Cleopatra had killed.

Charmion, her vengeance at last complete, also drinks poison. Olympus goes to his old nurse, Atoua, who also dies after hearing the news of Cleopatra's death.

Olympus surrenders to the council of High Priests, who condemn him to death after learning of his crimes and true identity.

Cleopatra

Fox Film Corporation; Released October 14, 1917; 11 reels; DIRECTOR: J. Gordon Edwards; SCENARIO: Adrian Johnson (from Shakespeare and Sardou)*; PHOTOGRAPHY: Rial Schellinger, John W. Boyle

CAST: Theda Bara (Cleopatra), Fritz Leiber (Caesar), Thurston Hall (Marc Antony), Henri deVries (Octavius), Art Acord (Kephren), Albert Roscoe (Pharon), Dorothy Drake (Charmian), Dell Duncan (Iras), Hector V. Sarno (Messenger), Herschel Mayall (Ventidius), Genevieve Blinn (Octavia)

Haggard won £5,000 ($25,000) in a lawsuit charging plagiarism from his 1889 novel of the same name.

One of the most sought after "lost films" of the silent era, *Cleopatra* was also Theda Bara's most elaborate vehicle. In the planning stages since late 1915, this production's "hype" has managed to survive over the years even if the film itself has not. Fox's publicity department worked overtime on this epic. For starters, the press was informed that a 2,500-year-old inscription in a Theban tomb had been discovered that predicted the coming of Theda Bara. It was at this time that some studio wag noticed that the actress' name was an anagram of "Arab Death"; one can imagine the field day that publicity had with *that* tid bit. Theda herself got into the swing of things, doing her own historical research at New York's Metropolitan Museum of Art before entraining for the West Coast, claiming that she *was* the reincarnation of the Siren of the Nile, and refusing to eat before a statuette of Amen-Ra was placed on her table.

Shot in the summer of 1917, *Cleopatra*'s sets cost a reported $500,000. These included a full-size Sphinx and reasonable facsimiles of the

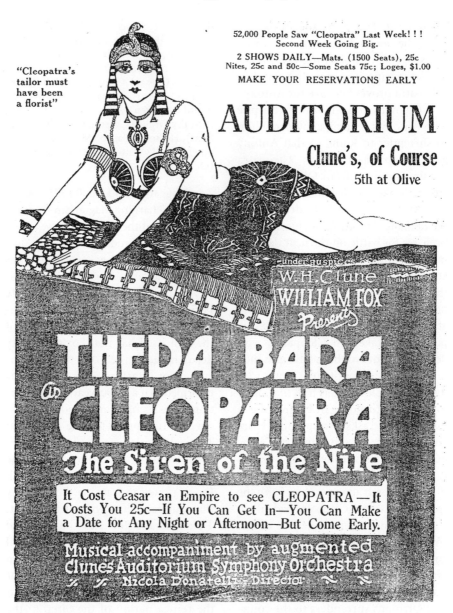

Cleopatra (Fox, 1917). Newspaper ad.

pyramids in Ventura County, canals and the Alexandria waterfront in Venice, and a fleet of Roman triremes and Egyptian warships for the recreation of the battle of Actium, in Balboa harbor. Some 30,000 extras, recruited from the local environs, were used in the battle scenes. Bara wore 50 different costumes, most of which left little of her anatomy to the viewer's imagination.

Cleopatra (Fox, 1917). Albert Roscoe, Theda Bara.

At the premiere at Clune's Auditorium in Los Angeles (where D.W. Griffith's monumental *The Birth of a Nation* (1915) had also premiered) a specially written score was performed by a full symphony orchestra. Bara was in attendance and received cheers and flowers from her devoted fans at the film's conclusion. The critics, however, were divided, either praising the film to the skies or castigating its excesses.

When *Cleopatra* was road shown, Bara made personal appearances; box office records were broken in New York, Washington, D.C., Buffalo, and Schenectady. It eventually became the year's top grosser.

The Moving Picture World, November 3, 1917 (Edward Weitzel):

There have been many mimic Cleopatras since the birth of the drama but never before has a feigned "Serpent of the Nile" been given such a massive and artistic setting as the one furnished by William Fox for the ten-part production in which Theda Bara acts the Egyptian vampire. The scope of the story embraces many of the historical facts used by Shakespeare in writing both *Julius Caesar* and *Antony and Cleopatra*, and it is evident that Adrian Johnson, the author of the scenario, has gone to the English poet for most of his incidents, rather than to Plutarch. The author has furnished some original material, however, and has also borrowed a character and a striking scene from Sardou's drama on the same subject. Several of the subtitles are from Shakespeare.

The result of this literary patchwork is a lucid and fairly authentic

Cleopatra (Fox, 1917). Theda Bara.

Cleopatra (Fox, 1917). Theda Bara.

account of the love affair between Cleopatra and Julius Caesar, and the Egyptian queen's overmastering passion for Mark Antony. The scenes shift from Alexandria to Imperial Rome, and several historical moments that have been immortalized by the brush of some famous artist, are reproduced with impressive fidelity. The most important of these are the murder of Julius Caesar in the Capitol, the first meeting between Cleopatra and Caesar, and the triumphant return of the enchantress in her barge with Antony a willing captive.

Opening with the lady's conquest of Caesar and his return to Rome, the action busies itself with a fictitious love affair between Cleopatra and a gentleman of the house of Pharaoh, while fate is disposing of Julius and setting the stage for the entry of Mark Antony into the life of the Egyptian. The meeting between the two, the sudden and violent love engendered in both, Antony's return to Rome, his marriage with Octavia, the weary waiting of Cleopatra, the reuniting of the lovers, the interference of Octavius Caesar in behalf of his sister, the battle against the forces of Antony and Cleopatra by those belonging to Octavius, the sea fight at Actium and the deaths of the Egyptian queen and her Roman, all these historical situations are thrown on the screen with an accuracy that necessitated the employing of one of the largest forces of actors, extra people and other essential workers ever used in a photo-spectacle, and the building of a correspondingly large number of

Cleopatra (Fox, 1917). Theda Bara.

edifices of ancient Rome and Egypt, with streets, waterways and interiors that truthfully reflect the period.

J. Gordon Edwards, who directed the production, has held his work well in hand and brought out a series of rapidly shifting pictures that tell the story with a force in keeping with the subject and the ambitious attempt to make it live on the screen. Toward the end the action would be strengthened by condensing it, the movement up to this point having been firm and engrossing.

The cast is exceptionally able. Theda Bara as Cleopatra is always satisfactory to the eye, save that a certain grade of spectators will criticize unfavorably the very frank display of her physical charms and some of the seductive wiles she uses to ensnare her lovers. Technically her acting commands respect without ever reaching any great tragic outburst, and she is best in the lighter scenes of the part. Her dressing of the Egyptian is remarkable for the variety and beauty of the garments employed.

A gratifying feature appertaining to the male members of the cast is their ability to wear the costumes demanded by the time. This is notable so in the case of Fritz Leiber, who plays Julius Caesar, and of Thurston Hall, the Antony; of Herschel Mayall, the Ventidus, and of Henri De Vries, the Octavius Caesar. All four are to be credited with impersonations of the first rank.

Dawn
(novel, 1884)

SYNOPSIS: Philip and George Caresfoot are cousins who obviously do not get along, for on page one the former is beating the hell out of the latter, calling him a liar. Philip's father,

Devil Caresfoot, enters and asks what has happened. George tells him not to blame Philip because the latter felt he had been wronged. Philip continues calling his cousin a liar, then admits to gambling away £10 he was supposed to put in the bank. Devil decides it is time his son got some discipline and knowledge, so he sends him off to Oxford. At the same time, George is to be apprenticed to a law firm.

Philip's only friend, a neighbor's daughter named Maria Lee, is expected to become his wife. She, however, moves to the isle of Jersey to be with her aunt.

Philip goes to Oxford for three years. Upon his return, he meets a beautiful young German woman named Hilda who is on her way to become a companion for a young Englishwoman in order to learn the language. That turns out to be Maria, who had returned while Philip was away.

Philip later learns that his father has not much time to live, and would like to see his son married to Maria.

One afternoon at Miss Lee's, Philip asks Hilda to meet him that night. Maria confronts him and he promises to marry her. He asks her not to tell anyone, even Hilda, just yet. She agrees. At their tryst, Philip decides to end his flirtation with Hilda, but when she tells him that she is returning to Germany for good, he loses his resolve. He proposes marriage, but asks her to keep their union secret until after his father's death. They are married in London, where they take an apartment. Soon after, Devil Caresfoot throws a lavish dinner at which he announces his son's engagement to Maria. Philip later tells his father that he can never marry Maria. Devil gives his son an ultimatum: either he marries Maria or he will be disinherited.

George Caresfoot spots Hilda in London one day. Doing some checking, he discovers the marriage and writes an anonymous letter of warning about Philip to Hilda.

After some months, unable to stand the deception any longer, Hilda goes to Devil Caresfoot and tells him of her marriage to Philip. When the latter confronts his son, he has a heart attack. Philip notes his father's old will on a table and withholds his father's medicine until he swears to change his mind about disinheriting him. Devil calls his son a murderer and a liar and expires.

As a doctor examines the body, the right hand moves, pointing at Philip, who becomes frightened. The doctor explains that it is the final slackening of muscle tension.

That night, Hilda gives birth to a girl who is named Angela. Philip then discovers that a new will had been made, naming his cousin George as heir to the bulk of the estate; he had let his father die to no purpose.

Aware that she is dying, Hilda calls for Maria and tells her everything. Maria had received a letter from George telling of Philip's perfidy. When he begs her forgiveness, she refuses it and leaves him for good. On her deathbed, Hilda makes Philip promise to take care of the child, mend his ways and marry Maria. She then dies peacefully at dawn.

George meets with Mrs. Bellamy, a scheming woman who had instigated his letters to the two women. She is also in love with George and now asks for her intimate letters to him. He refuses, giving her jewelry instead, for he wants a hold over her. Furious, she returns home to work her wiles on her meek husband.

Fast-forward almost ten years: Angela has become an inquisitive and intelligent child. One Mr. Fraser undertakes to round out her education. Another decade passes; greedy Philip has amassed a considerable fortune and asks his daughter to try to buy the property which George inherited.

Meanwhile, Mr. Bellamy has become a knight through his wife's machinations. He visits George and secretly makes impressions of the lock and key to George's safe, for the latter is ready to use the letters against Mrs. Bellamy.

Enter Arthur Heigham, George's ward. After meeting Angela accidentally while fishing, he falls in love with her. His stay at George's ended, Arthur is invited by Philip to stay at his home. He thus gets to spend much time with Angela.

Nasty cousin George has also fallen for Angela, however, and uses his hold over Lady Bellamy to get her to arrange his marriage to the young woman. Before she can, though, George contracts typhus.

Nursed back to health by Lady Bellamy, he continues to scheme, for he still desires Angela. Philip offers to buy his land; Lady Bellamy tells him that he must make a choice — sell the land or give up Angela. He refuses to do the former. George has her speak to Philip. She tells him of George's refusal to sell, but also reveals his desire for Angela. Philip can ask for the land as a price for Angela; he refuses, stating that the girl is practically engaged to Arthur. Lady Bellamy gives him one week to decide; his greed surfaces, so that when Arthur asks for Angela's hand, Philip says he needs a week to decide.

Lady Bellamy devises a scheme whereby George can have Angela and Philip his land without the latter feeling responsible. Part of the plan stipulates that Arthur must refuse to see or write to Angela for the space of a year as proof of his love. He and Angela agree to this without enthusiasm.

Arthur goes to Madeira; aboard ship he meets Mildred Carr, a young widow who owns a residence on Madeira. Over time she falls in love with Arthur.

Back in England, George, Philip and Lady Bellamy all try to get Angela to forget Arthur. Philip has a change of heart and makes a deal with George that if he can win Angela on his own, Philip will pay a certain sum for his estate.

When Lord Bellamy learns of all this, he takes his wife to Madeira, for now he has a plan. Noting how Mildred Carr seems to care for Arthur, the pair tries to get her to try to win him. Lady Bellamy tricks Arthur into giving her the engagement ring given him by Angela. She promises to tell Angela as much about him as possible upon her return to England. Eventually Mildred tells Arthur of her love, but he refuses her and leaves the island.

Back in England on Christmas Day, Lady Bellamy interrupts Angela at dinner to inform her that Arthur is dead. She shows her the ring and a death certificate in Portuguese. Angela refuses to believe her until the old witch shows her a letter of farewell from Arthur. After getting over her initial shock, Angela turns to charity work.

George then develops consumption. It is feared that he will die, so everyone gets on Angela's case to marry him. Realizing the situation and how everyone feels, Angela finally consents, but stipulates that the marriage is to be in name only.

The night after the wedding, George goes to Angela's room and reveals that he is not dying; that was just a ruse to gain her consent. She runs from her room. Seeing her father on the landing below, she calls, to him, but he fails to hear her. A moment later, flames appear below. Angela threatens to jump from the balcony if George gets any closer.

After traveling about on the Continent, Arthur arrives in London one week before the year of separation is up and begins to make wedding arrangements. On his way to Angela's he meets Pigott, her old nurse, who had been turned out earlier. She tells him of the girl's marriage to George. Struck dumb, he loses control of himself. Meeting Angela farther on, he berates her severely. She is so shocked to see him alive that she faints. Arthur places her on a bench; George suddenly appears, having fled from the fire. He witnessed their little scene together and goes after Arthur, who throttles and curses him, but lets him go. George then confronts Angela, who is just awakening from her faint. He strikes her with a riding crop; as he does so a second time, Arthur's dog, which had been given to Angela, attacks him. Knocked into the water, George's head strikes a rock and he drowns. Angela passes out again and awakens completely mad.

During George's confinement, Lord Bellamy had managed to steal back his wife's letters to George. He now tells her that he must expose her, though he offers to look after her. She refuses his aid and leaves him. She later takes poison. When her doctor arrives, he attempts to revive her with an electric battery. He succeeds, but she is completely paralyzed.

Arthur goes to hell with himself and winds up back on Madeira. There he asks for Mildred's hand, but she refuses, because he is asking her on the rebound after losing Angela.

Angela eventually regains her sanity, but becomes subject to strange dreams and visions. Meeting her father at her mother's grave one day, she agrees to move back in with him temporarily. She goes to visit Lady Bellamy, who tells her where Arthur can be found. Angela writes to Arthur, enclosing proof of all that had transpired since his first departure. She arrives on Madeira soon after the package and the two lovers are reunited.

If you followed all of the above, you are a better man than I — or a soap opera aficionado!

Dawn

Lucoque Productions (Great Britain); Released 1917; 5,500 feet; DIRECTOR: H. Lisle Lucoque; SCREENPLAY: Pauline Lewis

CAST: Madeleine Seymour (Angela Caresfoot), Karina (Mildred Carr), Hubert Carter (Devil Caresfoot), Edward Combermere (George Caresfoot), R. Heaton Grey (Philip Caresfoot), Annie Esmond (Mrs. Bellamy), Frank Harris (Mr. Bellamy), George Snazelle (Arthur Heigham)

The only known existing print of this film rests comfortably at the Nederlands Filmmuseum in Amsterdam, should any among you care to make the trip.

Jess
(novel, 1887)

SYNOPSIS: On his way to a new job at Silas Croft's ostrich farm in the Transvaal, South Africa, Capt. John Neil encounters a young woman on horseback being chased by an ostrich. The bird gets the better of the two until they fight it together. Neil breaks the bird's neck. The girl turns out to be Bessie, Silas Croft's niece. Now horseless, the pair must walk a mile to the farm. On the way, they meet a native leading their horses, as well as Bessie's sister Jess.

After Capt. Neil and Silas Croft meet, the latter tells the soldier the girls' history. They are the daughters of his worthless half-brother. Their mother took them from England, but died en route; he has taken care of them ever since. One day the half-brother came looking for the girl and Silas thrashed him. The brother vowed vengeance, but died from a burst blood vessel while on a drinking spree before he could exact it.

Neil settles in to work at the farm. He meets a half-Boer, half-English man named Frank Muller, who is despised by the Crofts, and who considers himself a Briton.

After six weeks, Capt. Neil proves satisfactory in his work and pays Silas Croft £1000 for a half-interest in the farm, as per their arrangement. He also gets along very well with the Crofts and their native workers.

Frank Muller proposes marriage to Bessie. She rejects him and he blames the presence of Capt. Neil, then vows to have Bessie without fail.

Over time, Jess begins to have feelings for Neil, and he for her, though neither speaks of it. Bessie tells Jess of Muller's proposal and also that she's been in love with John ever since their first meeting, and now feels he loves her as well. Jess is crushed, but does not show it. She goes to visit a school fellow of hers in Pretoria for two months. Neil and Bessie ride with her part of the way. When she is alone with Neil, Jess asks him to protect Bessie from Frank Muller and he agrees. Later that day, John catches Muller beating Jantje, a native who works for Silas Croft. He steps in and beats Muller before a group of whites and natives. Croft later says that he has made a bad enemy.

Neil eventually proposes marriage to Bessie; she admits her love for him, but feels unworthy.

News of Boer unrest against British rule fuels Muller's ambition to rule a Boer free state after the British are overthrown. Still desiring Bessie, he goes to Silas Croft, saying he is willing to protect him in case of war, but only if he can have Bessie. Croft replies that he has no say in the matter; the girl must decide. Muller reveals that he has

already been rejected, and Croft banishes him from the property. Muller threatens to burn the place and kill Croft and Neil if necessary. On his way home, he encounters Bessie. Again he proposes and is again rejected. Becoming angry, he grabs her, but is frightened off by a trick of Jantje, who had been spying upon him. Later, John and Bessie receive Silas' blessing for their marriage.

Just before Christmas, word reaches the Croft farm that the Boers have declared war on the British and have already annihilated a British force. John takes a wagon and a Swazi boy named Mouti to bring Jess back from Pretoria. He has to bluff his way past two Boer guard posts, and is also shot at, but he manages to get through to the beleaguered city.

Jess had been thinking about leaving Pretoria, until she got her sister's letter announcing her engagement to John. She is happy for Bessie, but resolves never to see Capt. Neil again. On her return from a walk, she espies Neil in the cart as he enters the city. Arrangements are made for his stay, as it is believed he will be unable to leave until a British relief force arrives. John and Jess find an abandoned cottage in which to live. All during the siege, John goes out on sorties with the volunteers, in order to keep busy. One day Jess is told that he has been killed and she passes out. The report turns out to be false; John runs to Jess, and she falls sobbing into his arms when she awakes. Puzzled by this emotion, John asks and discovers that Jess loves him and he loves her. Jess reminds him about Bessie, and he departs, shame-faced.

Jess goes for a doctor when John limps back; he has been hit in the leg. The doctor ties the artery, but it breaks shortly thereafter and John begins bleeding profusely. The doctor returns and operates again. Jess nurses Neil until he recovers. They agree to forget what was said upon John's return, but both know that they cannot.

One day, a friend of the Croft family, Hans Coetzee, appears in Pretoria to arrange an exchange of prisoners. Jess asks him to procure passes for her and Capt. Neil. When he hesitates, Jess says she will speak to her uncle regarding a loan Coetzee still owes, so he agrees.

When he tells Muller of this, the latter gets the passes. He is going to be running the district in which the Crofts reside; his intention is to kill everyone except Bessie.

John and Jess depart with Mouti from Pretoria with an escort of two armed Boers. When they stop at a cottage to eat, Frank Muller appears. He explains it was he who procured the passes. Neil refuses to shake hands with him, and they almost come to blows.

Muller gives the two Boers orders to take the Britons to a certain spot at a river where they will be drowned; this failing, they are to be shot.

That night, a great storm erupts as the party reaches the river. Muller tells them where to cross the river. As they do so, a flash of lightning reveals the two Boers and Muller aiming their rifles at them. With the first volley, Mouti and one of the horses are killed. The other horses break free and the cart floats downriver. The Boers keep firing until they believe the cart has sunk. As

they ride away, a bolt of lightning kills Muller's men and he flees at the sight.

The cart catches against some rocks. Unaware the Boers are dead and Muller gone, Jess and John again reveal their love for each other. Jess, who cannot swim, begs John to swim to safety; he refuses. Just then the cart is torn loose; before it overturns, John grabs Jess around the waist and jumps free. After struggling in the water, he is able to climb onto a large flat rock and pulls Jess up with him. The next day they find two of their horses and the food bucket they had brought. They later discover the remains of the Boers.

Back at the Croft farm, Silas had run up the Union Jack on his flagpole, assured that his record in the area would keep him safe. Bessie gets a letter from Frank Muller, apprising her of Capt. Neil's death. She sets her dog on the messenger, a Kafiri witch doctor. When he returns to Muller, the latter is plotting to have Silas Croft tried for treason for flying the Union Jack, leaving the outcome of the trial without doubt. The witch doctor asks if he can be the one to shoot Silas.

Several weeks later, Muller and a band of armed men take Croft from his home. Muller again proposes to Bessie and is once more refused. This time, though, he says that if she persists in her refusal, her uncle will die. She still refuses; Muller says he can take her without marriage. Silas is tried and found guilty; the sentence is death.

Meantime, John and Jess continue their journey without incident until they run into a group of Boers. Their pass is not good there, and when the Boers notice that the Britons are riding on Boer saddles, the pair is arrested. Jess is soon set free, however. On her way home, her horse dies, but she is able to walk the rest of the way, as she is not far from the farm. Seeing no light in the house, she pauses, and Jantze appears and tells her of the events which had occurred in her absence. Bessie is being guarded in the wagon house. Jess and Jantze attempt to free her. As Jess reaches the building and finds a hole in the wall, Muller enters and renews his plea to Bessie. He tells her that Jess is also dead, so that she is now alone, except for her condemned uncle. She finally consents to become his wife, though adding that doing so will kill her.

Hearing this, Jess retreats to Jantze's hut to ponder the situation. She decides that only Muller's death can free them all. Unable to do the deed herself, Jess appeals to Jantze's wish for revenge on the Boers for the deaths of his parents and uncle. The Hottentot agrees with her plan.

When it comes time, however, Jantze refuses to go alone, so Jess accompanies him. The Hottentot draws his knife and enters Muller's tent, but loses his nerve. Jess takes his knife from him and enters the tent. As she is about to strike the sleeping Muller, he awakes. Thinking he is seeing Jess' spirit; he freezes in fear. Jess stabs him and flees.

All this time, John had been a prisoner of the Boers. Held in a house owned by an old woman, he manfully withstands the Boers' taunts and mistreatment. Admiring his courage, the old woman sets him free after the Boers have left. Neil walks all night until he finds a cave near the Croft farm and there falls asleep.

Meanwhile, Jess had been running across the veldt until she reached the same cave wherein John was sleeping. She knows she is dying of exhaustion and wishes only to see John one more time. Finding the sleeping British officer, she kisses him three times. "Then at last the end came. There was a great flashing of light before her eyes and the roaring as of a thousand seas within her ears, and her head sunk [sic] gently on her lover's breast as on a pillow; there she died and passed upward toward the wider life and larger liberty, or perhaps downward into the depths of an eternal sleep."

John awakens next morning to find the body of Jess atop him. He carries her to the Croft farm, where she is buried. With Muller dead, the Boers depart without carrying out the sentence on Silas Croft. The Britons decide to return to England; there John and Bessie are wed.

Jess

Thanhouser; 3 reels; Reel One (*A Sister's Sacrifice*) released May 21, 1912; Reels Two (*Through the Boer Lines*) and Three (*Jess, the Avenger*) released May 28, 1912; DIRECTOR: George O. Nicholls; ASSISTANT DIRECTORS: David H. Thompson, Carl LeViness; PHOTOGRAPHY: A.H. Moses, Jr.

CAST: Marguerite Snow (Jess), Florence LaBadie (Bess), James Cruze (Capt. John Neil), William Russell (Frank Muller), Harry Marks, Harry Spear

This was the first Thanhouser film to be distributed by the Film Supply Company of America, which handled the output of 12 studios. Thanhouser had previously released through the Motion Picture Distributing and Sales Company.

Jess (Thanhouser, 1912). Capt. Neil (James Cruze) and Jess (Marguerite Snow). (Courtesy BFI Stills, Posters and Designs.)

Originally planned as a two-reeler, *Jess* was expanded to three reels, with each reel containing a complete story, so that exhibitors were given the option of renting the reel (or reels) desired.

Besides filming at the studio site in New Rochelle, New York, the company utilized sites in New Jersey and in and around the old Spanish fort in St. Augustine, Florida.

James Cruze (1884–1942) and Marguerite Snow (1889–1958) frequently appeared together in Thanhouser productions (see also the entry for the 1911 version of *She*). Thanhouser's two most popular players, they were married in 1913 in a ceremony which was filmed. Both left Thanhouser in 1915, and they

divorced in 1922. While Snow's career petered out by the mid–20s, Cruze went on to become a highly regarded director, helming such productions as *The Covered Wagon* (1923), *Hollywood* (1923) and *Old Ironsides* (1926). In both 1926 and 1929 he was listed among the world's top ten directors. He later formed two production companies, but was bankrupt by 1932 and died penniless.

The following review makes this appear a fairly faithful adaptation, although it does not say how Jess avenged her uncle. It also states that Jess and John were on their way *to* Pretoria when attacked; in the book, they are *leaving* Pretoria.

The Moving Picture World , May 18, 1912:

Jess

Thanhouser Does Rider Haggard's
Story in Three Reels.
An Ambitious Production

"Jess," from the adventure story by H. Rider Haggard, is now a Thanhouser "classic." It is in three remarkable reels. The sun-kissed sands of Africa fairly glisten and the desert winds whirl almost out of the picture and around the spectators. Such an exhibition of realism, fidelity to nature and stirring character portrayals are rarely seen on the screen. "Jess," sympathetic, heroic, self-sacrificing, makes an appeal such as is difficult to shake off. She worms her way gradually but irresistibly and stands out in relief, a noble martyr to love and self-sacrifice. The exhibition of pantomime in portraying these varying emotions and characteristics is a revelation.

The title role is taken by Marguerite Snow. Flo LaBadie plays the sister, Bess. James Cruze is powerful in the part of Captain John Neil, the Englishman, and William Russell gets real hatred from you as Muller, the treacherous Boer. Miss Snow and Mr. Cruze seem to take their lives in their hands in the scene depicting their escape from Muller through the ford. The wagon in which they cross the stream is overturned by the strong current and Mr. Cruze pulls Miss Snow from under the vehicle just in the nick of time, and swims with her to safety. It is a deed of daring that is not encountered in the motion pictures every day.

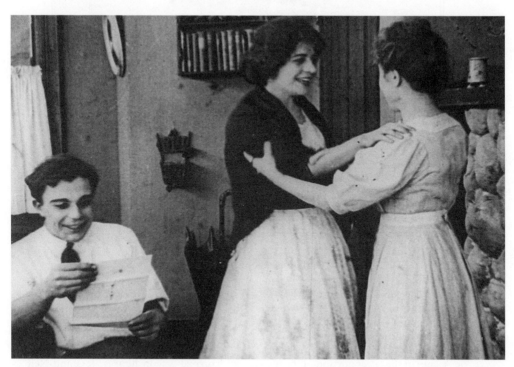

Jess (Thanhouser, 1912). James Cruze, Marguerite Snow, Florence La Badie. (Courtesy BFI Stills, Posters and Designs.)

Jess (Thanhouser, 1912). Trade paper ad.

The subject is so filmed that the love story of "Jess" and "Neil" is given in the first reel ... and the story of their wartime adventures appears in the second and third reels.... The fire scenes in the latter portion of the picture, showing the destruction of Silas Croft's home, are very realistic....

The picture takes on its highest degree of interest when Muller, whom Jess had rejected, is shown plotting the destruction of Jess and the man she loves, Neil. It is here that the overturned wagon figures. Jess and Neil are on their way to Pretoria, under official Boer protection supposedly, when Muller tricks the escort into thinking that Oom Paul Kruger wishes the couple killed. Crossing the stream, the Boer escort fire upon the pair and it is in the attempt to evade the musketry that the incident of the overturned cart occurs.

Jess and Neil become separated and the girl reaches the farm of Croft, her uncle, alone. There she finds that the villain Muller has been ahead of her, and that her uncle is a prisoner on a charge of treason. Muller, who is military head of the district, tells Bess that Croft will be convicted and hanged unless Bess consents to marry him. The girl, however, refuses; the court-martial is held and, when Jess arrives, her uncle is under sentence to die at dawn, a few hours away.

There is no one to whom she can appeal, and Jess, grief-stricken, decides to be her own avenger. And vengeance is hers in a way that is highly dramatic and highly moving — picturesque. The whole story is full of life and holds the spectator's interest every minute.

Jess

Kennedy Features, Inc., for World/Criterion; Released February 18, 1914; 4 reels; DIRECTOR: unknown; SCENARIO: Arthur Maude

CAST: Constance Crawley (Jess), Arthur Maude (John Neil)

From the following review, it can be ascertained that this production was extremely faithful to the source material.

Motography, February 21, 1914:

Jess—A Story of South Africa

When Kennedy Features were first conceived an announcement was made to the effect that photography was to be featured in all films released under this brand, and certainly *Jess*, the four-part production in which

Constance Crawley and Arthur Maude are starred, lives up to the announcement.

Action a-plenty abounds in the picture and the battle scenes showing hand to hand conflicts between the British and the Boers are thrilling in the extreme. As the story runs:

Silas Croft, an Englishman, has taken up farming in South Africa and has been unusually successful. His sister in England, ill, widowed, and left with two little girls — Jess and Bess — starts for South Africa to make her home with him. The sister, however, is stricken with death just after landing from the steamer and the two little girls are sent on to the brother.

Jess is the older of the two children and when the mother dies she entrusts the care and happiness of the younger child to the sister, scarcely older. Gladly received and tenderly reared by their uncle, Silas Croft, the girls grow to beautiful and gracious young womanhood on his farm.

Sixteen years after their arrival in South Africa, John Neil, a young Englishman who has been an army officer, comes from England to learn South African farming and selects Silas Croft as his school-master. Both Jess and Bess fall in love with John Neil. Neil really loves Jess, but she, believing herself bound by the promise given her dead mother, makes John think she cares nothing for him and goes on a visit to Pretoria, then the principal city of South Africa, so that John may forget her and turn to Bess.

Shortly after the departure of Jess for Pretoria occurs the first revolution of the Boers against the British Government. Bess has an admirer, Frank Mueller, a wealthy and influential Boer, whom she hates and fears. Mueller knows that Bess is in love with John and plans to get rid of him.

Pretoria, held by the English, is surrounded by Boer troops and

Mueller, now a high officer of the Boer army, writes to Jess that her uncle is ill and needs her. John Neil has gone to Pretoria and Mueller is sure that he will accompany Jess on the trip home. Mueller sends a pass and two of his men to act as an escort. Jess and Neil start, but once outside of the British lines, they are taken captive by Mueller who laughs at the way they have fallen into his simple trap. Mueller attempts to kill both, but both escape. While in danger, Jess has confessed her love for John.

Now upon the screen is shown the fighting which took place around Pretoria. For week after week the Boers besieged and the British defended this city. The fighting is shown with strict regard for historical accuracy....

Failing in his plan to kill John Neil, Mueller captures Silas Croft and gives Bess the alternative of seeing her uncle die or of marrying him. She chooses to save her uncle but before the marriage is performed Jess surprises Mueller while he is asleep and stabs him to death; releasing her uncle and Bess.

Fleeing, Jess rejoins John in a cave near the farm. John is asleep when she returns to him and does not awaken until morning and when he does awake Jess is dead of exhaustion.

The British troops arrive, saving Bess and her uncle and John Neil as well. Bess and John are married and return to England. The drama closes with a view of the English home of the Neils, which is all happiness, but in a tableau it is shown that no matter what comes Jess will never be forgotten by either her sister, to whom she gave all, or by John Neil, who loved her very truly.

Heart and Soul

Fox Film Corporation; Released May 21, 1917; 5 reels; Based on *Jess; DIRECTOR*:

J. Gordon Edwards; *SCENARIO*: Adrian Johnson; *PHOTOGRAPHY*: Philip Rosen

CAST: Theda Bara (Jess), Edwin Holt (Silas Croft), Claire Whitney (Bess), Walter Law (Drummond), Harry S. Hilliard (John Neil), Glen White (Pedro), Alice Gale (Mammy), John Webb Dillon (Sancho), Margaret Laird (Jess, in Prologue), Kittens Reichert (Bess, in Prologue).

One of Theda Bara's many lost films, this picture was also one of her few box office failures. This was undoubtedly due to the fact that she played a good woman instead of her stock-in-trade of a vamp. A large plantation was built and 10,000 sugar canes were planted, just to be destroyed by fire at the film's climax. The locale was changed from South Africa to Hawaii.

Motography, June 2, 1917:

There is excitement all through this, which as a melodrama with thrills and surface action is very passable. Daring horseback riding, thrilling rescues, violent scenes, villainous brutality and the like are all there and the audience...will be kept on edge by the very swing of the action. But the story itself fails to register as a thoroughly prepared, logical sequence of dramatic events. The villain is so villainous that he is practically blind to reason. In fact, he has more ambition than reason.

Miss Bara's part as the self-sacrificing sister certainly does not stand out as the featured role.

The settings...taken in a very beautiful section of the South, lend a great deal of charm to the picture.

The Moving Picture World, June 9, 1917:

The Rider Haggard South African story of *Jess*, which furnishes the foundation for *Heart and Soul*, another five-reel Fox screen drama, is made up of excellent dramatic material. The author of the scenario has thought it expedient to shift the location to one of the Sandwich Islands… This slight departure from the physical facts of the country in no way interferes with the entertaining qualities of the picture. There is plenty of action in *Heart and Soul,* and the heroic sacrifice made by the heroine, that her younger sister may marry the man they both love, is a bit of honest drama which commands the respect and sympathy of everyone.

The drama is well acted. Fortunately for Theda Bara, she has little lovemaking to do. The gentler passions are not along the lines of her best endeavors. She atones for this, however, by the feeling she puts into the rest of her work, and her death scene is thoroughly artistic. Harry Hilliard is a vigorous and likable hero … J. Gordon Edwards directs the picture and again shows his ability to handle large bodies of extra people and to make the most of the individual efforts of the leading actors. The production is impressive.

King Solomon's Mines
(novel, 1885)

SYNOPSIS: Aging hunter and guide Allan Quatermain (who also acts as narrator and author of the manuscript) encounters two fellow Englishmen, Sir Henry Curtis and Capt. John Good, aboard a ship. The former is tall, solidly built, blond-haired; the latter short, stout and dark. Curtis needs someone to lead a safari in search of his brother. Quatermain reveals that he has heard of the brother, that he was in search of King Solomon's Mines. After swearing

Heart and Soul (Fox, 1917). Theda Bara.

the pair to secrecy, he tells them the legend of the mines. He obtained a map of the region from a dying Portuguese adventurer who had failed in his attempt to locate the mines, but lived to struggle far enough to reach Quatermain.

Curtis agrees to pay all expenses, and refuses a share in any treasure that is discovered. Quatermain wants the money for his son Harry's medical education in England, which Curtis pays in advance.

The party makes ready, adding two Zulus named Goza and Tom, a Hottentot servant named Ventvogel and another, smaller Zulu named Khiva, who speaks fluent English. Before they set out, they are joined by another Zulu named Umbopa, who appears out of nowhere, offering his services. Curtis takes him as a servant.

When Good is threatened by a bull elephant during a hunt, Khiva gives his life saving Good's. The party almost dies of thirst in a desert before reaching Sheba's Breasts, the two mountains which mark the boundary of the land they seek. They climb the left one, but Ventvogel dies of exposure on its peak. They find a cave at the summit and a white man's corpse within it. Curtis ascertains that it is not his brother. They return down the mountain and begin their trek up the ancient Solomon's Road.

They are discovered by a band of Kukuanas, the natives of the region, in their camp. Good, trouser-less, false teeth-less and monocled, draws the attention of the warriors, who marvel at his white legs. He also had been shaving and was only half-finished when interrupted. Quatermain gives them a demonstration of the power of his rifle and the white men are declared to be gods by the Kukuanas. They are led by a veteran warrior named Infadoos and Scragga, the son of the Kukuana king Twala, to the latter's village.

Twala is an evil king, and looks it, with but one eye in a face none too pretty to begin with. His foremost supporter is a shriveled old woman of indeterminate age named Gagool, who wields terrible power. She it was who had Twala made king. He was the weaker of twin boys born to the former queen. The Kukuana custom is to kill the weaker twin, but his mother hid him. Infadoos was his younger brother, born of another woman. When the former king died, Infadoos' brother Imotu was made king. He had a son named Ignosi. After a severe famine, the people were discontented, and Gagool saw her chance to make Twala king. She declared that Imotu was no king, and revealed the existence of Twala, who bore the symbol of Kukuana kingship, a snake tattoo about his waist. Imotu was ill at the time, yet Twala killed him and was declared king. Imotu's wife fled with their son and was never again seen.

As Twala is saluted by his warriors, one of the latter accidentally drops his shield. Twala orders his son Scragga to kill him, which he does, with relish. Like father, like son. Quatermain then informs Twala that the whites have come from the stars to see his land. Quatermain again shows the power of his rifle by shooting an ox. He offers his rifle to Twala, but with the stipulation that he not use it to kill men. If he does, the rifle will kill *him*. The hunter gives another demonstration by shattering a spearhead with a shot.

Gagool is described as "made up of a collection of deep, yellow wrinkles. Set in the wrinkles was a sunken slit that represented the mouth, beneath which the chin curved outward to a point. There was no nose to speak of … a pair of large black eyes, still full of fire and intelligence … which gleamed … like jewels in a charnel house. As for the skull … its wrinkled scalp moved and contracted like the hood of a cobra." Gagool prophesies that much blood, rivers of it, will soon flow. "Blood is good, the red blood is bright. There is no smell like the smell of new-shed blood…" She questions the aim of the white men, and shows her suspicion of Umbopa. Before she can force him to show his hand, though, she falls to the ground in an epileptic fit.

When they are alone, Quatermain asks Infadoos why Twala has not been overthrown. The old warrior tells him that Scragga would then rule, and he is even worse than Twala. Umbopa interrupts, asking Infadoos how he knows Ignosi is dead. Infadoos replies that it was assumed, since he has never returned. Umbopa then tells Infadoos of the child's fate. He and his mother were led to the land of Amazulu by some nomads who had found the pair wandering in a desert. They lived with the Amazulu for many years, until the mother died. Then Ignosi became a wanderer. He served as a soldier and servant for years, biding his time until he met some white men who sought the land of the Kukuanas and joined up

with them. Umbopa then removes his *moocha* (girdle), revealing a blue snake tattoo about his mid-section. Infadoos recognizes him as the true Kukuana king. He and the whites agree to help him gain the throne. In exchange, Umbopa agrees to let the whites have as much of Solomon's treasure as they can find.

The whites are then presented with some ancient chain mail and battle axes by Twala. That night the "smelling out of the witches" ceremony is held.

The ritual begins as Gagool dances into a frenzy, chanting, "What is the lot of man born of woman?" and receiving the reply "Death!" from the assembled warriors. She then begins pointing out alleged evil-doers among the fighting men. Those chosen are instantly slain with spears by 12 large warriors. When she points at Umbopa, Quatermain calls out that Umbopa is his dog, and that by shedding his blood that of the whites is also shed. By the laws of hospitality he claims protection for Umbopa. Twala refuses; as the executioners advance, Umbopa raises his spear and Quatermain covers Twala with a revolver; Good and Curtis also draw their weapons. Twala yields and allows Umbopa to be spared.

Later, Infadoos brings three chiefs to see Umbopa's tattoo, in an effort to win their support. They see it, but want a greater sign that the power of the white gods will be with them. The whites confer. Good has an idea and checks his almanac, discovering that there is to be a total eclipse on the following day. The whites inform the chiefs that they will put out the sun on the morrow as proof of their power. The chiefs agree to help Umbopa. Sir Henry has Umbopa promise that he will put an end to the witch-hunting once he is king.

That evening a dance of all the young women of the tribe is held. After each has danced individually, Twala asks Good to select the fairest from among them. He does so, only to discover the woman is to be sacrificed to the trio of stone colossi which guard the mines. The woman, Foulata, pleads for her life. Good makes a move towards her and she clasps his legs and begs him to save her. Quatermain interrupts, stating that the white gods will not tolerate such a sacrifice. When Twala becomes angered, the Englishman threatens to put out the sun. Gagool says that if the sun is put out, the young woman shall go free; if not, the whites shall die along with her.

Seeing the eclipse beginning, Quatermain gestures toward the sun while reciting passages from *The Ingoldsby Legends*. The Kukuanas cower in fear as the moon makes its way across the sun. Scragga tries to spear Curtis, but his blade is deflected by Curtis' chain mail coat. The latter grabs the spear and slays Scragga.

When the eclipse becomes full, the whites, Ignosi, and Foulata flee from the village. Arriving at an outpost, Ignosi assembles his troops for battle on the morrow. Twala sends a messenger with terms, which are refused.

The next day a tremendous battle is fought, involving tens of thousands of warriors. Twala's forces are finally driven off. Quatermain is knocked senseless at the end of the attack.

Ignosi's army finds itself low on water. It is decided to attack Twala's camp.

Another fearful struggle ensues with both sides giving their all. Suddenly Twala himself appears and challenges Sir Henry Curtis to solo combat. After exchanging but a few strokes, they are swept up by the larger conflict. Eventually Twala's forces are scattered. Good is badly beaten by a Kukuana warrior, but is saved by his armor.

Twala surrenders to Ignosi, and is allowed the chief's prerogative of choosing how he will die. He wishes to die fighting and selects Sir Henry as his opponent. After a terrific fight, Sir Henry prevails, striking Twala's head from his body with a battle axe.

Ignosi is proclaimed king. Good becomes feverish and is tended by Foulata until he is well. Quatermain reminds Ignosi of his promise to take the whites to the mines. Only Gagool knows the way, however. Ignosi tells her she will die if she does not lead the whites to the mines. She agrees, but reminds them of the last white man who attempted to take the treasure. Betrayed by a woman, he was lost in the mountains and died.

Gagool leads the whites and Foulata to the mines, which are guarded by three seated stone colossi, one female and two male. Inside is a gigantic cavern full of stalactites. A smaller inner chamber contains a stone table around which sit the bodies of 27 former Kukuana kings which are slowly being turned into stalagmites by water dripping from the ceiling. At the head of the table is a 15-foot tall skeleton holding a spear poised for striking. The treasure chamber is hidden behind a great rock which opens and closes by a lever with counterbalances. The treasure itself is in yet another chamber behind a painted wooden door. The whites enter while Foulata waits outside with Gagool. They find much ivory, boxes of ancient gold coins and, in a small recess, stone boxes full of uncut diamonds. While they are thus occupied, Gagool sneaks out and tries to close the rock, but Foulata tries to prevent her. The old witch fatally stabs the young woman, but the rock falls on her, crushing her to death. Foulata professes her love for Good as she dies. Thus the miscegenation issue is nicely avoided, while Foulata's sacrifice gives her character some depth and nobility, a rare concept in Victorian literature.

The whites are trapped inside overnight before they realize that the air is still fresh, proving the existence of an opening somewhere. A stone ring in a rock is found in the floor, and it takes the strength of all three to open it. Beneath it is a stairway. Quatermain grabs a handful of diamonds before descending the steps. Finding a passage with two forks, they take one but are stopped at an underground river. They retrace their steps and take the other fork. They eventually find an opening in the side of the mountain and escape. After resting, they try to find the opening again, but are unsuccessful.

Returning to Ignosi's village, they say farewell to their friend. He is angered until Quatermain explains about their homesickness. They depart Kukuanaland past a grateful people. Good is asked by a young girl to show his white legs again (he had recovered his trousers earlier). He refuses at first, then compromises by rolling his pants up to his knees. Infadoos leads the party out of Kukuanland by a different route than that by which they entered. When he leaves them, Good gives him a spare monocle. The whites are then led by five native guides across the desert.

After travelling three days, they encounter a white man living in a hut with a black man. The former turns out to be Sir Henry's brother George; the latter was his servant, Jim. He had started for the mines two years earlier, but had his leg crushed in an accident and decided to stay where he was. Having plenty of ammunition, they survived on game.

Curtis and Good return to England with the diamonds. Curtis writes to Quatermain and convinces him to come to England. The guide agrees, wishing to visit his son and see to the publication of his book.

King Solomon's Mines

African Film Productions (South Africa); Released November 21, 1918; 8 reels; DIRECTOR: Horace L. Lucoque; PHOTOGRAPHY: W. Bowden

CAST: Hal Lawrence (Allan Quatermain), H. J. Hamlin (Sir Henry Curtis), Ray Brown (Capt. John Good, R.N.), Umpikayiboni (Umbopa), Edna Joyce (Queen of Sheba), Frank Fillis (Captain of the Guard), Phyllis Solomon (Leader of Dance Troupe), Vivien Talleur, Bertie Solomon

British director-producer Lucoque was invited by Harold Shaw of African Film Productions to helm this initial photoplay in that country's effort to improve the quality of its filmic output. *Allan Quatermain* [q.v.] was

King Solomon's Mines (African Films, 1918). Unknown actress, Ray Brown, unknown actress, H.J. Hamlin, Hal Lawrence. (Courtesy BFI Stills, Posters and Designs.)

announced simultaneously as his next project. The sole copy of this film is in the South African National Film, Video and Sound Archive.

King Solomon's Mines

Gaumont-General Film Distributors (Great Britain); Released June 1937; 80 minutes; DIRECTORS: Robert Stevenson, Geoffrey Barkas; SCREENPLAY: Michael Hogan, Roland Pertwee; PHOTOGRAPHY: Glen MacWilliams, Cyril J. Knowles (African exteriors); MUSIC: Mischa Spoliansky; COSTUME DESIGN: Marianne; EDITOR: Michael Gordon; ART DIRECTOR: Alfred Junge; MUSICAL DIRECTOR: Louis Levy; LYRICS: Eric Maschwitz; SOUND: A. Birch; SONGS ("Ho! Ho!" and "Climbing Up"): Eric Maschwitz, Mischa Spoliansky

CAST: Paul Robeson (Umbopa), Cedric Hardwicke (Allan Quartermain), Roland Young (Commander Good), John Loder (Sir Henry Curtis), Anna Lee (Kathy O'Brien), Arthur Sinclair (Patrick O'Brien), Robert Adams (Twala), Arthur Goullet (Sylvestra), Ecce Homo Toto (Infadoos), Makubalo Hlubi (Kapse), Mjujwa (Scragga), Sydney Fairbrother (Gagool), Alfred Goddard (Red), Frederick Leister (Wholesaler)

This was the first sound film to be made in Haggard's native land. Gaumont produced what is the best adaptation of a Rider Haggard work to date. Directed by Robert Stevenson in Britain and Geoffrey Barkas in Africa, the second version of *King Solomon's*

Mines is notable for its fidelity to the book, fast pacing and excellent casting. Sir Cedric Hardwicke made a very believable Allan Quatermain (though here called *Quartermain*), African-American singer-actor Paul Robeson was an excellent Umbopa, British leading man John Loder was a stalwart Sir Henry Curtis, Roland Young an eccentric Capt. Good, and Anna Lee (Stevenson's wife) the feisty daughter of an Irish adventurer, characters created for this production. They convince Quartermain to allow them to travel with him. On the way they find a wagon with a dying Portuguese and an African inside. The former babbles about having a map of King Solomon's Mines, which turns out to be true. He does not survive the night, and the Irishman finds the map and takes off alone to find the fabled mines. The African, Umbopa, attaches himself to Quartermain's party. The girl later steals Quartermain's wagon and goes after him with Umbopa. When she is caught, Good and Curtis decide to go on ahead with her, and since Quartermain has a contract with Curtis, he goes too. After crossing a great desert, they reach the land of the Kukuanas. From here on the film follows its source material closely, with certain omissions.

King Solomon's Mines (African Films, 1918). Lobby card. (Courtesy BFI Stills, Posters and Designs.)

Very impressive is diminutive British actress Sydney Fairbrother as Gagool, a character based on an actual minion of the great Zulu chief Shaka, who was likely the inspiration for the cruel chief Twala. At the smelling-out ritual, she marks Umbopa for death, but Quartermain jumps in front of him and fires his rifle, halting the executioners and causing Twala to flee with his followers. The remainder of the warriors pledge allegiance to Umbopa, who has shown them his snake tattoo, proving him to be their rightful ruler.

This is the only sound version to include the incident of the solar eclipse, although it is done spontaneously here, not promised beforehand. The subsequent battle between the forces of Umbopa and Twala is excitingly presented as the two massed armies jab at each other with spears and hack away with axes at close quarters. Equally well staged is the confrontation between Twala and Sir Henry Curtis, with the Englishman victorious.

Foulata is omitted, as is the dance of the young women. British society being as backward as America's then, a romantic relationship between a

King Solomon's Mines (Gaumont-British, 1937). Umbopa (Paul Robeson, center) and his men prepare for another onslaught. (Courtesy BFI Stills, Posters and Designs.)

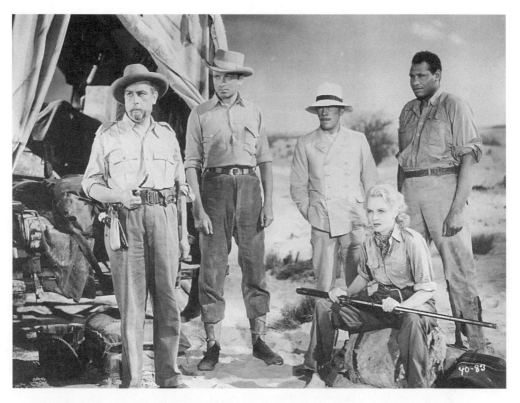

King Solomon's Mines (Gaumont-British, 1937). Cedric Hardwicke. John Loder, Roland Young, Anna Lee, Paul Robeson. (Courtesy BFI Stills, Posters and Designs.)

black and a white could not be shown on screen. It's a wonder the producers allowed the white substitute for Foulata to be Irish, given the relations between Britain and Ireland. Here, though, Curtis is the object of her affection.

Further luster was added to this production by the very convincing set of a volcano's interior, with jets of flame and bubbling lava surrounding the characters as they make their escape from certain death. Although such an episode is not in the book, it makes for exciting viewing, while having the characters sit in darkness overnight hardly would have. The girl's father is

found in the mines with a broken leg. Gagool traps the party inside, but Umbopa rescues them as the volcano convulses, killing Gagool in the process.

The art direction was handled by Alfred Junge, who had worked previously at Ufa, Germany's most prestigious film studio. Later, in the '40s, he would do some fine work for the team of Michael Powell and Emeric Pressburger.

It should be noted that while this production included two of the three stone colossi guarding the entrance to the mines, all subsequent versions of *King Solomon's Mines* do not. *All* sound versions have omitted the stone table inside around which sat a giant skeleton and the bodies of 27 former kings of the local tribe slowly being turned into stalagmites by water dripping from the cavern ceiling.

The New York Times, July 3, 1937 (Frank S. Nugent)

> Robert Stevenson's capable direction and a sincere Anglo-American cast ... has done rather more than muddle through.... Sir Cedric Hardwicke ... is the doughty Allan Quatermain ... cajoled into leading a pocket-size expedition into unknown Africa ... an exciting make-believe, which doesn't have to be taken seriously to be enjoyed.

King Solomon's Mines

MGM; Released November 1950; 101 minutes; *DIRECTORS:* Compton Bennett, Andrew Morton; *PRODUCER:* Sam Zimbalist; *SCREENPLAY:* Helen Deutsch; *PHOTOGRAPHY:* Robert Surtees; *EDITORS:* Conrad A. Nervig, Ralph F. Winters; *ART DIRECTORS:* Cedric Gibbons, Paul Groesse; *COSTUME DESIGN:* Walter Plunkett; *SET DECORATORS:* Keogh Gleason, Edwin B. Willis; *COLOR CONSULTANTS:* James Good, Henri Jaffa; *RECORDING SUPERVISOR:* Douglas Shearer; Produced in Africa (Belgian Congo, Tanganyika, Uganda, Kenya)

CAST: Stewart Granger (Allan Quatermain), Deborah Kerr (Elizabeth Curtis), Richard Carlson (John Good), Hugo Haas (Smith), Lowell Gilmore (Eric Masters), Kimursi (Khiva), Siriaque (Umbopa), Sekaryongo (Chief Gagool), Baziga (King Twala), Corp. Munto Anampio (Chief Bilu), Gutare (Kafa), Ivargwema (Blue Star), Benempinga (Black Circle), John Banner (Austin), Henry Rowland (Traum)

ACADEMY AWARDS: Best Editing; Best Cinematography (color).

NOMINATION: Best Production.

This production is notable for a number of firsts. It was the first adaptation of a Haggard work to be filmed in color; the first to win an Academy Award (actually two); and the first Haggard-based film to be made since before the War. The latter fact obviously affected the screenplay. With the monumental carnage of the war still seared into many memories, the massive battle among the Kukuanas (here called Kaluanas) was jettisoned, leaving Umbopa and Twala to fight for the throne in solo hand-to-hand combat. As Quatermain explains to Mrs. Curtis and Good, it is the tribal custom because "it saves war and bloodshed." It was Stewart Granger's (1913–1993) first American film after a number of movies in his native England.

Other differences include Henry Curtis being the sought-for adventurer and the seeker being his wife; John Good here is merely Mrs. Curtis' brother. The old female witch Gagool is a male witch doctor of the same name, and the "smelling-out" ritual does not occur. Umbopa does not appear until very late in the proceedings, shortly before the safari reaches the territory within which lie King Solomon's Mines. Twala has no facial disfigurement, and of course, there is no Foulata. The action takes place in 1897, 12 years after Haggard penned the novel. Released in the first year of the prudish and wholesome 50s, the mountains called "Sheba's Breasts" in the novel became "The White Twins."

These differences aside, the entire mood of Rider Haggard's work is lost due to the realistic approach taken by the filmmakers. For the score, native

King Solomon's Mines (MGM, 1950). Kimursi, Richard Carlson, Deborah Kerr, Stewart Granger. (Courtesy Collectors Book Store.)

music was used throughout. Actual Watusi tribesmen played the roles of Umbopa and the other Kaluanas (Kukuanas). As an adventure film, this *King Solomon's Mines* is a fine one, but it is not H. Rider Haggard. The one minuscule bow to the book's fantasy elements is a brief shot of a corpse encased in ice within the mines.

The five-month shooting schedule on the Dark Continent produced extensive footage of African fauna, which added much to the film's interest (one reason it became a world-wide box office hit). It also came in handy for later MGM productions based on the works of Haggard.

The New York Times, November 10, 1950 (Bosley Crowther):

There is more than a trace of outright hokum in this thriller ... but there is also an ample abundance of scenic novelty and beauty to compensate. ... Metro has brought into the film such a riot of ethnic illustration, natural history and anthropology that a skeptic can go with the safari just for the sights to be seen.

King Solomon's Mines (M-G-M, 1950). Deborah Kerr, Richard Carlson, Stewart Granger. (Courtesy Collectors Book Store.)

Watusi

MGM; Released July 1959; 85 minutes; Technicolor; Based on *King Solomon's Mines*; DIRECTOR: Kurt Neumann; PRODUCER: Al Zimbalist; SCREENPLAY: James Clavell; PHOTOGRAPHY: Harold E. Wellman; EDITOR: William B. Gulick; ART DIRECTORS: Malcolm Brown, William A. Horning; ASSISTANT DIRECTOR: William Shanks; MAKEUP: William Tuttle; HAIR STYLES: Sydney Guilaroff; SPECIAL EFFECTS: Lee LeBlanc; CAMERA OPERATOR: Fred J. Koenekamp

CAST: George Montgomery (Harry Quartermain), Taina Elg (Erica Neuler), David Farrar (Rick Cobb), Rex Ingram (Umbopa), Dan Seymour (Mohamet), Robert Goodwin (Jim-Jim), Anthony M. Davis (Amtaga), Paul Thompson (Gagool), Harold Dyrenforth (Wilhelm)

The working title of this production was *Return to King Solomon's Mines*. This film contains so much unused and stock footage from *King Solomon's Mines* (1950) [q.v.] that it would be indistinguishable from the earlier film except for the cast. Even then, the actors from the other picture are seen in several long shots. The wafer-thin plot is almost identical as well. The native music *is* identical.

Here, Harry Quartermain (again that extra "r"), the son of Allan, who is

Top: *Watusi* (MGM, 1959). Taina Elg, George Montgomery. Bottom: *Watusi* (MGM, 1959). George Montgomery, Taina Elg, David Farrar. (Courtesy Collectors Book Store.)

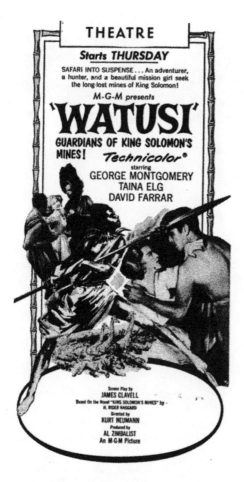

THEATRE

Starts THURSDAY

SAFARI INTO SUSPENSE... An adventurer,
a hunter, and a beautiful mission girl seek
the long-lost mines of King Solomon!

M-G-M presents

'WATUSI'

GUARDIANS OF KING SOLOMON'S
MINES! *Technicolor®*

starring
GEORGE MONTGOMERY
TAINA ELG
DAVID FARRAR

Screen Play by
JAMES CLAVELL
Based On the Novel "KING SOLOMON'S MINES" by
H. RIDER HAGGARD
Directed by
KURT NEUMANN
Produced by
AL ZIMBALIST
An M-G-M Picture

Watusi (MGM, 1959). Newspaper ad.

now dead, has come to Africa to try his luck at finding the fabled mines of King Solomon. He teams up with a fellow named Cobb, who is living in his father's old house. Right away the screenwriter has tampered with the Quatermain family history as set down by Haggard. In the novel *Allan Quatermain*, it is mentioned that Allan's son Harry has died of smallpox, so he predeceased his father. A mother, stepmother and sister are also spoken of in this film, whereas in the books only Allan's wife appears. It seems that Harry's stepmother and younger sister were U-boat victims during WWI, explaining his hatred for Germans even after the war. The rescued daughter of a slain German missionary is the love interest, although only after she saves Harry's life, which causes him to forget his bias.

The party treks through desert, veldt and Watusi country courtesy of the earlier film, reaches the same Watusi village, and is led to the mines where a teetering rock must be crossed to reach the treasure. They are in and out quicker than you can say "up the creek in Mozambique." On the way Cobb and Harry had both fallen for the woman; after their adventure, the rivalry is settled when Cobb decides to return to England and the woman and Harry opt for Africa.

Watusi is a minor effort and best avoided by Haggard enthusiasts.

The New York Times, July 2, 1959 (Howard Thompson):

> [*Watusi*] is no improvement on *King Solomon's Mines*.... With some logic, a large portion of the original picture's African footage has been borrowed wholesale ... and the three principals draped against it.

Drums of Africa

MGM; Released July 1963; 92 minutes; DIRECTOR: James B. Clark; PRODUCERS: Al Zimbalist, Philip Krasner; SCREENPLAY: Robin Estridge, Arthur Hoerl; PHOTOGRAPHY: Paul C. Vogel; EDITOR: Ben Lewis; MUSIC: Johnny Mandel; SPECIAL EFFECTS: Robert R. Hoag; ART DIRECTORS: George W. Davis, Addison Hehr;

Top: *Drums of Africa* (MGM, 1963). Frankie Avalon, Mariette Hartley. Bottom: *Drums of Africa* (MGM, 1963). Frankie Avalon, Torin Thatcher, Mariette Hartley, Lloyd Bochner. (Courtesy Collectors Book Store.)

SET DECORATORS: Henry Grace, Jack Mills; MUSIC AND LYRICS ("The River Love") by Russell Faith and Robert Marcucci, sung by Frankie Avalon

CAST: Frankie Avalon (Brian Ferrers), Lloyd Bochner (David Moore), Mariette Hartley (Ruth Knight), Torin Thatcher (Jack Cuortemayn), Michael Pate (Viledo), Hari Rhodes (Kasongo), George Sawaya (Arab), Ron Whelan (Ship Captain), Peter Mamakos (Chavera)

This film is not available on video as of this writing, and is rarely shown on television. It is known to contain much stock footage from *King Solomon's Mines* (1950) [q.v.].

The New York Times, July 4, 1963 (Howard Thompson):

> "...[A] leathery engineer ... representing progress clashes with a stubborn old native "protector" ... evil slave traders provide a melodramatic finish.

King Solomon's Mines

Cannon Group; Released November 1985; 100 minutes; DIRECTOR: J. Lee Thompson; PRODUCERS: Yoram Globus, Menahem Golan; ASSOCIATE PRODUCER: Rony Yacov; SCREENPLAY: Gene Quintano, James R. Silke; PHOTOGRAPHY: Alex Phillips; MUSIC: Jerry Goldsmith; PRODUCTION DESIGN: Luciano Spadoni; SET DECORATOR: Nelle Giorgetti; PRODUCTION ASSOCIATE: Avi Lerner; COSTUME DESIGN: Tony Pueo; EDITOR: John Shirley; MAKEUP: Walter Cossa

CAST: Richard Chamberlain (Allan Quatermain), Sharon Stone (Jesse Huston), Herbert Lom (Col. Bockner), John Rhys-Davies (Dogati), June Bathelezi (Gagoola), Sam Williams (Umbopo), Shai K. Ophir (Kassam), Mick Lesley (Dorfman), Vincent Van Der Byl (Shack), Bob Greer (Hamid), Oliver Tengende (Bushiri), Neville Thomas (German Thomas), Isiah Murert (Rug Carrier), Rocky Green, Calvin Johns, Isaac Mabhikwa, Brian Kagure, Stanley Norris (Silent Ones), Anna Ditano (Camp Follower), Andrew Whaley (German)

This production was obviously made to cash in on the craze caused by the 1981 film *Raiders of the Lost Ark* , which itself was inspired by the serials made by Republic in the 30s and 40s. It also aspired to higher comic heights than the earlier film, with only sporadic success.

Once again a female character not in the novel is introduced, this time Jesse Huston, who is seeking her father, an archaeologist. The story is set in a fictional African country during World War I. The villains of the piece are the German military, depicted as comic Wagner-loving sputterers, and a Turk played by Welsh actor John Rhys-Davies, who was also in *Raiders of the Lost Ark*.

The opening is straight out of the earlier film, featuring two comic chases through an open-air marketplace. The stunts throughout the film are outrageous, not the least of which is having Allan Quatermain dragged behind a speeding train by a chain; managing to get his feet onto the rails, he stands and climbs back onto the train, with nary a scratch to show for it. The woman's father is being held captive by the Germans, who want the route to King Solomon's Mines. They are also after her to use her as leverage to get the old man to talk. She is a bungler, so eventually she is caught and the old man tells the Germans what they want to know.

She and Quatermain try to outrace the Germans to the mines, a sequence

King Solomon's Mines (Cannon, 1985). Richard Chamberlain. (Courtesy Collectors Book Store.)

which fills the middle of the film. They first steal a German plane; forced down, they are captured by a tribe of cannibals from whom they escape after being cooked in a giant pot. They then meet a tribe of natives who live upside-down in trees. With the Germans right behind them, Quatermain and the woman forge ahead until captured by another unfriendly tribe ruled by a very old woman named Gagoola. We are getting closer to Haggard here; this Gagoola is a frightful creature right in keeping with Rider's character. She orders her warriors to tie up Quatermain and suspend him over a pit full of hungry crocodiles. Umbopo appears and reveals himself as Twala(!), the rightful ruler of the Kukuanas, baring

his chest and showing his tattoo. Meanwhile, Quatermain manages to free himself just as the Germans attack the village.

Gagoola has two men grab Jesse and they take a secret passage to the mines. Inside, the old hag tries to "hot-pot" Jesse, a device borrowed from *She*. Umbopo and Quatermain rescue her and the chief takes them to a large cavern containing the bodies of several former Kukuana queens (another difference from the novel) encased in ice. Quatermain and Jesse then discover the treasure chamber, but are trapped therein by Gagoola. They are inadvertently rescued from the trap-filled chamber by the German officer, who has followed them looking for the

Top: *King Solomon's Mines* (Cannon, 1985). Richard Chamberlain, Sharon Stone. Bottom: *King Solomon's Mines* (Cannon, 1985). Sharon Stone, Richard Chamberlain. (Courtesy Collectors Book Store.)

diamonds. His greed leads to his doom when he forces Quatermain and the girl to give up the diamonds they had taken. Meanwhile Umbopo pursues Gagoola, who jumps into a fiery pit to escape him.

Umbopo assumes the chieftainship of the Kukuanas while Quatermain and Jesse go off together, each with one huge diamond.

Filming began on location in Harare, Zimbabwe, in January 1985. The cast and crew had to withstand both political unrest and the worst rainstorms in the country's history. A second film, *Allan Quatermain and the Lost City of Gold* [q.v.], was shot during the company's stay, but not released until 1987.

Variety, November 23, 1985:

> Cannon has tried to update the hero of the H. Rider Haggard novel for today's impatient audiences ... generally good production values and snappy effects directed by J. Lee Thompson ... clumsy with logic ... making the action hopelessly cartoonish.

Moon of Israel
(novel, 1918)

SYNOPSIS: Narration by an Egyptian scribe named Ana opens the book; he remains as the narrator and a major character throughout.

Born on the same day as Seti, prince of Egypt and heir to the throne, his life becomes intertwined with the son of the Pharaoh after the latter summons him to court because of the fame of his stories. In disguise, Seti and Ana go among the people to observe their situation. Coming upon a group of Hebrew slaves, they see an old straggler being beaten by an overseer. The old man turns on the latter and kills him with a wooden spade. Other overseers attack him until a soldier arrives and draws his sword. Suddenly a young woman appears from the crowd and stands over the old man, begging for mercy. She appeals to Seti, although she does not know him, and he tells the soldier to stay his arm. The soldier responds by cursing and striking Seti; in the same motion he slays the old man. Seti summons his bodyguards who had been following behind him, and a melee results until Seti reveals his identity. He holds court then and there and tries the soldier. The woman states that she is the daughter of the dead man. The prince condemns the soldier and he is instantly beheaded.

Seti offers Ana the post of private librarian for one month. Ana accepts. The two seal their brotherhood with an oath and by splitting an alabaster cup, each taking half of it.

At Pharaoh's palace, Moses and another Hebrew appear to ask Pharaoh to let the Israelites leave Egypt. As their reason, they ask Seti to tell Pharaoh of the previous night's events; he refuses. The daughter of the dead man, Merapi, known as the Moon of Israel, steps forth and relates the incident. Seti corroborates her story. Pharaoh says the Israelites must now work harder and supply their own straw for brickmaking. Moses curses him and his country and departs.

Pharaoh orders Seti, his cousin Amenmeses and Ana to go to Goshen to observe the Hebrews' situation. First, however, he decrees that Seti shall marry his half-sister Userti. Before they depart, she has an audience with Ana. Feeling she can trust him, Userti gives Ana a mail shirt and sword with which to protect the prince. Seti is warned by two court magicians that the trip to Goshen will bring danger to his body, heart and throne.

While in Goshen, Seti must rule on the case of an Egyptian soldier molesting a Hebrew girl. The Hebrews are unsatisfied with his verdict; that night, the soldier is murdered and the family of the girl disappears.

Seti and Ana come upon Merapi praying in the desert. Her foot is injured, so Seti takes her back to Goshen in his chariot. On the way, they encounter Merapi's fiancé Laban, who is looking for his betrothed. Amenmeses also appears, as he has been searching for Seti. Laban has words with the Egyptians.

When Seti accidentally enters a Hebrew temple, he is attacked. A priest stops them and says that if Seti had deliberately entered, Jahveh would strike him dead in a minute. Still alive after one minute, he is allowed to leave.

As Seti and Ana ride through some rocky terrain, Merapi suddenly appears and warns them of an ambush. As they try to turn, they are attacked by 30 or 40 Hebrews, who kill their horses. Seti's two guards are killed, leaving only him and Ana, who sends the charioteer to get help. In the resulting fight, Merapi kills a man about to kill Seti and is herself wounded. Just then the Egyptian guard arrives.

Ana lies unconscious for three days; when he awakes, he sees Merapi. She has been given a home in Egypt, for she has betrayed her people.

When Seti makes his report to Pharaoh, they disagree over the status of the Hebrews; Seti wants to set them free, Pharaoh wants them kept enslaved. Userti suggests that Merapi test her god against Amon Ra, the chief Egyptian god. If she is not killed by Amon, Seti promises to study the religious question. If Merapi's god does nothing to Amon, though, she is to be handed over to Amon's priests.

At the appointed time, Merapi appears in the temple. Priests pray to Amon; a wind arises and blows off Merapi's wimple and scarab clasp, but she is unharmed. She then prays to her god; another wind arises and blows the statue of Amon to dust.

Pharaoh again argues with Seti about the Hebrews; the prince remains firm. His father disinherits him, but not Userti. He names Amenmeses as his successor. Seti and Merapi move to Memphis. When Pharaoh dies, Amenmeses is crowned. At the coronation, when a certain statue does not bow as the new Pharaoh passes, it is seen as a sign of disapproval. Once more the Hebrew prophets appear and appeal for freedom for their people, but are again refused.

In Memphis one night, Seti tells Merapi of the prophecy regarding her. She declares her love for Seti, but says it cannot be due to laws forbidding marriage between Hebrews and Gentiles. The Egyptian replies that all relationships run risks, which he is willing to take. Merapi then submits.

Meanwhile, in Thebes, Ana encounters his former wife, now ruined by riotous living. Without revealing his identity, he gives her some gold and she departs. During his absence, the prophets had returned and turned the waters of the Nile to blood. All the fish died and the water was unfit to drink.

Plagues of frogs, lice and flies follow. Only Seti's house, where he lives with Merapi and their newborn son, is spared. More plagues follow; still Seti's house is spared. The people begin to feel that he is right in setting the Hebrews free. Ki comes to Seti seeking shelter, for he has been stripped of his title by Pharaoh for disagreeing with him. Amenmeses becomes worried that Seti will regain the throne, so he sends assassins to kill him, but they are thwarted.

Still more plagues strike the country. The people besiege Seti's home and demand that Merapi pray for release from the plagues. They dress her as Isis and force her to pray. When she does, the sun returns. Laban appears and curses Merapi and her child.

Seti sends Ana and another to Pharaoh to beg one last time for the release of the Hebrews. He says he will not because he cannot. Unrest increases throughout the land.

One night Seti's son tells his parents of a dream he had wherein a lady came and took him to a star. Animals then begin dying all around. The child arises, stares upward for a moment, then drops backward, dead. At the same time, all the first born of Egypt are dying. Pharaoh finally allows the Hebrews to leave Egypt.

Merapi's uncle visits Merapi and asks her to join her people, saying that if she does not, she will die. She chooses to remain with Seti.

Meanwhile, Userti stirs up the Egyptian people against the Israelites. Pharaoh goes in pursuit of them with his army. Merapi has a dream about her people which includes a pillar of fire, the Red Sea crossing and the destruction of Pharaoh and his host, but does not understand it. When she has it interpreted, Seti rushes to warn Amenmeses, but the Pharaoh dismisses the warning as a trick to save the Israelites. Ana loudly announces the dream in the camp and many soldiers desert. The next day Seti and his party witness the parting of the Red Sea and the death of Pharaoh and his army. Just then, Seti and Ana see a vision of Merapi calling for help. Seti immediately rushes back to Memphis in his chariot.

Arriving there, he finds Merapi and a man upon a flaming pyre. Laban is also there, cursing Merapi and all Egyptians; Ki has him thrown onto the pyre. Seti rescues Merapi as Ki steals away; he is caught and brought before Seti. Merapi relates all that transpired while Seti was away. Ki made her an offer to be Queen of Egypt if she would reveal her source of magic to him. She said she had none, and everyone turned against her. A stranger came to take her to Seti, but they are captured along the way. The stranger is revealed as Laban. Ki puts Merapi in prison and ask her many questions, but she gives no answers. Then he built the pyre for her.

Seti judges Ki, then asks the people for a verdict. "Death!" is the unanimous cry. Ki tells Seti he will never be happy before he is consigned to the flames. Merapi dies three days later. After her funeral, Seti takes his place as Pharaoh, with Userti as his queen. Six years later, Seti and Ana see Merapi and her son in a vision; the next day Seti is found dead.

Die Sklavenkönigin
The Slave Queen

United States and Great Britain: *Moon of Israel*; Sascha Films (Austria); Released October 24, 1924; 12 reels; Distributed in the United States by F.B.O. Pictures Corp. (1927); Based on *Moon of Israel*; DIRECTOR: Mihaly Kertesz [Michael Curtiz]; PRODUCER: Alexander Kolowrat; SCENARIO: Ladislaus Vajda; PHOTOGRAPHY: Gustave Ucicky, Max Nekut; MUSIC: Björn Maseng; ART AND SET DECORATORS: Arthur Berger, Emil Stepanek; COSTUMES: Remigius Geyling; ASSISTANT DIRECTOR: Arthur Gottlein

CAST: Maria Corda (Merapi, Moon of Israel), Adelqui Miller (Prince Seti), Arelette Marchal (Userti), Ferdinand Onno (Ana), Oscar Beregi (Amenneses), Henry Mar (Moses), Adolph Wiesse (Pharaoh Menapta), Reinhold Haeussermann (Pampasa, Seti's Tutor), Georges Haryton (Laban), Emil Hayse (Ki, the High Priest), Boris Baranoff (Merapi's father), Hans Thimig

One of Kertesz' early efforts, *Die Sklavenkönigin* is not a "run of DeMille" epic; it contains more action than the American director ever included. The sets and costumes match DeMille's, for as every film fan knows, only God could *surpass* DeMille. The crowds are handled equally well and may actually outnumber those appearing in the American's films, given the economic situation in Europe at the time, with its rampant inflation and unemployment. Location shooting was done at the Laaerberg, a mountainous area outside Vienna which was popular with filmmakers.

The director's noted visual style is apparent even at this early date. He utilizes a variety of camera angles and artistically composes his shots. As "Michael Curtiz" in the United States, he would later helm such classics as *The Adventures of Robin Hood* (1938), *Yankee Doodle Dandy* (1942) and *Casablanca* (1942).

The print owned by this writer has German intertitles; however, he shall do his best to convey the plot from the visuals.

Opening with a shot of four trumpeters atop a statue, Kertesz pulls back his camera to a wide-angle shot of a very large crowd arranged before a temple. Prince Seti decides to go among the slaves in disguise, the better to observe actual conditions. He witnesses an overseer beating an old man, who retaliates in vain, unlike in the novel, where he kills the overseer. Seti keeps him from killing the man, receiving a blow to the face. The overseer then kills the man. Revealing his identity, Seti tries the man on the spot. Unlike the book, there is no soldier involved in this incident, only the overseer, who is taken away. He had earlier been making a pass at a Hebrew woman. She is the daughter of the dead man.

The remainder of the film is faithful to its source, save for some minor points. At the ambush of Seti, he and Ana initially use bows to fight the Hebrews, and their horses are not killed, but unhitched by the charioteer, who still *runs* for help, rather than riding one of the horses. Not to worry; he finds a cavalry troop in time.

Top: *Moon of Israel* (Sascha Film, 1924). Bottom: *Moon of Israel* (Sascha Film, 1924). Maria Corda, Adelphi Millar. (Courtesy BFI Stills, Posters and Designs.)

At the Temple of Amon, when the Egyptian priests pray, nothing happens to Merapi. When she prays, not only is the statue destroyed, but a hailstorm occurs.

In the film, Menaptah's death occurs immediately after his heart attack, instead of his lingering for a few hours.

Only a couple of the plagues are depicted in the film, and when the last occurs, only an owl dies before the son of Seti.

When Seti gives warning to Amenmeses, the latter barely reacts and Seti departs peacefully. Ana does not proclaim the dream aloud and no soldiers are seen deserting. The parting of the Red Sea is technically the equal of DeMille's depiction of it in *The Ten Commandments* (1923), no doubt because it was accomplished in the same way. Seti does not see the vision of Merapi in danger until that night.

In Memphis, it is Ana who orders Ki's death. After her rescue by Seti, Merapi dies in his arms, and the film ends.

Hopefully, this film will become available with English intertitles, for it is definitely worth viewing, both as a faithful adaptation of a Haggard work and an example of silent film spectacle.

National Board of Review Magazine, July 1927:

The price of Red Sea crossings is coming down. When one of them is thrown in as a mere incident in a romantic love affair between a Jewish slave maiden and a son of a Pharaoh, the mind harks back almost incredulously to the prodigious publicity noises which emanated from the DeMille studios while *The Ten Commandments* was in process.

Not that we mean to detract from DeMille's pioneer effort. His crossing was ... the first, a notable demonstration of the theory that the movies can cross anything. After that as in the case of the first flight across the ocean, all subsequent performances are bound to seem easier. Yet just to see it done again, that sudden parting of an immense mass of water and the confident, dry-shod advance of a people strong in their faith, is worthwhile and the *Moon of Israel* gains in appeal by the repetition.

Nor is the crossing of the Red Sea the only thing that makes *Moon of Israel* memorable. Imaginative direction and the fine handling of crowds mark all the spectacle scenes andleave a vivid impression of the splendor and magnificence of Egyptian civilization under the rule of the Pharaohs. It is in this combination of noteworthy mass effects and an intriguing love story that the strength of the picture lies.

... The outstanding piece of acting in *Moon of Israel* is contributed by Marie [*sic*] Corda in the part of Merapi. This talented actress has already become known to American audiences through her interpretation of the frivolous wife in *Madame Wants No Children*.... Her performance here shows that she has dramatic as well as comedic appeal. She succeeds admir-ably in conveying the pathos of her part and showing the conflict between her love for Seti and her loyalty for her people.

Mr. Meeson's Will
(novel, 1888)

SYNOPSIS: Meeson & Co. is a large publishing house, mainly of religious books. One day a young authoress named Augusta Smithers comes to Mr. Meeson for an accounting of her novel. Reviewing the terms of her agreement with the firm, she feels she has been cheated and will write no more books for the company. Meeson's nephew Eustace is present at the interview and takes the woman's side. He tells off his uncle and is fired and removed from the old man's will. Mr. Meeson goes to his solicitor, tears up his old will and dictates a new one.

Miss Smithers had gone to Meeson for extra money because she had sold the rights to her book for a flat sum and was unable to support herself and her younger sister on it. Her sister becomes ill and a doctor recommends that she move to a warm climate. After leaving Meeson, Augusta goes to a bank for a loan, but is refused. Her sister dies that night.

Ten days later, Eustace visits Augusta. He tells her of his argument with his uncle, and she is flattered. She apologizes for having made a scene, explaining that she needed money badly. Eustace asks why and she shows him her sister's body in the child's bedroom. Eustace is shocked and apologizes for intruding at such a time.

Miss Smithers decides to go to New Zealand, where she has a clergyman relative. There she would be free of Meeson's contract. Eustace finds out too late about her departure. On board the *S.S. Kangaroo*, Augusta runs into Mr. Meeson, who at that moment is seasick. He recognizes her and warns her not to try to write anything in New Zealand, for he has agents there and in Australia.

The captain discovers she is aboard and gives her the cabin of the second officer. He then introduces the young woman to Lady Holmhurst, who has read her book three times. When she introduces Augusta to her husband, who is talking to Meeson, the writer snubs the publisher. Augusta later tells Lady Holmhurst of her relationship with Meeson, and the latter promises to somehow get her contract torn up. Meeson is thereafter snubbed by everyone on board. A New Zealander named Mr. Tombey professes his love to Miss Smithers.

One night the *Kangaroo* collides with a whaling ship which had no lights, cutting it in two. The *Kangaroo* also suffers damage, causing it to sink. The passengers panic; the lifeboats are only enough for 300 people, and there are 1,000 aboard. Augusta gets into a boat with the Holmhurst's little son, while Meeson jumps into the sea and is taken aboard a boat.

A boat containing Lady Holmhurst and 20 others is picked up by a sealing whaler. Taken to the Australian coast, these survivors are sent back to England.

A boat with Smithers, Meeson, the boy and two sailors sights land the next morning: Kerguelen Land, an uninhabited island. Reaching the shore, the occupants find two ramshackle huts. Augusta and the boy move into one, the men take the other. There is plenty of food and water. During the night,

Meeson goes to Augusta's hut and asks to be let in; the two sailors have been drinking in his hut, and he could not abide them. The writer allows him to enter.

The next morning, Augusta is shocked by the publisher's appearance; he is dying. Full of remorse, he wishes to amend his will and make Eustace his heir again. Augusta reminds him there are enough witnesses present, so why not write a new will? There is neither paper nor pencil to be found, however. Meeson gets the idea to write it in blood on linen, but there is no linen. Noticing a tattoo on one of the sailors, Miss Smithers has the idea of tattooing the will upon the other sailor. He refuses, though, because he hates Meeson, and suggests it be done on the child. Augusta is outraged by this suggestion and offers to have the will tattooed upon herself. Using a cuttlefish for ink, one sailor writes "I leave all of my property to Eustace Meeson" across Augusta's shoulders. The two sailors sign as witnesses. Augusta goes to her hut and passes out.

The next day, Meeson is worse; he begins hallucinating that his former employees are coming for him, and he dies. She informs the sailors, but they are too drunk to care. That night she hears them singing; suddenly there is a yell and then silence.

Miss Smithers finds the bodies of the sailors in the water the next morning. After a week on the island, she and the boy are picked up by an American ship. The captain's wife is British and befriends her. Eventually they reach the Azores, whence they get passage to Southampton. Arriving there, Miss Smithers and the boy find they are a *cause celebre*, news of the *Kangaroo*'s sinking having already reached Britain. Augusta reads a newspaper with an article pertaining to Mr. Meeson. The courts had assumed him drowned and made his last written will the legal one. At Waterloo Station the pair is again met by a crowd; among them is Lady Holmhurst, who takes her son and blesses Augusta.

In the meantime, Eustace Meeson has taken a job as a proofreader. He feels he has lost Augusta as well as his uncle's money. When he reads of her survival, he takes a carriage to Waterloo Station and catches Augusta as she is leaving in a cab. They make a date to meet at Lady Holmhurst's the next morning. At that time Augusta relates her adventures to Eustace and shows him the will tattooed on her back. He thanks her and informs her that probate can be revoked by producing a subsequent will.

When they are alone, Eustace professes his love for Augusta, but she does not respond. When Eustace tells Lady Holmhurst they are engaged, she remains quiet.

Eustace hires his twin friends — one a solicitor, the other a barrister — to take his case. It is decided that Miss Smithers will have to be registered with other wills, which is out of the question. To remedy this, it is arranged to have the young woman remain in the presence of an officer of the court until the trial, thus satisfying the legal requirement. Eustace insists on being present also, fearing that the court officer will fall in love with the beauteous Augusta.

Miss Smithers is examined by the court officer and it is decided that a photographic copy of the will be made to be filed. The next day, while out shopping, Augusta is horrified to see copies of the photo being sold in the street and appearing in newspapers. She is spotted, and pressed so hard by a crowd that she has to be rescued by two policemen and a gentleman who get her away in a cab. Meanwhile, Eustace also finds copies of the photo in every photo shop he passes and threatens the photographer. He takes legal action to have all the photos withdrawn, since the will is evidence in a pending case.

The defendants wish to settle out of court; they offer the plaintiffs half the property and will pay court costs. Eustace is satisfied with this, but Augusta is not, for she sees the defendants are afraid.

At the hearing, the plaintiffs' lawyer becomes very nervous as he speaks. One of the defendants' lawyers feels sorry for him and creates a diversion. The resulting laughter relaxes the lawyer and he continues. When Augusta is called to the stand, one of the opposing lawyers objects to her giving testimony, since she is a document, the will being upon her body. Her lawyer argues that signatures could not be tattooed since they could not be recognized as such, and that the plaintiff's case would be ended by disallowing Miss Smithers' testimony. The judge rules for the plaintiffs since the skin is not a whole person; technically, they could be separated. Augusta is sworn in and exhibits the will on her back to the judge and lawyers.

After more witnesses are called and give testimony, the judge weighs the case and decides in favor of the plaintiffs. Ten days later, Eustace and Augusta are wed. Not long afterwards, Eustace buys his uncle's firm. He gives Augusta her contract, upon which he has written "Cancelled." He then calls all the employees together and announces that sweeping changes will be made in company policy toward them and all authors.

Mr. Meeson's Will

Thanhouser; Released November 6, 1915; 3 reels; DIRECTOR: Frederick R. Sullivan; ASSISTANT DIRECTOR: Perry Horton; PHOTOGRAPHY: Charles Wilbur Hoffman

CAST: Florence LaBadie (Augusta Smithers), Justus D. Barnes (Mr. Meeson), Bert Delaney (Eustace Meeson), Ethyle Cooke (Lady Holmhurst), Dorothy Benham (Dickie Holmhurst), Lawrence Swinburne (Mr. Tombey), Charles S. Gould, Samuel Niblack

Originally planned as a four-reel Mutual Masterpiece, this film was re-edited and released as a Than-O-Play. It was filmed at Charleston, South Carolina, and Far Rockaway, New York; the locales in the film are England and New Zealand.

The Moving Picture World, October 30, 1915:

This is a three-part adaptation of a book by H. Rider Haggard. Flo La Badie plays the feminine lead with good effect. The story is ... a rather improbable proposition and has not in it the realism that the present day public craves. Nevertheless, it is an adaptation of a well-known literary work, and as such will be accepted as above the ordinary.

Mr. Meeson's Will (Thanhouser, 1915)
Poster. (Courtesy Ned Thanhouser.)

The Grasp of Greed

Bluebird-Universal; Released July 17, 1916; 5 reels; Based on *Mr. Meeson's Will*; DIRECTOR: Joseph DeGrasse; SCENARIO AND ADAPTATION: Ida May Park

CAST: C. Normand Hammond (John Meeson), Jay Belasco (Eustace), Louise Lovely (Alice Gordon), Gretchen Lederer (Lady Holmhurst), Lon Chaney (Jimmie)

The Moving Picture World, July 22, 1916 (Margaret I. MacDonald):

> The story of *John Meeson's Will*, written by H. Rider Haggard, is one of the old-fashioned, incredible sort that is difficult for the modern mind to become reconciled to and the joker will not overlook the opportunity for a laugh when the judge orders said will to be produced in court, considering that it is tattooed on a young lady's shapely back. The back utilized in this production belongs to Louise Lovely, and will be appreciated as a perfect specimen.
>
> Joseph De Grasse directed the picture and has succeeded in establishing what seems to be the proper atmosphere. But Miss Lovely must be reprimanded for dressing the role of Alice Gordon in modern garments, while the masculine element of the play sports those of at least half a century ago. Some fine effects have been obtained in the earlier portion of the picture, notably in the scenes having to do with the home life of Alice, and the death of her little sister. Here Miss Lovely exhibits her ability for emotional work.

Motion Picture News July 15, 1916:

> Wills have been more or less prominent in motion picture since their inception. But this is probably the first time a document of such legal importance has been tattooed on the smooth white back of a young lady. This is the most prominent feature of *The Grasp of Greed*.... The picture builds up well ... but when the young lady's back is exposed to view and the judge proclaims that it must be passed around the court ... there is no more seriousness in the picture.... Lon Chaney in a comedy role is excellent.

She
(novel, 1887)

SYNOPSIS : Horace Holly, a singularly homely college student, is made the sole guardian of his only friend's five-year-old son. The friend, Vincey, is coughing badly and says he will not survive the night. He tells Holly of his ancient lineage, traceable to the twenty-ninth dynasty of Egypt. That ancestor, a priest named Kallikrates, took vows of celibacy and then fled Egypt with a princess. They were the only survivors of a shipwreck on the African coast and were cared for by a beautiful white woman who was the iron-handed ruler of a savage race. For reasons which Vincey would not divulge at the time, his ancestor was murdered by the white queen. His wife escaped to Athens, where she bore a son. Five hundred years later, the family moved to Rome. Centuries later they settled in England, and took up respectable occupations.

Some years ago, Vincey undertook an expedition in connection with the box he has with him. He met his wife in Athens, and she died giving birth to their son Leo. Vincey asks Holly to be Leo's guardian until Leo's twenty-fifth birthday. He is then to open the iron box, read the contents and allow Leo to decide whether or not he will undertake the quest mentioned therein. A sum of money is also bequeathed to the boy. Holly swears to assume all responsibilities.

The next morning, Holly's valet informs him of Vincey's death. Leo moves in with Holly, who hires a young male attendant named Job to assist him.

On Leo's twenty-fifth birthday, the box is opened, revealing a casket. Inside this is an ancient Egyptian box made of silver. Inside that is a letter from Leo's father, two rolls of parchment, a piece of ancient Greek pottery, an ivory miniature of Leo's mother and a scarab with an inscription. The latter translates to "Royal Son of Ra." The letter tells of Leo's father's journey to an unknown region of Africa. From a native he learned of a tribe of people living in a region surrounded by mountains and swamps. They spoke a dialect of Arabic and were ruled by a white woman who held the power of life and death. For lack of provisions, he could not go on. He traveled to Greece, where he met Leo's mother, who died in childbirth. Vincey studied Arabic with the intention of returning to Africa, but his health failed and he did not live. He gives his son the choice of following up on the legend or of destroying all reference to it. Holly advises Leo against making the trip, feeling that Vincey was raving due to his illness.

Translating the writing on the potsherd, they read the story of Kallikrates as told by his wife, Amenartas. After breaking his vows to be with her, the couple fled southward, spending two years along the coast of Libya, "where by a river is a great rock carven like the head of an Ethiopian." They then came to "a hollow mountain, where a great city had been and fallen and where there are caves which no man hath seen the end and they brought us to the Queen of the people who place pots upon the heads of strangers, who is a magician having a knowledge of all things, and life and loveliness that does not die." This queen fell in love with Kallikrates and wished to kill Amenartas, but the priest refused her advances. The queen then led the pair to a great pit which held the Pillar of Life. She stood in the flames and came out unharmed and even more beautiful. She swore to make Kallikrates immortal if he would kill his wife. He again refused her. The queen then killed Kallikrates and banished Amenartas from her domain. She gave birth to a son aboard ship before reaching Athens. Amenartas begs her son to find and slay the woman in revenge for his father. She adds a proviso: "If thou dost fear or fail, this I say to all of thy seed who come after thee, till at last a brave man be found among them who shall bathe in the fire and sit in the place of the Pharaohs." The parchments tell of the Vincey family history.

Holly believes in the relics' authenticity, but feels the story of the immortal queen is nonsense. He is sure that Vincey was not in his right mind when he wrote the letter and when he appeared the night of his death. Leo is determined to see the matter through, however, even if he must do so alone. He says he will at least get some good shooting out of it. This sways Holly; Job agrees to accompany them. Three months later they are on their way.

The last part of their sea voyage is made in an Arab dhow, which is wrecked by a squall off the central African coast. Leo almost drowns; the Britons and the Arab captain are the only other survivors. The next morning, they see the rock shaped like an Ethiopian's head nearby.

They discover a swamp and evidence of an ancient mooring place. They embark upon the river in the swamp in the whaling boat they had brought along. Forced to abandon the boat due to shallow water, they continue on foot, pulling the boat. They soon realize they are not on a river, but an ancient canal. One night, Holly is awakened by a man with a spear who speaks an Arabic dialect, who asks who he is. Holly explains, then hears another voice ask, "What color are they?" Told they are white, the voice says, "Slay them not. Four moons since word came from 'She-who must-be-obeyed : White men come; if white men come, kill them not.' Let them be brought to the house of 'She-who-must-be-obeyed.' Bring forth the men and let that which they have with them be brought forth also."

A party of 50 light-skinned men clad in leopard skin girdles become visible. The Arab, Mahomet, is almost killed for having dark skin, but is spared by the man in the shadows. The whites are carried in litters, but Mahomet is made to run. Hours later, Holly is questioned by a white-bearded man named Billali. He says his people are the Amahagger, the People of the Rocks. They arrive at "a vast cup of earth, four to six miles in extent, and molded to the shape of a Roman amphitheater. The sides of this great cup were rocky, clothed with bush, but its center was of the richest meadowland, studded with single trees of magnificent growth, and watered by meandering brooks." In this valley they encounter the women of the cave-dwelling tribe. One, Ustane, goes up to

Leo and kisses him; he returns the embrace. (They later find out this is how Amahagger women choose their mates.)

Holly questions Billali about "She," but learns little, save that she is apparently very old. Billali leaves them to consult with "She" as to her wishes regarding the whites. Leo feels "She" may be the woman described on the piece of pottery in the casket.

Job attracts the attention of one of the Amahagger women, but he rejects her. A few days later, the visitors are invited to a feast. There the Amahagger try to place a red-hot pot upon Mahomet's head. Holly fires, killing both the woman and Mahomet. The tribesmen attack the outsiders. The latter make a stand upon a ledge at one end of the cave. Holly and Job empty their pistols, then fight with knives. Leo is overwhelmed and about to be killed when Ustane shields him with her body. The men are ready to kill both; Leo is stabbed in his side with a spear. As Holly passes out, he hears a voice call out "Cease!"

Holly awakes to see Ustane tending Leo, Job and Billali, whose men are tying up some Amahagger men. Billali tells Holly that "She's" vengeance will be terrible.

Three days later they leave the cave to travel to visit "She." On the way, Holly saves Billali from drowning in a swamp. They come to a huge solitary mountain of smooth, bare rock. Billali tells Holly it is the abode of "She." He continues with the history of the area: The plain was once a giant lake which was drained by the original inhabitants, who built the mighty city of Kor. They also cut passages throughout the mountain and built the road across the plain, which was originally used as a canal.

The outsiders are blindfolded before entering the mountain. On the other side of the rock wall, their blindfolds are removed. On the plain beyond, they are surrounded by curious Amahagger. They enter a cave in which bas-reliefs with the same design as on Amahagger pottery cover the walls. A mute leads them to their chambers.

While awaiting an audience with "She," they find more bas-reliefs which depict the embalming and burial methods of the ancients. Meanwhile, Leo becomes delirious from his wound.

Holly finds Leo's scarab ring and dons it just before Billali appears to usher him into She's presence. As they enter She's chamber, Billali gets down on his knees and warns Holly to do likewise, or be blasted by the queen. Holly chooses to remain on his feet. Upon reaching a curtain, Billali prostrates himself; Holly becomes fearful. A snow-white hand appears through the curtain and a silvery voice asks him in classical Arabic why he is so afraid. A moment later, a tall figure covered from head to ankle in a translucent gauzy material emerges from behind the curtain. Holly is able to discern a female figure through the material. The figure again asks Holly why he is afraid and turns, revealing a perfectly rounded white arm and long raven hair. She then asks him why he came hither and how is it that he speaks her language. Noticing Billali, she chastises him for the attack of his people upon the strangers. The old man explains the situation and that he has brought the guilty parties to be judged by She. She forgives him, but warns him to keep his people under better control.

She then allows Holly into her private chamber and interviews him. She tells him her name is Ayesha (there is a footnote here giving the pronunciation as "Assha"). She tells Holly of some of her history, including her stoning in Jerusalem prior to the arrival of the Messiah. The Briton wonders at this, for that was 2,000 years ago. She does not reply to his questions. Ayesha states that the only reason she lives there is that she awaits the return of her lover whom she is sure will come back to her, no matter how long it takes.

She reveals to Holly how she knew of the strangers' coming by showing him a scene of his journey in a font-like vessel filled with water. Ayesha tells him that the past can be viewed in the font, but not the future. She inquires after Leo and learns that his fever is in its third day. She says she will wait one more day before trying her curative powers on him. Allowed one last question, Holly asks to see Ayesha's face. The queen warns him that her beauty is overpowering, but he persists. She begins to undo the wrappings she wears. "Now robed only in a garb of clinging white that did but serve to show the rich and imperial shape, instinct with a life that was more than life, and with a certain serpent-like grace which was more than human. On her little feet were sandals, fastened with studs of gold. Then came ankles more perfect than sculptor ever dreamed of. About her waist her white

kirtle was fastened by a double-headed snake of solid gold, above which her gracious form swelled up in lines as pure as they were lovely, till the kirtle ended at the snowy argent of her breast.... I gazed above ... at her face, and — I do not romance — shrank back blinded and amazed. I have heard of the beauty of celestial beings, now I saw it; only this beauty, with all its awful loveliness and purity, was *evil*— or rather, at the time, it impressed me as evil. How am I to describe it? I cannot — simply I cannot. The man does not live whose pen could convey a sense of what I saw. I might talk of the great changing eyes of deepest, softest black, of the tinted face, of the broad and noble brow, on which the hair grew low, and delicate, straight features. But, beautiful, surpassingly beautiful as were all these, her loveliness did not lie in them. It lay rather ... in a visible majesty, in an imperial grace, in a godlike stamp of softened power, which shone upon that radiant countenance like a living halo.... Though the face before me was that of a young woman of certainly not more than 30 years, in perfect health and the first flush of ripened beauty, yet it bore stamped upon it a seal of unutterable experience, and of deep acquaintance with grief and passion." In short, she was not bad-looking.

Before Ayesha covers herself, a look of horror overspreads her features as she notices the scarab on Holly's finger. She demands to know where he got it. Terrified, Holly can only say that he found it. Ayesha says she knew of one like it, only that one hung around the neck of the one she loved. With that, the audience ends.

That night, Holly discovers a passageway in the rock wall of his chamber. He follows it to the chamber with the curtains, which is lit by a white fire that burns without smoke. He espies Ayesha kneeling by a corpse. She stands, and the bodice of her robe falls to her waist. She begins a litany of curses against an unnamed woman. She addresses the corpse as Kallikrates and attempts to re-animate it, but desists. "To what purpose? Of what service is it to recall the semblance of life when it cannot recall the spirit?.... The life in thee would be *my* life, and not *thy* life, Kallikrates!" She kneels next to the body and Holly returns through the passage.

The following day She sits in judgment of the Amahagger men who attacked the strangers. Holly relates the events, which are confirmed by Billali. A leader of the Amahagger explains their side and asks for mercy. She condemns them all to the cave of torture; those who survive after two days will be slain. Clearly a no-win situation.

Ayesha next shows Holly the wonders of the mountain's interior, beginning with the statue of Kor's greatest king over her daïs. A wall inscription tells of a great plague which decimated the city. Those who survived it died from starvation from the famine which followed. Ayesha shows Holly a great pit into which the bodies of the plague victims were thrown — a hill of human skeletons. She continues to a small chamber which is filled with figures wrapped in yellow linen. The queen unwraps one to reveal the perfectly preserved body of a woman and an infant. They view a few more before Ayesha takes Holly to her chamber for more conversation. She unveils again, and Holly falls to his knees before her. The queen expresses a wish to see Leo.

Holly goes ahead and is met by Job and Ustane, who tell him that Leo is near death. Holly runs to him; Ayesha soon arrives and commands Job and Ustane to leave. The girl refuses; Ayesha merely says, "Go!" and Ustane crawls from the chamber. Upon seeing his face, She staggers backward "as though she had been shot or stabbed" and turns on Holly, reviling him for not telling her that Leo was her lost Kallikrates. Realizing then that Holly was unaware of that fact, She gives him a phial and tells him to pour it down Leo's throat. She tells Holly that Leo will sleep for 12 hours and awake recovered.

Ayesha remembers Ustane and asks Holly who she is to Leo, and is told that according to Amahagger custom, they are man and wife. The queen says Ustane must die. Holly enters into a moral argument with her. He reminds the queen that Ustane saved Leo's life during the Amahagger attack. Ayesha orders Holly to bring Ustane before her. She tells the girl that the Amahagger marriage custom does not extend to strangers and dismisses her. Ustane defies the queen and Ayesha swiftly touches her upon the head, leaving three white marks in her hair and dazing her. Ustane departs and Ayesha warns Holly not to tell Leo how she left and as little as possible about herself.

Holly and Leo are taken to a new chamber which abuts Ayesha's. The next morning, Ayesha is standing over Leo when he awakes; he embraces her, thinking that she is Ustane. She tells him that the girl has left to visit someone and that she has replaced her. Leo returns to sleep; upon awakening he begins asking questions of Holly. The latter, remembering Ayesha's words, tells him little. In an audience with Ayesha, Leo is told that Ustane is merely a fickle savage.

Ayesha then takes the pair on a tour of the caves, including the font upon which She can project one's thoughts. That evening, She invites them to a dance outside the caves.

Dark figures bearing flaming corpses rush onto the plateau. After arranging them in a huge bonfire, one figure grabs an arm and uses it to light mummies hung as lamps about the area. Two lines of dancers enter, one of men, one of women; they begin a sort of fiendish can-can. This develops into a drama about an attempted murder, with the victim buried alive and struggling in the grave. One large woman breaks from the group and runs toward the audience, calling for a black goat. She falls to the ground in an epileptic fit. The others say she has a demon and go to get a black goat. Returning with one, they cut its throat and give its blood to the woman, who drinks it and becomes calm again.

The dancers depart, then return dressed in the skins of various animals. Each one imitates the sound and the motion of that particular animal. Holly and Leo ask to be excused and proceed to examine the mummy lamps. When they are in shadow, a dancer in a leopard skin rushes past them into the darkest area. They follow, and discover the dancer to be Ustane. She begs Leo

to flee with her. As she embraces him, however, the sound of laughter reveals the presence of Ayesha. With her are Billali and two mutes.

They retire to Ayesha's chamber and She and Ustane argue over who shall have Leo. Ustane brazenly defies her queen. The latter stands and stretches her arm toward the girl, who clasps her head and screams, then drops dead upon the floor. Realizing what has happened, Leo springs toward Ayesha, but she gestures at him and he falls backward. She begs his forgiveness, but he threatens to kill her. Ayesha calls him Kallikrates; Leo answers that he is not the Egyptian priest, but his descendant. He refuses to have anything to do with her, but She reminds him that he has not seen her for a very long time. She unveils; Leo takes one look at her and exclaims, "Oh, great heaven! Art thou a woman?" Ayesha motions toward Leo and he succumbs.

Later, in Ayesha's bed chamber, the pair sees two beds of stone, on one of which lies a mummy. Ayesha unwraps it to reveal Leo's double. She then bids Holly open its garment, disclosing a puncture wound. Ayesha relates her history to Leo, then pours some acid upon the corpse, which is dissolved completely. The queen takes a handful of the ashes and flings them into the air. "Dust to dust!— The past to the past!— the lost to the lost!— Kallikrates is dead, and is born again!"

When Holly and Leo are alone, the latter gives vent to his feelings, and they both admit that they are forever bound by Ayesha's wondrous beauty.

Ayesha informs Leo that they cannot be lovers until he is like her. She promises to take him to the Place of Life, so that he may become like her. She makes Holly the same offer, but he declines. She expresses her desire to leave Kor and go with Leo to his country, where they shall rule together. The Britons are astounded; Holly tries to dissuade the queen, to no avail.

They begin their trip to the place of Life, with Ayesha being carried by six mutes in a litter, while Billali and the Britons walk. They view the ancient ruins of Kor at sunset and in the moonlight. In the inner court of a shrine is a marble globe about 20 feet in diameter with a female figure atop it, nude save for a veil over its face. Ayesha says it is the symbol of Truth.

Outside again, they come to a cliff face; Ayesha dismisses Billali and her bearers, bidding them wait at this spot. She begins her ascent up the rock wall, followed by Leo, Holly and Job, who carries a wooden plank. About 50 feet up is a cave, which She enters. Inside is a narrow walkway over a bottomless chasm. While buffeted by strong winds, they cross the walkway, though the men must do so on hands and knees. At the end of the walkway, Ayesha pauses. She explains that soon there will be light. Shortly, the setting sun provides the light. Opposite is a cone-shaped rock with a large balancing rock atop it. They use the plank to cross to this rock. Just after Job crawls across, the plank falls into the abyss.

Reaching a small chamber, they re-light their lamps. Ayesha relates how a hermit who had once lived there was the one who discovered the flame of life. He would not avail himself of its powers, nor would he allow her to do

so. She waited until he died and bathed in it, becoming and remaining youthful. When she bid Kallikrates do likewise, he turned away, and she killed him in her fury.

Ayesha then asks Leo for forgiveness for her evil doings and to declare his love for her, which he does. They pass through more tunnels and chambers; a light (accompanied by a sound like thunder) flashes up ahead. They enter a chamber of smooth rock walls with a floor of white sand, which glows with a rose-colored light. The thunder ceases, but at one end of the chamber, "with a grinding and crashing noise ... there flamed out an awful cloud or pillar of fire, like a rainbow many-colored and like the lightning bright." They approach the end of the cavern; the multi-colored flame passes and disappears again. She tells Leo to bathe in the flame when it reappears. He is unsure, but agrees. She needs to be sure of his resolve and says she will enter the flame first in order to assure him of its safety. Leo again agrees, as does Holly. As the flame again approaches, Ayesha disrobes and shakes her voluminous hair about her, clasping it with her solid gold snake. She kisses Leo on the forehead and enters the fire. The flames run up and down her figure and hair and even into her mouth. When she finishes bathing, though, her expression suddenly changes. She emerges a different woman, her frame thinner, her voice and vision weaker. Her hair falls out and she begins to shrivel until she is all withered. Her last words to Leo, whom She calls Kallikrates, are to forget her not, that She will come again and be even more beautiful. She dies, and the men swoon.

Holly awakens to find Job dead of terror. Leo is well, but his hair has turned gray. They watch the flame pass once more before they leave. All goes well until they reach the balancing rock and have to jump to reach the walkway. Holly goes first, but misses, holding on by one hand. Leo jumps past him and pulls him up onto the walkway. They make it safely down the cliff and meet Billali and the mutes.

Holly tells the old man of She's death. Billali replies that without She, Holly and Leo will be food for the Amahagger. Holly reminds the old one of his debt for having saved his life; Billali conceives a plan whereby the Britons are escorted from Kor through the swamps. Upon reaching the other side, Billali bids the pair farewell.

Holly and Leo eventually reach the Zambesi River, and after a few more adventures only referred to by Holly, they board a boat for England and home.

La Danse du Feu/La Colonne de Feu

Dance of Fire / Pillar of Fire

Star Film (Paris, France); Released 1899; 1 minute; Scenes comique et fantasmagoriques No. 188; DIRECTOR AND SCENARIO: Georges Méliès; Based on the climax of She

CAST: Georges Méliès, Jeanne d'Alcy, Mlle. Barral

Georges Méliès (1861–1938), a producer of stage illusions, became enchanted by the new medium of motion pictures after viewing the initial offerings of the Lumière brothers in Paris in 1896. He immediately saw the commercial potential in movies and set out to become a filmmaker. In his films, utilizing the simple device of stopping the camera at the desired moment, he changed humans into all kinds of creatures and objects and back again. Combining this technique with double exposures and black backgrounds, Méliès created hundreds of short films over the next 18 years. While he himself never progressed technically, he led the way for all the special effects men to follow.

In *The Pillar of Fire*, Ayesha was portrayed by Méliès' wife, Jeanne d'Alcy.

She

Edison Manufacturing Company; Released November 13, 1908; 1000 feet; DIRECTOR: Edwin S. Porter; PRODUCTION DESIGNER: Ralph Murphy

CAST: Florence Auer (Ayesha), William Ranous (Leo Vincey).

Edwin S. Porter, the Edison director who is credited with creating the narrative form in American film with *The Great Train Robbery* (1903), was the first American filmmaker to tackle Haggard. He created this one-reel picture featuring actress Florence Auer as Ayesha, the queen who refused to become a senior citizen.

Moving Picture World, for November 14, 1908:

Synopsis of Scenes: "A mysterious metal box is bequeathed to Leo, a young Englishman, to be opened on his twenty-fifth birthday.

It is opened in the presence of his guardian and his servant. They find an Egyptian tablet 2,000 years old. The guardian, a linguist, interprets it. It tells how, 2,000 years before, an Egyptian princess and her husband, traveling in Africa, meet a mysterious woman, a queen, called "She," with power over Life and Death.

"She" falls in love with the prince, and, in jealous fury, kills him. "She" sends the princess out of the country. "She" has the body entombed to await his reincarnation. The princess leaves an account of her adventure on a tablet; bequeaths it to her descendants, that one may some day find "She," wrest the secret from her, and avenge the ancient wrong.

Leo determines to seek "She." The three reach Africa, where they are met by men from "She," who has seen their arrival in a vision.

While awaiting the chief's return, Leo is kissed by Ustane, a beautiful maiden, and she thereby becomes his wife. The Englishmen are set upon by the natives and are only saved by the chief's arrival. He conducts them to "She," who finds in Leo the reincarnation of the prince.

Leo is overcome by the wondrous beauty of "She." "She" prevails upon Leo to bathe in the "Pillar of Life," a mysterious fire, but he hesitates and "She," to encourage him, enters the flame, becomes young and radiant, but gradually grows old before his eyes until her form is entirely consumed. [From this synopsis, it is obvious that this production, while very short, is a faithful adaptation of the novel's major events.]

She

Thanhouser; Released December 26, 1911; 2 reels; DIRECTOR: George O. Nichols
CAST: Marguerite Snow (Ayesha), James Cruze (Leo Vincey/Kallikrates), William C. Cooper (Horace Holly), Irma Taylor (Ustane), Viola Alberti (The Pharaoh's daughter), Harry Benham (Billali), Alphonse Ethier (Job), Marie Eline (Leo Vincey as a Youth)

This version of Rider Haggard's most popular novel was filmed by the Thanhouser Company of New Rochelle, New York, and was their first two-reel production. It also marked the first pairing of Marguerite Snow and future director James Cruze, who would later marry. (See entry for the 1912 film *Jess.*)

Covering the events of the novel chronologically, beginning in ancient Egypt in 350 B.C., it depicts only the highlights. Amenartas convinces Kallikrates to leave Egypt with her. They journey along the African coast, eventually reaching the domain of "She." Ayesha offers Kallikrates a chance to bathe in the Flame of Life, but he is loyal to Amenartas, and Ayesha slays him. Amenartas flees with her infant son, vowing vengeance on "She." Ayesha keeps the body of her dead love in a niche in a cave. Jumping ahead to the nineteenth century, the film shows Holly being entrusted with the young Leo Vincey and a chest; the elder Vincey is not shown. On Leo's twenty-fifth birthday, Holly opens the chest and a letter and map are discovered. The letter implores Leo to go to Africa and take vengeance on "She." He and Holly leave immediately and reach the territory ruled by Ayesha. An old man leads them directly to the royal cavern of "She." Neither the Amahagger nor Billali are named; the former are merely extras. Leo springs at Ayesha, but she unveils and overcomes him with her beauty. She then offers him a chance to kill her with a knife, but he cannot. Ayesha shows Leo the body of Kallikrates before she destroys it. She then leads Leo and Holly to the site of the Flame of Life. As she enters the flame, its quality changes and she shrinks and shrivels until she is no more. The Britons return to England and destroy all evidence of their fantastic adventure.

The scenes in which the protagonists travel to and from the city of Kor were most likely shot on Long Island Sound, a stone's throw from the Thanhouser studio. Intertitles serve only to describe forthcoming action; the "dialogue" being delivered by wild gesticulation on the part of the actors. The interiors are somewhat lacking in detail, and the camera remains stationary throughout, which was the norm for the time. The latter fact proved a distinct hindrance in the climactic scene in which Ayesha shrivels and perishes in the magic flame. Miss Snow appears to be replaced by either a child or a midget in makeup. The character of Ustane is barely noticeable.

This is a serious attempt of translating Haggard to the screen, its shortcomings notwithstanding.

The Moving Picture World, December 23, 1911:

> A story like *She* ... is a natural temptation to an ambitious and capable maker of films and ... the Thanhouser Company have succumbed to the temptation in a two-reel production. About two years ago, when the two- and three-reel production was still regarded as a curiosity, the Edison Company made a motion picture version of the story in one reel. It was an artistic masterpiece, and despite the fact that only the few who had read the story could thoroughly understand and enjoy the picture, it gained no small popularity and was justly considered one of the early moving picture classics. The Thanhousers in filming popular fiction and well-known dramas ... are guided by a controlling desire to make the story clear to the general public, only a very small portion of whom may safely be presumed to have read Ibsen or Haggard or even Dickens.... [T]hey have succeeded in making a mysterious and complicated novel very plain to the average moving picture patron and in so doing they have at the same time kept up their high standard of art and dignity in rendering this strange piece of fiction into moving pictures.

> The story deals with the mysteries of Egyptian worship, with the tricks and wonders of that magic, which even in the most ancient times has surrounded the land of the Pharaohs with a certain indefinable awesome spell. Of course there are scores of stories touching upon the strange worship and the veiled ritual of old Egypt, but none of them have the bold stroke of the English writer who, himself a traveler on the dark continent, joined the old and the new together and by giving the main story a distinctly modern setting and introducing besides mysterious high priests and priestesses and savage tribes, a blond young Englishman of 25, very much a child of our own days, he has invested the novel with an unusual interest. Before we realize it we have forgotten the improbabilities of the tale and begin to believe in reincarnation, in the fires of youth and the flames of death and actually enjoy being mystified.

> To picture this weird tale in its entirety would be impossible. The Thanhouser company has not attempted this, but have taken the thread of the story from the initial causes and has pictured the events in their logical sequence, giving us a better interpretation than would otherwise be obtained in pictures....

The scene in the Cave of Fire is most convincing and an excellent interpretation of the storied description of that awful climax. Passing over the terrifying adventures attending the escape of Vincey and Holly from the city of Kor, the reel concludes with Vincey seated in his London home, a melancholy figure, as he consigns the records of Kallikrates to the flames of his hearth fire....

His Egyptian Affinity

Nestor/Universal; Released August 27, 1915; 2 reels; Based on *She*; DIRECTOR: Al Christie

CAST: Victoria Ford (Egyptian Princess), Eddie Lyons (Her Lover).

A spoof of the novel, this short appears to have the major elements contained in Haggard's work with a few differences: Here the princess dreams of the future 2000 years hence. She and her lover have been reincarnated and are chased by a Bedouin chief across the desert.

Moving Picture World August 28, 1915:

> A farce comedy, well produced, and enacted in an enthusiastic manner. The play is full of rapid action, and has evidently been produced at some expense. It deals ... with a subject almost wholly Oriental, where a spring touched in a sarcophagus 2000 years later than the opening scenes, causes the dead to return and the feud of the past is recommenced and finished with a flourish....

She

Barker Motion Picture Photography (Great Britain); Released March 14,1916; 1645 meters; DIRECTORS: Will Barker, H. Lisle Lucoque; SCENARIO: Nellie E. Lucoque; PRODUCTION DESIGNER: Lancelot Speed

CAST: Alice Delysia (Ayesha), Henry Victor (Leo Vincey), Sidney Bland (Horace Holly), Blanche Forsythe (Ustane), Jack Denton (Job), J. Hastings Batson (Billali)

This was the second film directed by Lucoque after he had formed his own production company, Lucoque Ltd., in January 1915 with a capital of £6,000. He immediately negotiated with Haggard's agent and was able to purchase the film rights to six of his novels for seven years. *She* was co-directed and produced by William H. Barker, who had made his reputation by supplying footage of the Grand National horse race, run annually in Liverpool, to theaters in London on the day of the race. Earlier, in 1897, he had collaborated with early film apparatus inventor William Friese-Greene on the filming of Queen Victoria's Golden Jubilee. In 1904 he built the first studio at Ealing. In 1911 he paid noted stage actor Sir Herbert Beerbohm Tree £1000 for one day's filming of *Henry VIII*, which he then exhibited at high admission prices. Two years later he produced an epic two-hour version of the popular play *East Lynne*. He quit the film industry shortly after his association with Lucoque. He died in 1951 at the age of 84.

The title role was played by Alice Delysia (1889–1979), a Parisian-born revue star of the Moulin Rouge who made some films in Britain. Henry Victor (1888–1945), who played Leo, was born in London but raised in Germany. He went on to a long career as a character actor in Great Britain and the United States.

Henry Victor as Leo Vincey

Jack Denton as Job (his servant)

Sydney Bland as Horace Holly

Alice Delysia as She

Hastings Batson as Billali

Blanche Forsythe as Ustane

Top: *She* (Barker Motion Photography, 1916). Alice Delysia, Hastings Batson, Sydney Bland.
Bottom: *She* (Barker Motion Photography, 1916). Henry Victor, Alice Delysia. Opposite
page: *She* (Barker Motin Photography, 1916). Henry Victor, Jack Denton, Sydney Bland,
Hastings Batson, Alice Delysia, Blanche Forsythe. (Courtesy BFI Stills, Posters and Designs.)

She

Fox Film Corporation; Released April 22, 1917; 5 reels; DIRECTOR: Kenean Buel; PRODUCER: William Fox; SCENARIO: Mary Murillo; PHOTOGRAPHY: Frank G. Kugler

CAST: Valeska Suratt (Ayesha), Ben Taggart (Leo Vincey), Miriam Feuche (Ustane), Tom Burrough (Holly), Wigney Percival (Billali), Martin Reagan (Job)

Valeska Suratt (1882–1962) was one of Theda Bara's chief rivals for the vamp crown. Like Bara, she hailed from the midwest, having been born in Terre Haute, Indiana. She originally signed with the Lasky Company in 1914, working for them until November 30, 1916. One of the stipulations in her contract gave her the right to choose her own wardrobe and supporting players.

The Moving Picture World, May 5, 1917 (Edward Weitzel):

> The opportunity for spectacular effect and weird suggestion in *She* ... explains its selection for picturization by the Fox company.... The linking together of two widely separated periods in the world's history is skillfully accomplished, and the character of Ayesha, the white queen of a tribe of savages, that know her by the comprehensive title of "She-who-must-be-obeyed," is an attractive one for any woman. The further fact that she has bathed in the flame of life and will never grow old is also largely in her favor. The story need not be recalled here. As set down by Haggard, its full realization would be a very complicated and elaborate affair. Mary Murillo has managed to condense it into five reels and made everything reasonably clear. Kenean Buel's direction of the production has many points of excellence; the one note he has failed to sound is the eyrie [*sic*] feeling that pervades the original

> work. Valeska Suratt's performance of the ancient queen is also untouched with the same important quality. Her dressing of the character is in keeping with the author's conception, but her entire performance is uninspired, a defect for which ease and freedom of movement and close attention to the task in hand does not fully atone. The Leo of Ben. L. Taggart is another quite ordinary performance. Miriam Feuche is an appealing Ustane, Tom Burrough plays Holly convincingly, and Wigney Percival acts Billali to good effect.... The ensemble scenes are well handled.

She

(aka Mirakel Der Liebe)

Europaische Film-Allianz/Warton Hall; Released May 5, 1925; 98 minutes; DIRECTOR: Leander de Cordova; PRODUCER: George Berthold Samuelson; SCENARIO: Walter Summers; PHOTOGRAPHY: Sidney Blythe; ART DIRECTOR: Heinrich Richter; MUSICAL ARRANGEMENTS: W.L. Trytel (from the opera "Sadko" by Nicolai Rimsky-Korsakov)

CAST: Betty Blythe (Ayesha), Carlyle Blackwell (Leo Vincey/Kallikrates), Henry George (Horace Holly), Mary Odette (Ustane), Marjorie Statler (Amenartes), Tom Reynolds (Job), Jerrold Robertshaw (Billali), Alexander Butler (Mahomet), Dorothy Barclay (Slave)

This production turned out to be Lucoque's last, as he went bankrupt shortly afterwards. His health having failed as well, he handed the directorial reins to his friend Leander de Cordova, then committed suicide in November 1925. He had renewed his rights to *She* as well as acquiring those for *Mr. Meeson's Will*, which he never filmed, owing to his financial troubles.

The intertitles were allegedly

She (Europaisch Film-Allianz, 1925). Betty Blythe as Ayesha.

She (Europaisch Film-Allianz, 1925). Mary Odette, Carlyle Blackwell.

written by Haggard himself, but this writer has yet to find any proof.

Taking advantage of the cooperation then in practice by German studios of sharing their superior facilities, this picture was filmed in an airplane hangar situated on the outskirts of Berlin. Unfortunately, the company did not have the state-of-the-art technical skill of the Germans, so the effects work suffered. However, it is faithful to the source material, and is the last time that Holly was portrayed as an ugly man, as he is described in the book. It is also the final time that Ayesha killed Ustane herself, rather than delegating the task.

Los Angeles–born Betty Blythe (1893–1972), who had had a great success wearing very revealing costumes in the title role of *The Queen of Sheba*

four years earlier, reappeared in all her Rubenesque glory in similarly daring costumes. Unfortunately for Blythe, it was the middle of winter and the hangar was unheated, causing her to suffer from exposure. It was for her art, however, so she put on a bold (and nearly bare) front and carried on in the best tradition of the theater.

Her co-star was early American matinee idol Carlyle Blackwell (c. 1884–1955), a one-time stage actor who made many films for Vitagraph, Kalem and World Pictures in the teens. In 1922 he moved to England, where he remained for the next 14 years, functioning as actor, director and producer.

Variety, July 7, 1926:

The scenes are merely a series of mythical, mystical strangeness that

She (EuropaischFilm-Allianz, 1925). Betty Blythe, Carlyle Blackwell.

She (EuropaischFilm-Allianz, 1925). Tom Reynolds, Henry George, Carlyle Blackwell, Betty Blythe.

never convince ... and only result in this picture being another slam against the British film industry.

She

RKO; Released July 25, 1935; 95 minutes; *DIRECTORS*: Irving Pichel, Lansing G. Holden; *PRODUCER*: Merian C. Cooper; *ASSOCIATE PRODUCER*: Shirley C. Burden; *SCREENPLAY*: Dudley Nichols, Ruth Rose; From the Novel by H. Rider Haggard; *PHOTOGRAPHY*: J. Roy Hunt; *MUSIC*: Max Steiner; *SET DECORATOR*: Thomas Little; *EDITOR*: Ted Cheesman; *FIRST ASSISTANT DIRECTOR*: Harry D'Arcy; *MAKEUP*: Carl Axcelle; *ASSISTANT CAMERAMAN*: Charles Burke; *SOUND*: John L. Cass; *ART DIRECTORS*: Van Nest Polglase; Alfred Herman; *SECOND ASSISTANT DIRECTOR*: Charles Kerr; *SPECIAL EFFECTS*: Vernon L. Walker;

ORCHESTRATION: Maurice DePackh; *DANCE DIRECTOR*: Benjamin Zemach; *OPTICAL EFFECTS*: Linwood G. Dunn; *MATTE PHOTOGRAPHY*: Guy Newhard; *MATTE PAINTER*: Mario Larrinaga; *PRODUCTION ILLUSTRATORS*: George Russell, Lansing Holden, Harold Miles, R. Doulton Stott, Dennis Holden; *SOUND EFFECTS*: Lee Steiner; *HAIR STYLES*: Hollis Barnes; *TECHNICAL ADVISOR*: Dr. Luido Gorgastin

CAST: Helen Gahagan (Ayesha), Randolph Scott (Leo Vincey), Nigel Bruce (Holly), Helen Mack (Tanya Dugmore), Lumsden Hare (Dugmore), Gustav von Seyffertitz (Billali), Julius Adler (High Priest), Samuel S. Hinds (John Vincey), Noble Johnson (Amahaggar Chief), Bill Wolfe, Arnold Grey (Priests), Jim Thorpe (Captain of the Guard), Ray Corrigan, Jerry Frank (Guards)

Dance
Direction for the "Hall of Kings" sequence

As in the silent era, Haggard's *She*
was the first of his works to be adapted
in the sound period. The most visually
striking of the Haggard adaptations,
this eighth version of his most popular
work was created by the team of Ernest
B. Schoedsack and Merian C. Cooper
for RKO in 1935. Just two years earlier
this duo had given the world what is
arguably the most original film ever
made, *King Kong*. Probably due to the
surfeit of jungle pictures produced at
that time, writers Dudley Nichols and
Ruth Rose (Mrs. Schoedsack) altered
the setting from Africa to the Arctic.
They also changed Ayesha's original
lover from an ancient Egyptian priest to
a fifteenth century Englishman, thus
making the queen only 500 years old, a
mere infant compared to Haggard's
2000-year-old character. Van Nest Polglase and Alfred Herman fashioned
some memorable art deco sets, ably
abetted by the matte illustrations of
Mario Larrinaga and a team of artists,
which gave this production its "must-
see" reputation. This picture became
the first Haggard adaptation to receive
an Academy Award nomination, albeit
for a minor and short-lived award, that
of Dance Direction. The nominee was
Benjamin Zemach, for his imaginative
choreography for the Hall of Kings
dance number.

Besides the different setting, this
version omits the Ethiopian Head landmark and the Arab sailors. It also offers
two original characters, a man named
Dugmore and his daughter Tanya, who
becomes a substitute for Ustane. Leo is
an American here, and it is his uncle

John who tells him of the family legend. He is dying of radium poisoning
from attempting to reproduce the
magic element in the Flame of Life. He
has a letter, written in the fifteenth century by the widow of John Vincey,
which in effect retells the legend as set
forth in the novel, only in a different
period and region. Uncle John gives
Leo a gold figurine of a woman in
flame. After explaining everything, the
uncle dies.

Leo and Holly journey northward.
They encounter a man named Dugmore and his daughter Tanya at an outpost. They ask him to supply porters
for the rest of their trip. He is uninter-
ested until they show him the gold
figurine. His greed makes him find
porters and join the expedition. He is
killed in an avalanche which reveals an
opening through a mountain. Leo,
Holly and Tanya enter and find themselves in the caves of the Amahagger.
From this point, the film follows the
main thread of the novel closely. The
sequence of the nocturnal dances is
omitted, as is Leo's opportunity to kill
Ayesha. Instead, he rescues Tanya from
being sacrificed and they escape with
Holly from the Hall of Kings. Eluding
the guards, they stumble upon the
chamber wherein exists the Flame of
Life. She is already there, and offers Leo
the chance to become immortal. He
refuses; Ayesha asks if she bathes first
and is unharmed, will he then enter,
and Leo agrees.

She enters the flame, and rapidly
ages, calling to Leo as in the book,
before finally falling to the ground,
dead. The entire return trip is omitted;
Holly, Leo and Tanya are shown in a

She (RKO, 1935). Nigel Bruce, Helen Mack, Randolph Scott, Noble Johnson.

comfortable British home in the final scene.

In her only film performance, stage actress Helen Gahagan gave an acceptable portrayal of the superannuated sovereign Ayesha (herein called "Hash-A-Mo-Tep"), convincingly showing all the moods of the mercurial monarch. She gave the order for execution and declared her love for Leo Vincey with equal feeling. Years later, when she ran for the U.S. House of Representatives, Miss Gahagan attempted to buy up all prints of this film, figuring no one would vote for a candidate who was so blasé about handing down the death penalty. Fortunately, she was unsuc-cessful, although for many years the picture was unavailable. It was not until 1996 that it was seen on television and released on videocassette.

The other leads — Randolph Scott as Leo Vincey, Nigel Bruce as Holly and Helen Mack as Tanya — struggle against rather weak dialogue, a frequent shortcoming of Schoedsack-Cooper productions. The producers had originally wanted Joel McCrea and Frances Dee for the roles of Leo Vincey and Tanya Dugmore, but they were not available, so they got Scott on loan from Paramount and took a chance on relative newcomer Mack, a former child actress who made her debut as

She (RKO, 1935). Randolph Scott, Helen Gahagan, Helen Mack. (Courtesy Collectors Book Store.)

Gloria Swanson's daughter in *Zaza* (1924). The film lost $180,000, possibly from the cost of the impressive sets — the Hall of Kings covered 34,000 square feet and was 40 feet high.

One of Haggard's best lines is paraphrased in this film. In the book, after She has condemned the Amahagger who had harmed the outsiders, She says to Leo, "How thinkest thou that I rule this people? I have but a regiment of guards to do my bidding. Therefore it is not by force. It is by terror. My empire is of the imagination." In the film, Hash-A-Mo-Tep asks Leo, "How do you think I rule these people? It's not by force, it's by terror. My empire is of the imagination." The last sentence could be said to apply to Haggard himself, as the author of so many romance novels.

This version of *She* stands as a fine example of pure spectacle, and, despite the differences with the novel, manages to capture the fantasy element as few other filmizations of Haggard's works have.

Variety, July 26, 1935:

Some of the sequences are stunning.... Story blame belongs with basic yarn, and not with the treatment.

The London Times, October 31, 1935:

[N]either the actors nor the director seems able to believe … in their story. At times the fable … becomes a heavily improving allegory of love, death and immortality…. [T]he immortal queen's palace … is decorated like a night-club….

Malika Salomi

Comedy Pictures (India); Released May 1953; Based on *She*; SCREENPLAY-DIRECTOR: Mohammed Hussein; PHOTOGRAPHY: V. Karmat; MUSIC: Muhammad Iqbal, K. Dayal

CAST: Krishna Kumari (Ustane), Rupa Varman (Ayesha), Kamran (Leo), Amrit, Helen, Sheikh, Shafi, Nanda, Kamal Mohan

This film gave the "Indian film treatment" to Haggard's most popular novel, for it was replete with dances and

Top: *She* (RKO, 1935). Helen Gahagan, Randolph Scott. Bottom: *She* (RKO, 1935). The Hall of Kings. (Courtesy Collectors Book Store.)

sentimental songs. The setting was a country bazaar and the Amahaggers wore satin capes; they were probably in a higher tax bracket than their literary cousins.

She

Hammer-Seven Arts Twentieth Century-Fox (Great Britain); Released May 1965; 106 minutes; DIRECTOR: Robert Day; PRODUCERS: Michael Carreras, Aida Young; SCREENPLAY: David T. Chantler; PHOTOGRAPHY: Harry Waxman; MUSIC: James Bernard; ART DIRECTOR: Robert Jones; EDITOR: Eric Boyd-Perkins; ASSISTANT DIRECTOR: Bruce Sharman; SPECIAL EFFECTS: George Blackwell; MUSICAL SUPERVISOR: Philip Martell; SOUND: Claude Hitchcock; CHOREOGRAPHY: Cristyne Lawson; PRODUCTION MANAGER: R.L.M. Davidson

CAST: Ursula Andress (Ayesha), John Richardson (Leo Vincey), Peter Cushing (Horace Holly), Christopher Lee (Billali), Bernard Cribbins (Job), Rosenda Monteros (Ustane), Andre Morell (Haumeid), Julie Mendez, Lisa Peake, Soraya (Night Club Dancers)

Hammer Films, a minor British outfit, became known for their horror films beginning in the late 50s with successful adaptations of *Frankenstein* and *Dracula*. Their version of *She* is a horror of a different sort, as it unmercifully mistreats the spirit of Haggard's classic tale.

It begins in Palestine in 1918, 30 years after the book's publication. Holly, Vincey and Job are World War I veterans out for a night on the town in

She (Hammer, 1965). Ursula Andress, Christopher Lee, John Richardson. (Courtesy Collectors Book Store.)

She (Hammer, 1965). John Richardson, Ursula Andress. (Courtesy Collectors Book Store.)

a noisy night club replete with belly dancers. A native stares oddly at Leo and returns with a young beauty clad in veil and diaphanous outfit. She attracts the attention of the English trio, but it is Leo who goes to her table and introduces himself. She gives her name as Ustane and lures Leo into an alley where he is knocked unconscious just after the girl kisses him and has a change of heart about her task. A black-bearded Billali appears and congratulates Ustane for a job well done. Leo awakes in a roomy apartment guarded by muscular Nubians. Moments later, a *blonde* Ayesha appears, *sans* veil, and kisses Leo. She calls herself "Ai-ee-sha" instead of "Assha," proving that the screenwriter did not read the book's footnotes, if indeed he more than skimmed the novel. All this in the film's opening ten minutes; so much for fidelity to the source material. The backgrounds of Holly and Vincey are only touched upon while Leo's family history, the iron box and its contents are deleted entirely.

Leo and Ayesha kiss some more and she gives him a ring and a map, promising him all that he desires if he will journey to her land. The map is to guide him there; by returning the ring to her, he will prove himself to be the one for whom she has waited 2000 years. No explanation is given as to how Ayesha and her entourage got to Palestine, nor how they will return to their homeland. Anyone still wishing to view this picture, read on.

Holly examines the ring, positive it is Egyptian circa 1000 B.C. because it bears the insignia of the high priest of Isis. Looking at the map, he is certain that the city marked is the legendary city of Kuma (instead of Kor). He recalls the legend of a band of rich Egyptians who were exiled for the murder of the high priest committed by their leader. Leo is all afire to go, and Holly and Job are right behind him, yet another departure from the novel.

As they cross the Desert of Lost Souls, they have their water bags slashed and are attacked by Tuaregs, who steal their camels and wound Leo. With stiff upper lips, the party proceeds on foot. Ustane suddenly appears with water, saying she has never been far away since she knew of the situation.

Ustane explains that she had been trained to be Ayesha's handmaiden until her father became involved in some trouble. He was demoted to overseer of Ayesha's slaves, the Amahagger, a people "who live in the shadow of the Ethiopian Head." This last is the sole reference to the geographical landmark so important in the novel. She tries to dissuade the trio from continuing, but being British, they must carry on.

Leo becomes feverish and weak from his wound. They are discovered by a band of Amahagger warriors, who take the party to their cave dwellings. There the Amahagger attempt to sacrifice Leo, but Billali appears with some of Ayesha's army and takes the outsiders and 15 Amahagger to Kuma.

At this point, the film begins to show some fidelity to its inspiration. Ayesha meets with Leo and stimulates his memory; a flashback shows Kallikrates kissing a woman and being stabbed to death by Ayesha. Leo still doesn't believe himself to be the reincarnation of the Egyptian priest.

Meanwhile, the Amahagger warriors are brought before the queen, who has them thrown into a fiery pit.

Ayesha shows the Britons the ruins of Kuma and tells Leo about an old mystic who met her party in the desert, but told only her about the Flame of Life. She takes Leo to the latter and gives him the choice of bathing in it.

Ustane decides it best that she leave; when she says goodbye to Leo, she kisses him. Ayesha witnesses this scene and misunderstands it, being the jealous type. The queen is about to have Ustane dropped into the fiery pit, but Leo objects. Ayesha offers him the chance to save the girl by stabbing her (Ayesha) with the same dagger she used to kill Kallikrates. Leo takes the dagger, but is unable to strike. Holly and Job are told to return to their world, for Leo has made his choice and will remain in Kuma.

Ayesha takes Leo to an inner room containing a stone slab. Atop the slab lies a still human form. Leo is amazed to see his double; now he believes that Kallikrates was his ancestor. Ayesha pours a vial of some liquid over the corpse, dissolving it.

Ustane is killed and her ashes brought to her father. At this, the Amahagger revolt. Meanwhile, Ayesha and Leo prepare to bathe in the Flame of Life. A fireball falls from the sky into the Flame, turning it blue and cold. Billali suddenly appears. He also wishes to become immortal. He and Leo fight with swords; Billali knocks down Leo and heads for the Flame, but Ayesha kills him first. She and Vincey enter the Flame together. The queen suddenly begins to age rapidly; she dies without speaking, unlike in the novel. Holly and Job have arrived in the meantime. The Flame becomes hot again and Vincey cannot re-enter it. He bemoans the fact that he will live forever without his beloved Ayesha. Presumably the Amahagger triumphed over Ayesha's army, though this is not shown.

The sets are unimaginative, looking more like your Uncle Fred's cluttered attic than an ancient city. The ethereal music used as Ayesha's theme is a weak attempt to capture the mood of the source material. Actors portraying the Amahagger are blacks, another difference from the book.

Ursula Andress acts as if she were afraid of spoiling her makeup, so frozen do her features remain. Among the leads, only Peter Cushing seems sincere. As Ustane, Rosenda Monteros convincingly conveys the young woman's love for Leo and understanding of her situation. This version of *She* is strictly for Andress and Cushing fans.

The New York Times, Sept. 2, 1965 (Bosley Crowther):

> [E]verything about this picture … looks old and distinctly unmodern. It lacks style, sophistication, humor, sense and, above all, a reason for being, since it isn't even as good (excepting that it is in color) as the last re-make of *She* done with Helen Gahagan in 1935….

The Vengeance of She

Hammer-Seven Arts/Twentieth Century-Fox (Great Britain); Released May 1968; Color by DeLuxe; 101 minutes; DIRECTOR: Cliff Owen; PRODUCER: Aida Young; SCREENPLAY: Peter O'Donnell, based on characters created by H. Rider Haggard; MUSIC AND SPECIAL MUSICAL

The Vengeance of She (Hammer, 1968). John Richardson, Andre Morell, Olinka Berova. (Courtesy Collectors Book Store.)

The Vengeance of She (Hammer, 1968). John Richardson, Olinka Berova. (Courtesy Collectors Book Store.)

EFFECTS COMPOSED BY Mario Nascimbene; MUSICAL SUPERVISOR: Philip Martell; PHOTOGRAPHY: Wolf Suschitzky; SUPERVISING EDITOR: James Needs; PRODUCTION DESIGNER: Lionel Couch; COSTUME DESIGNER: Carl Toms; PRODUCTION MANAGER: Dennis Bertera; EDITOR: Raymond Poulton; ASSISTANT DIRECTOR: Terence Clegg; CAMERA OPERATOR: Ray Sturgess; SOUND RECORDIST: Bill Rowe; SOUND EDITORS: Roy Hyde, Jack Knight; CONTINUITY: Phyllis Townshend; MAKEUP: Michael Morris; HAIR STYLIST: Mervyn Medalle; WARDROBE MISTRESS: Rosemary Burrows; SPECIAL EFFECTS: Bob Cuff; RITUAL SEQUENCES DESIGNER: Andrew Low; RECORDING DIRECTOR: A.W. Lumkin

Cast: John Richardson (Kallikrates), Olinka Berova (Carol), Edward Judd (Philip), Colin Blakely (George), Jill Melford (Sheila), George Sewell (Harry), Andre Morell (Kassim), Noel Willman (Za-Tor), Derek Godfrey (Man-Hari), Danielle Noel (Sharna), Gerald Lawson (The Seer), Derrick Sherwin (No. 1), William Lyon Brown (Magua), Charles O'Rourke (Servant), Zohra Segal (Putri), Christine Pockett (Dancer), Dervis Ward (Lorry Driver)

A misbegotten picture made to cash in on the box office success of the previous film, this production utilized the leftover sets and costumes from the lost city and its lack of style. A young European woman is lured to Kuma by the powers of a mystic acting under Kallikrates' orders. Followed there by a psychiatrist whom she had encountered on her journey, she is told she is the reincarnation of Ayesha come to regain her throne. Her mind is controlled by the mystic, who believes he will be allowed to bathe in the magic flame for finding her. As she is about to enter the flame, her slaves revolt and the psychiatrist is freed. He runs to the chamber of the flame and breaks the mystic's hold on the woman. When Kallikrates realizes she is not really the reincarnation of Ayesha, he enters the flame and dies. The city is then destroyed by fire and earthquakes as the woman and psychiatrist escape. Sound familiar? Another film to avoid.

The New York Times, May 30, 1968 (Vincent Canby):

> [A] scriptwriter's mindless sequel to Haggard's African adventure classic, *She* ... [Olinka] Berova, who looks like a young Ursula Andress ... plays an innocent European girl ... drawn to the lost African city of Kuma to succeed to the queendom of Miss Andress....

She

Paul Raleigh/Thys Heyns Film & Television Ltd., Johannesburg for Blue Flower Productions Ltd., Capetown (South Africa); Color Original Air Date: January 1980; 240 minutes; SCREENPLAY-DIRECTOR: Peter Thornton; PHOTOGRAPHY: Hanro Mohr

CAST: Wendy Gilmore (Ayesha), Kenneth Hendel (Horace Holly), Giles Ridley (Leo Vincey), Len Sparrowhawk (Job), Victor Melleney (Billali), Janet Krohn (Ustane)

EPISODES: 1. The Head of the Ethiopian 2. The People of the Rocks 3. The Hot Pot 4. Ayesha 5. The Tombs of Kor 6. She 7. The Chasm 8. The Fire of Life.

This is the only made-for-television version of *She* ever produced. Ayesha was played by an Australian journalist and architect(!) named Wendy Gilmore, who gave the character the proper attribute of scholarly knowledge of the occult sciences.

She

Royal Film/American National Entertainment; Filmed in 1982, reviewed in 1985; not released theatrically; 106 minutes; Eastmancolor; DIRECTOR: Avi Nesher; PRODUCER: Helen Sarlui; ASSOCIATE PRODUCER: Renato Dandi; SCREENPLAY: Avi Nesher; PHOTOGRAPHY: Sandro Mancori; ART DIRECTORS: Ennio Michettoni, Umberto Turco; EDITOR: Nicholas Wentworth; MUSIC: Justin Hayward, Motorhead, Rick Wakeman; COSTUMES: Ivana Massetti; SPECIAL EFFECTS: Armando Grilli

CAST: Sandahl Bergman (She), David Goss (Tom), Quin Kessler (Shandra), Harrison Muller, Jr. (Dick), Elena Wiedermann (Hari), Gordon Mitchell (Hector), Laurie Sherman (Taphir), Andrew McLeay (Tark), Cyrus Elias (Kram), David Brandon (Pretty Boy), Susan Adler (Pretty Girl), Gregory Snegoff (Godan), Maria Quasimodo (Moona), Mary D'Astin (Eva), Mario Pedone (Rudolph), Donald Hodson (Robel), David Traylor (Xenon)

An obviously troubled production, this picture lay dormant for three years and was never released theatrically. Having seen it, this writer deems the latter a wise move. Set in some future time, this "She" is a fighter, not a scholar. Every so often She must prove her ability by battling other warriors. If victorious, She is allowed to bathe in a cavern pool which heals her wounds. She becomes involved with two men, one of whom has a sister who has been captured by a warlord. Along the way to his stronghold, the trio encounters a number of silly-looking and mentally deficient individuals, including a family of vampires. At one point, She sums up the plot in one sentence: "This has nothing to do with sense." This travesty has been seen on television and is available on video; *why* remains a mystery.

Variety, December 22, 1985:

> Resemblance to H. Rider Haggard's *She* is quite remote, with Bergman skinny-dipping in a hot springs bathtub to be rejuvenated ... Special effects are minimized and acting is generally poor.

Stella Fregelius
(novel, 1904)

SYNOPSIS: Morris Monk invents a form of wireless communication which he calls an aerophone. With it he hopes to revolutionize the communications field. His indolent young cousin Mary Porson begins to drift away from him as the years go by, even though she was the only person with whom the aerophone worked.

Morris' father and Mary's father make plans to have the two youngsters marry. Since Mary stands to inherit her father's fortune, it will be an advantageous match, for Morris' father is nearly bankrupt. When Col. Monk broaches the subject to his son, Morris is not hopeful, but agrees to ask Mary for her hand.

The night after a dinner party at the Monks', Morris proposes and Mary accepts him. At the party it is learned that the local rector is trading places with one up north, in the interest of his wife's health. The new rector's name is Fregelius, a widower of Danish descent and the father of a daughter named Stella.

When Mary's father suffers a stroke, Col. Monk feels an earlier marriage date would be expedient. Mary rejects the idea, feeling that her father needs her.

A steamer is wrecked on shore near Monksland. One badly injured man is brought to the house by some sailors and Morris admits him. A doctor is sent for and he sets the broken leg of the delirious man, who calls for "Stella." Recalling the dinner party, Morris asks the man if he means Stella Fregelius, and he receives a positive answer before the man passes out. He figures the man to be the new rector and he wonders where she is, as no woman is present. Thinking she may still be aboard the ship, Morris takes a small boat to search for her. As he nears the reef, he hears a woman singing. When dawn breaks, he spots the prow of the ship. Upon the forecastle, supporting herself by a wire rope, is a dark-haired woman in a red cloak. She ceases her singing when she sees Morris. Despite the danger, he goes aboard and takes her off the doomed vessel. They row away from the ship shortly before it goes under. Talking with her afterwards, Morris learns the woman is a believer in fate and feels that they were destined to meet. A storm begins as they sail and they drift for a full day and night. Morris learns of Stella's past, that her mother died when she was 14 (she is now 24) and her twin sister died at 17. When they finally reach land, they stop briefly at Dead Church, a ruined structure on the coast. All the time they were together, Stella seemed to know

Morris' thoughts. They reach Monks-land, where they bathe and are fed.

Mr. Fregelius' injuries are bad enough to keep him bed ridden for two months. When he learns of the circumstances under which his daughter was found, the old man is disturbed. He explains to Morris that Stella's grandmother, mother and sister all sang the same song she was singing at one time and all were dead within a year.

During her stay at Monksland, Stella assists Morris with his aerophone and hits upon the means to make it function properly. In the meantime, a neighbor, Stephen Layard, begins paying court to Stella. When he finally proposes, he is rejected and takes it very badly. When Mr. Fregelius learns of this, he is also disappointed. Morris assumes Stella has accepted Layard when she doesn't answer his inquiry about him. He receives a letter from Mary, who is in Beaulieu, France, with her ill father, and has decided to spend two weeks there.

Stella sings and plays violin for Morris; it is then he learns that she has rejected Layard. He postpones his trip to France.

The next day, Morris gets a letter from Mary apprising him of her father's passing. She asks him to cancel his visit, as she will be staying with a friend in a convent for one month in mourning. A letter from his father brings the same news and also tells him to remain at home, for as co-executor of his uncle's will, he will be kept busy with legal matters.

One night, after Morris helps Stella get settled in her new home, they are returning to Monksland on foot when a gale hits. Morris stoops to adjust Stella's hood just as a cart bearing Stephen Layard and his spiteful sister passes. The couple is caught in the glare of the cart's lamp; the Layards believe Morris to be kissing Stella and continue on their way.

Miss Layard tells Col. Monk of the incident, but he refuses to believe his son kissed Stella. Fearing the story has already been spread about, Col. Monk asks Mr. Fregelius to speak to Stella. She decides it is time to leave so that Morris cannot be hurt by scandal. She decides to go to London to seek work.

Col. Monk also speaks to his son and is reassured that nothing has occurred between him and Stella, and that he intends to marry Mary.

The Fregeliuses leave Monksland and move into the Rectory. That night, with a storm brewing, Morris meets Stella at the Dead Church and they admit their love for each other. Stella says she knows that they will be together in the afterlife. Taking Morris' hand, she "weds" him spiritually, stating she will be waiting for him. This causes the man to think they may be near death now. Sensing his thoughts, Stella tells him, "Remember always, far and near, it is the same thing; time is nothing; this oath of ours cannot be touched by time or earthly change."

Morris leaves the church first, for the two must not be seen together. Stella faints after he is gone. Unable to sleep that night, Morris goes to his workshop, where he is startled by the bell of his aerophone. It is Stella; she is still in the Dead Church. The sea water is rising from the gale. Morris renews his vows of love; Stella begins singing the song she sang the night they first met. The sound of crashing stone signals the end; the aerophone in the Dead Church is destroyed and Morris hears no more.

When news of the circumstances of Stella's death gets about, Morris becomes famous, for his aerophone has proven itself. He takes care of Mr. Fregelius, who is broken in spirit after the death of his daughter. Mary returns and Morris tells her everything. She understands fully. Within three months they are married. Morris becomes wealthy from his invention and Mary gives birth to a boy and later a girl.

In time, Mary tries to get Morris to forget Stella altogether. She feels she has succeeded, when actually she has not. Morris visits Mr. Fregelius regularly and orders a monument made for the dead woman.

The rector allows Morris to have Stella's diary. Morris reads it eagerly, especially the parts concerned with mysticism. He gets the idea to invent an aerophone which will allow him to communicate with the spirit world.

On the fourth anniversary of Stella's death, Morris goes to his lab and envisions Stella and hears music. He does not see her again until New Year's Eve. He becomes obsessed with Stella's spirit to the detriment of his mortal self. One day Mary finds him sitting in his workshop — dead.

Stella

Master's Films (Great Britain); Released May 1921; 5,500 feet; Based on *Stella Fregelius; DIRECTOR*: Edwin J. Collins
CAST: Molly Adair (Stella Fregelius),

Manning Hayes (Morris Monk), Charles Vane (Stephen Layard), Betty Farquhar (Mary Porson)

Swallow
(novel, 1899)

SYNOPSIS: This is a tale of the Boers in the Cape Colony and Natal in the early nineteenth century. It is narrated by Suzanne Botmar, wife of Jan and mother of Suzanne, who is called "Swallow" by the local native tribe.

One day when she is seven, little Suzanne disappears while out playing. Her father searches in vain for her. The following night she reappears with a young boy. Both are soaked to the skin. Her mother undresses the boy, noting his thinness, the quality of his clothes and the fact that he speaks only English. Suzanne says that he is the brother she has always wanted and that she found him by the sea. She had dreamt of him the night before and knew just where to find him.

In due course, the Botmars engage an English-speaking tutor so that they may understand the boy. They learn that his name is Ralph Kenzie, and that he and his parents were on a ship from India bound for England when a storm wrecked the ship off the African coast. A number of passengers, including Ralph and his mother, got away in a boat. After reaching the shore, they died off one by one until only Ralph remained. Some natives fetch his mother's jewelry and Bible, and give the body a decent burial.

Ralph and Suzanne grow up together, forming a spiritual bond.

Stella (Masters Films, 1921). Charles Vane, Molly Adair.

After two years, the tutor joins the Botmar household, as he is no longer able to stand the activities at the home of the Van Voorens, his previous employers. When Ralph is 19, Jan learns of a Scottish lord and lawyer who are in the area looking for a boy who was believed lost in a shipwreck ten years before. They have heard that he was found by a local Boer family and have come for him.

Meanwhile, Swart Piet Van Vooren has been paying court to Suzanne. She will have nothing to do with him, for he is an evil half-breed who consorts with Kaffir witch doctors. Ralph likewise proposes to Suzanne. When they return home, Jan tells them about the Scots and the wealth to which Ralph is heir. The Englishman says he cares naught for that; Africa is his home. Jan insists that he go, but Ralph tells him of his determination to wed Suzanne and asks how he wishes to lose his daughter, for he will under any circumstances.

Before the Scots arrive, Jan and Ralph go onto the veldt, leaving Vrouw (Mrs.) Botmar to deal with the foreigners. They arrive with an interpreter and are told that Ralph lives there but is away at the moment. She then deliberately lies, saying that Ralph is not the man they seek, though his name is similar, and shows them acceptable proof of that fact.

Shortly afterward, young Suzanne meets the lawyer and tells him the truth. She tells her mother what she has done, but the Scots do not return, apparently satisfied with the first story they were told.

His father having died and left him all his property, Swart Piet again pays court to Suzanne, who rejects him outright.

One day, Suzanne happens upon Swart Piet about to hang a witch doctoress on a trumped-up charge of cattle theft. Suzanne yields to Piet's demand for a kiss and the black woman, Sihamba, is let go. Sihamba later thanks Suzanne for rescuing her and says she will serve the Boer girl for the rest of her days. Possessed of second sight, the witch doctoress speaks of a vision wherein she sees herself repaying Suzanne many years hence.

Upon hearing Suzanne's account of these events, Ralph goes after Van Vooren and beats him in a fight, having sworn to Suzanne that he would not kill the half-breed. Piet later ambushes Ralph, shooting him in the back. Ralph recovers, however. Weeks later, Piet sends a letter to Jan asking for his daughter's hand. Jan has Ralph reply that he would sooner see his daughter dead.

A native named Zinti accidentally overhears Piet plot to kidnap Suzanne and bring her to his new house, which is hidden in a far-off spot. He tells Sihamba what he heard and she rides past the ambush just in time to warn the Boers of the trap. They retreat to the open veldt (plain). It is then decided that Ralph and Suzanne will marry soon, for Van Vooren will not leave them alone.

After the couple is wed, they go to live by themselves. As they camp that night, Swart Piet surprises them, telling Ralph he intends to kill him and take Suzanne for his own. He gives the couple five minutes alone, then orders one of his men to shoot Ralph. None of the Kaffirs can bring himself to do the foul deed, so Piet himself shoots Ralph. Seeing him still alive, Piet throws the Englishman's body over a cliff into the sea.

Sihamba and Zinti had followed the newlyweds and happen upon Piet and his party on their way back. Guessing that Ralph had been killed, Sihamba looks for him anyway. She finds him still alive in a pool at the base of the cliff; he had only been shot in the shoulder. She tells the servants to take Ralph back to the Botmars' after Zinti has given them directions to Piet's hidden house. Sihamba and Zinti go there in an attempt to rescue Suzanne while awaiting a rescue party of Boers.

At Piet's stronghold, Sihamba finds Suzanne in a hut. The Boer girl is using a knife to fashion a noose. Fearing the worst, Sihamba drops into the hut and rescues Suzanne, who shows no enthusiasm, believing her husband to be dead. Sihamba tells her that he lives and they leave the hut. They join Zinti and continue until they spot a guard. Zinti covers him with a musket, but when the guard sees Suzanne escaping, he turns and runs, fearing Piet more than a gun. Zinti fires but misses. The trio reach their mounts and head for a mountain some distance away. Zinti's horse gives out, so he hides by the road. The women go on until Suzanne's horse also drops. She mounts behind Sihamba and they ford a river, reaching a land projection on the other side. Piet had caught up with them, but his horse did not dare to cross the swollen river. Reaching the mountain, the women enter the village of Sigwe. Sihamba tells their story and asks for protection until they reach the Botmar home, which is 100 miles away. Sigwe tells them of a dream one of his diviners had: A white swallow would fly before his army and make it victorious at little cost. Suzanne's native name is "Swallow," so he agrees to protect them if Suzanne will go with his army, which is about to attack an enemy in the north. With Swart Piet just behind them, she agrees. Sihamba says they will find a means of escape later. When the half-breed arrives and asks for the women, Sigwe puts him off, making him angry. Sihamba then mocks him and he fires at her, but misses. For this violent act against a guest, Sigwe has Piet and his men beaten and driven from the village. Zinti arrives and all three outsiders are guarded until it is time to march. That night, Suzanne appears in a vision to Ralph, whose fever breaks the next day.

Through Swallow's intervention, war is averted and differences settled. Sigwe does not allow her to leave, however, for the dream further showed bad luck for the Kaffirs if she does. They are allowed to visit Sihamba's tribe, though,

and they find the land devastated by drought and disease. The tribe has lost their leader and welcomes Sihamba, for she had been in line for the throne before she fell out with the tribe. Suzanne is also made a chieftainess.

Meanwhile, the British have been making life hard for the Boers. The Dutch settlers decided to pack up and trek elsewhere.

Attacked by Zulus, the Boers defeat them after a hard-fought battle. Ralph finds a man hiding among the wagons and prepares to shoot him, but the man begs for his life, claiming he is a slave to the Zulus and not one of them. Jan is all for killing the native until he realizes that he has witnessed this scene before, when he looked hard into Sihamba's eyes. He spares the man and later it is discovered that he is from Sihamba's village.

In the meantime, Suzanne had sent Zinti to tell her parents where she was. Through a series of misadventures, it takes him over a year to reach the Botmar house. Finding they have departed, he returns to Suzanne to tell her of the trek.

Swart Piet had been nearby all the time, awaiting an opportunity to seize Suzanne. He steals some Zulu cattle and mixes it in with Sihamba's herd.

News comes that a group of white people are camped not far off. Sihamba sends Zinti to see who they are. When he returns, a Zulu impi (regiment) has surrounded the mountain, but he gets through. He tells Sihamba that the whites are Boers, but he couldn't get any names. Sihamba refuses the terms offered her by Piet and three Zulu chieftains, preferring to defend her land.

At dawn the Zulus attack, but are held off until they discover a weak spot in the rock through which a river flows. They are kept from the village by a narrow passage, but control the water. Thirst begins to take its toll on Sihamba and her people. Some of her warriors meet with Piet, who agrees to let them go if he can have Swallow and Sihamba. They agree, since they are tired of fighting and believe Swallow has brought them misfortune. Sihamba curses them, but can do nothing else. She devises a plan whereby Suzanne may slip past the Zulus and Piet. She cuts the Boer girl's hair and paints her body so that she resembles a Kaffir woman. She tells Zinti to accompany Suzanne past the Zulus and then make for the Boer camp. Sihamba must stay on the mountain, for her small stature would betray her. They first take a Kaffir woman's corpse, paint it white and cover it with Swallow's cloak. They then place it in the spot where Suzanne used to sit atop a cliff, and where Piet can see her.

The tribe is released and Suzanne makes her escape. When she can go no farther, she sends Zinti to the Boers to bring help. The Kaffir guard at the Boer camp will not let Zinti past until morning, when the Dutch are awake. Hearing his news, the Botmars head for the mountain by ox-cart. As they near the place, Ralph goes ahead on foot, for the oxen are too slow. Reaching the first barrier, Ralph hears voices and finds Swart Piet threatening Sihamba with death. The Englishman leaps at the half-breed, brandishing a spear. The latter runs up the mountain, stabbing Sihamba as he passes. Ralph catches Piet at the top of the cliff where the corpse sits; after a brief fight, he runs Piet through with his spear. Piet falls to the rocks below.

The Botmars had arrived in time to see Ralph chasing Piet up the mountain. Jan goes after them, but his wife stays with Sihamba, who is dying. The witch doctoress assures the woman that Suzanne is safe, well on her way to the Boer camp at Natal. This is the same camp that the Zulus are about to attack, however. When Ralph and Jan hear this, the former mounts Jan's great horse and heads for Natal as Sihamba breathes her last.

Arriving at Natal, Ralph has to ride through the Zulus in order to save Suzanne. She climbs up behind him and they begin their flight. They are soon surrounded by warriors, and Ralph and his steed are wounded. The horse goes mad and races through the encircling men. Just before reaching the Boer camp, the horse collapses. Ralph warns the Boers of their danger and they are able to defeat the Zulus.

The book returns to old Suzanne Botmar's narrative many years later. Swallow died as she reached old age, and Ralph and his son fell fighting with the British at Isandlhwana. An addition is written by her great granddaughter, who by coincidence or fate, marries Ralph's descendant.

Swallow

African Film Productions (South Africa); Released March 31, 1922; DIRECTOR: H. Lisle Lucoque PHOTOGRAPHY: W. Bowden

CAST: Dick Cruickshanks (Jan Botmar), Ena Soutar (Wilhelmina Botmar),

Joan Morgan (Suzanne Botmar), Hayford Hobbs (Ralph Kenzie), M.A. Wetherell (Piet Van Vooren), Gladys Atkins (Sihamba)

Lucoque's final production made in South Africa, and another lost film.

Jan's wife's name was changed from Suzanne to Wilhemina, probably to avoid confusion with her daughter, whose name in the book is the same as hers.

Rudyard Kipling
Stage Adaptations

In the late nineteenth century, playwrights began writing in what was to become the cinematic style — episodic action, cross-cutting between scenes, and emphasis on the visual. All the while their work was highly romantic, being based largely upon the popular literature of the day.

Having both the requisite popularity and the necessary romantic flair, Kipling's works found their way to the stage in several notable performances. Kipling found champions in the likes of Robert Hilliard and British thespian Forbes Robertson, although none of his works required the fantastic sets and effects popular at the time.

Kipling attempted some plays of his own, but his only completed work for the stage was a collaboration with his daughter Elsie, *The Harbour Watch*. It was produced twice at the Royalty Theatre in 1913 without much success. Kipling ended up destroying much of his dramatic material, scattering the best bits among his poems and short stories. One such uncompleted play was entitled *Gow's Watch*. Four of its surviving fragments can be found in *Traffics and Discoveries*, *Deb-*its and Credits* and a chapter heading in *Kim*.

There was also an attempt by one F. Kinsey Peile to dramatize *The Man Who Would Be King* in three acts. The manuscript was sold at auction in 1935. It contained around 300 alterations, additions or suggestions in Kipling's own hand.

Captains Courageous

Ford's Theater, Washington, D.C., September 21, 1992. Two acts. Book and lyrics by Patrick Cook, based on the novel by Rudyard Kipling. Music by Frederic Freyer. Directed and choreographed by Graciela Daniele. Sets by Christopher Barecca.

CAST: John Dossett (Manuel), Mark Aldrich (Nate), Larry Alexander (Tom), Don Chastain (Captain), Frank DiPasquale (Simon), Michael Greenwood (Murphy), Walter Hudson (Long Jack), George Kmeck (Walters), Joseph Kolinski (Stevens), Michael Mandell (Doc), John Mineo (Hemans), Kel O'Neill (Harvey), Ric Ryder (Evans), Michael Shelle (Harris), Richard Thomsen (Ollie), John Leslie Wolfe (Peters)

MUSICAL NUMBERS: "Little Fish," "Nothin' to Do," "I'm Harvey Ellsworth Cheyne," "Ten Seconds/Not So Bad," "Anybody Else," "I Make Up This Song,"

191

"Right Here," "Lord, Could She Go," "That's Where I'm Bound," "Jonah," "You Never Saw," "Song of the Sea," "The Grand Banks," "One More Year," "Regular Fellas," "I'm Home," "I Make Up This Song" (reprise), "Song of the Sea" (reprise)

This world premiere production marked the twenty-fifth anniversary of the re-opening of historic Ford's Theater. Designer Barreca based his conception of the *We're Here* upon drawings for a once-famous schooner, *The Blue Nose*. The mainmast was 36 feet tall, and the crow's nest was situated 26 feet above the stage, while the foresail swung out over the audience.

The producers admitted that the 1937 MGM film was also an inspiration, hence the enlarged role of Manuel.

This production was also presented in Chester, Connecticut, from May 12 to June 5, 1994.

Variety, October 5, 1992:

[*Captains Courageous*] is full of good intentions. The chief weakness is Freyer's score, which fails to deliver a much needed ballad or even a memorable sea chantey.... [S]everal numbers display charm, on balance they are tedious and unimaginative.... John Dossett is on target as the patient Portuguese fisherman....

A Fool There Was

Liberty Theatre, New York March 24, 1909. Three acts, seven scenes. Adapted by Porter Emerson Browne from the poem "The Vampire" by Rudyard Kipling.

CAST: Mr. Hilliard (The Husband), Nannette Comstock (The Wife), "Boots" Wurster (The Child), Edna Conroy (The Sister), William Courtleigh (The Friend), S.K. Walker (The Secretary), George Clare (The Butler), Matt B. Snyder (The Ship's Captain), Willard Robertson (The Ship's Doctor), Fred Nicholls (The Ship's Stew-

ard), Arthur Row (The First Passenger), Hal Wilson (The Second Passenger), Chas. W. Haskins (The Third Passenger), John Livingston (The Fourth Passenger), Viola McVine (The Fifth Passenger), Cornella Pope (The Sixth Passenger), Phyllis Carrington (The Seventh Passenger), Grace Noble (The Eighth Passenger), May Clark (The Ninth Passenger), Sarah Coleman (The Tenth Passenger), Leroy Johnson (The Messenger), C. Russell Sage (Young Parmalee), Katharine Kaelred (The Woman)

A hugely successful play, Hilliard's production went on the road with essentially the same cast to such cities as Washington, D.C., Boston, Toledo and Atlantic City.

New York Times, March 25, 1909:

Mr. Hilliard acts the husband for all he is worth, giving him the proper vigor and virility ... driving the lesson home in a carefully delivered study of the enervating effects of rum and rose leaves.... Miss Kaelred is the kind of siren of whom one is ready to believe the worst.... She is quite open and frank about it.

A Fool There Was

Queen's Theatre, London, March 21, 1911.

CAST: Frank Cooper (The Husband), Chas. Bryant (The Friend), William F. Grant (The Secretary), H. Lawrence Leyton (Young Parmalee), Horton Cooper (The Butler), Kendal Chalmers (The Ship's Captain), Ernest Graham (The Ship's Doctor), Harold T. Richardson (The Ship's Steward), Margaret Halston (The Wife), Madge McIntosh (The Sister), Mattie Block (The Child), Katharine Kaelred (The Woman)

This was the only British adaptation of "The Vampire." It ran for over four months at the Queen's Theatre, then transferred to the Aldwych Theatre on August 5.

A Fool There Was

Poli's Theatre, Washington, D.C. (S. Z. Poli, proprietor), September 7, 1914. Three acts, six scenes. The Browne Adaptation. Directed by Harry Andrews.

CAST: *Given in the Order of Their Appearance on the Stage.* Doris Eaton (The Child), Stanley James (The Butler), William D. Corbett (The Friend), Louise Kent (The Wife), Carl Brickert (The Husband), Russell Fillmore (The Secretary), George Gillman (The First Passenger), Jerome Reimers (The Second Passenger), Ada Sherman (The Third Passenger), Harry Andrews (The Doctor), Hardy Meakin (The Steward), Jack Ellis (Young Parmalee), Miss Jewel (The Woman), Wm. H. Evarts (The Captain), Marie Carroll (The Sister)

The program billed the company as "The Popular Poli Players"; whether they were or whether the proprietor had a penchant for alliteration is not known. In any case, it must have been a cut-rate outfit, for only three passengers are listed, meaning either that they could not afford more players or a larger ship.

A Fool There Was

Castle Square Theater, Boston, February 19, 1917. Directed by Robert Campbell by arrangement with Robert Hilliard — Klaw and Erlanger.

CAST: William Courtleigh (The Husband), Hallet Thompson (The Friend), Frank B. Hersome (The Secretary), Walter Woodall (The Butler), Edward Clare (The Captain), James Brown (The Steward), Jack Walsh (Parmalee), Gerald O'Brien (Messenger), Edna Conroy (The Woman), Lillian Lee Anderson (The Wife), Tracy L'Engle (The Sister), Little Ethel Wickmann (The Child), Passengers, Sailors, Policemen, etc.

The Light That Failed

Daly's Theatre, New York, May 16, 1891. One act. Adapted by Courtenay Thorpe.

CAST: Courtenay Thorpe (Dick Heldar), Miss Baneker (Maisie)

New York Times, May 17, 1891:

Mr. Courtenay Thorpe tried his hand at putting a great deal [of Kipling's novel] ... into a one-act play.... It's no wonder that Mr. Thorpe failed under the circumstances. Nobody else could have done better with his restrictions.

The Light That Failed

Lyric Theatre, London, February 7, 1903. Adapted from Rudyard Kipling's novel by George Fleming. Scenery by J. Harker, W. T. Hemsley, Walter Hann. Costumers: Madame Filkes, B. J. Simmons & Co., Maurice Angel. Hats by Valeska. Music Director: Claude Fenigstein. Stage manager: Mr. Ian Robertson.

CAST: Forbes Robertson (Dick Helder [sic]), Aubrey Smith (Gilbert Belling Torpenhow), Sydney Valentine (J. G. Fordham "Nilghai"), Herbert Dansey (Leone Cassavetti), Ean MacDonald (Morton Mackenzie), Leon Quartermaine (James Vickery), Frank Bickley (G. B. Deenes), Cyril Vernon (F. Cecil Vincent), Arthur Harrold (Phil Raynor), William Farren, Jr. (Beeton), George M. Graham (A Young Man), Gertrude Elliott (Maisie), Nina Boucicault (Bessie Broke), Margaret Halston (The Red-Haired Girl), Minnie Griffin (Mrs. Haynes), Aimee DeBurgh (A Model), Marianne Caldwell (A French Bonne), Dinkie, a fox terrier (Himself)

The following statement appeared in the programme for this production: "This, the only authorized version of Mr. Kipling's book, has been secured by Mr. Forbes Robertson for England

and America, by arrangement with Miss Olga Nethersole."

British actor Forbes Robertson made a career of the part of Dick Heldar in the first two decades of this century, essaying the role on the stages of many cities, including New York, Baltimore, Boston, Detroit, Pittsburgh, Providence and Toledo, as well as London. His leading lady was Gertrude Elliott, who seems to have made a career of playing Maisie.

This adaptation utilized the original "happy" ending of the novel. The production transferred to the New Theatre on April 20, 1903 and was later revived at the Theatre Royal, Drury Lane, in 1913.

The Light That Failed

The Boston Stage Society, Castle Square Theatre, May 7, 1906. Three acts and a prologue. The George Fleming Adaptation. Produced under the personal stage direction of W. C. Masson.

CAST: Howell Hansel (Dick Heldar), John Waldron (Gilbert Belling Torpenhow), William McVay (J. G. Fordham "The Nilghai"), Mark Kent (Leone Cassavetti), Edward Wade (Morton Mackenzie), Stanley Drewitt (James Vickery of the *New York Thunderer*), Robert La Seuer (G. B. Deenes), Willard Howe (F. Cecil Vincent), John Beck (Phil Raynor), Frederick Murray (Dr. Barrymore), Bernard Fairfax (A Young Man), John Geary (Beeton, a Housekeeper), Lillian Kemble (Maisie), Elfrida Lasche (Bessie Broke), Louise Marcelli (The Red Haired Girl), Marion Calvert (Mrs. Haynes, a Charwoman), Florence Russell (A Model), Grace Foote (A French Bonne)

The Light That Failed

Empire Theatre, Providence, Rhode Island, February 16, 1914. Directed by E. M. Leonard.

CAST: Nina Saville (Mrs. Beeton), John T. Dwyer (Gilbert Torpenhow), John A. Preston (Phil Dessau "The Creature"), Homer Barton (Dick Heldar, Artist), Ethel Daggett (Bessie Broke), Thomas Mulgrew (Henry Canby), Marion Ruckert (Masie [sic]), Bertha Leigh Leonard (Nell Hading "The Red Haired Girl"), Thomas Mulgrew (Dr. Sedgwick), M. A. Kelly (Cassavetti), Arthur DeLord (Felix Friend)

H. Rider Haggard
Stage Adaptations

The spectacle arrived on American stages in the 1870s when famed impresario David Belasco started utilizing large numbers of extras, live animals and actual weapons such as cannons in his productions. Others followed his lead with equal success. Among them were such notables as actor-producer William Gillette, who would become known as the preeminent Sherlock Holmes.

From the spectacle, it was but a small technological step to presenting an interpretation of a work of fantasy such as Rider Haggard's *She*. Both Gillette and Belasco produced versions of *She*, although the latter based his version on the former's adaptation. Reviews mentioned flaming torches and fire-sprouting skeletons among the effects.

Like Kipling, Haggard tried his hand at writing his own plays. He toyed with a stage version of his 1910 romance of ancient Egypt, *Morning Star*, but never progressed beyond toying. He also submitted at least two scripts or suggested adaptations to W. B. Yeats in Dublin, who responded that "neither would be possible at the Abbey [Theatre]."

From his correspondence with Kipling, it would appear that Haggard also had an idea of adapting *Queen Sheba's Ring* for the stage, but nothing came of it. The film rights to this novel were purchased by H. Lisle Lucoque, but the film adaptation remained likewise unrealized.

Allan Quatermain, or The Sun Worshippers

Orpheum Theater, San Francisco, November 7, 1887. In five epochs and six tableaux by Inigo Tyrell. Music by Dionys Romandy.

CAST: Helen Dingeon (Nyleptha), Belle Thorne (Sorais), Chas. Drayton (Agon, High Priest of the Temple of the Sun), R.L. Franklin (Lord Nasta), Mr. MacFaden (Kara, Captain of the Royal Bodyguard), George Traverner (Sir Henry Curtis), R. Valerge (Capt. Good), Joseph Lynde (Allan Quatermain), Chas. Heywood (Alphonse), George Staley (Umslopogaas), Mr. Jasilin (Masai Elmoran)

Cleopatra

Union Square Theatre, New York, December 21, 1891. Five acts, nine scenes.

CAST: R. D. MacLean (Harmachis, Son of Amenemhat), W. S. Hart (Antony),

Maclyn Arbuckle (Brennus), Max von Mitzel (Dellius), Charles Grey (Amenemhat), Dearborn Bird (Sepa, Uncle to Harmachis), Augustus MacLean (Centurion), Oliver Taylor (Officer of Guard), Mark R. Robbins (Paulus), Alexander McKenzie (Eros), Morris Bauer (High Priest), Agnes Maynard (Charmion, daughter of Sepa), Ellen Dean (Atoua), Marie Prescott (Cleopatra), Soldiers, Greeks, Egyptians, Romans, Nubians, etc.

This production was also seen in Toledo, Ohio and Boston. The actor playing Antony was William S. Hart (1864–1946), who went on to great fame as one of filmdom's major western stars in the teens and 20s.

Dawn

Hollis Street Theatre, Boston, May 28–June 2, 1888. Prologue and four acts, six scenes. Adaptation by Justin Adams.
CAST: Frank Losee (Philip Caresfoot), Charles Stedman (George Caresfoot), W. F. Owen (John Bellamy, attorney), S.E. Springer (Devil Caresfoot), Miss Mary Shaw (Lady Bellamy), Miss Agnes Leavitt (Hilda Van Holtz), Mrs. M. A. Pennoyer (Pigott), Robert Taber (Arthur Preston), J. P. McAuliff (Jakes), E. D. Denison (Jim Brady), Miss Annie Louise Ames (Angela Caresfoot)

Devil Caresfoot

Vaudeville Theatre, London, July 12, 1887. Adapted by Haddon Chambers and Stanley Little from Dawn.
CAST: Charles Charrington (Devil Caresfoot), Janet Achurch (Angela Caresfoot), Fuller Mellish (Arthur), Lottie Venn (Mrs. Carr), Carlotta Anderson (Mrs. Bellamy),Royce Carleton (Philip Caresfoot), Charles Dodsworth (Sir John Bellamy), Eric Lewis (Lord Minister), J. Hamilton Knight (Rev. W. Fraser), John Carter (Pigott)

This production moved to the Strand Theatre, London on August 6, and from there to the Comedy Theatre, London on August 23.

Jess

Adelphi Theatre, London, March 25, 1890. Adaptation by Ewretta Lawrence and J. J. Bisgood.
CAST: Ewretta Lawrence (Jess), Helen Forsyth (Bess), J. D. Burridge (Silas Croft), C. Dalton (Frank Muller), Julian Cross (Hans Coetzee), Athol Ford (Jantze)

Mameena

Globe Theatre, London, October 30, 1914. Adapted by Oscar Asche from Child of Storm.
CAST: Lily Brayton (Mameena), Oscar Asche (Zikali)

The producer went to some trouble to acquire authentic props for this drama set in Zululand, finding them in South Africa. Apparently the emphasis was placed on these artifacts and the visual effects, for Haggard himself said that the play lacked drama. After a run of 113 performances, the play was shut down due to the exigencies caused by World War I. It lost £8,000. The Globe Theatre is now known as the Gielgud Theatre.

She

San Francisco, 1887. Four acts. Adapted by William Gillette.

Gillette added characters to the story; including a clock salesman named Martin Brown (for comic relief) and an old hag named Dillyesha.

She

Tivoli Opera House San Francisco, July 11, 1887. Adaptation by Richard C. White. Directed by James O. Barrows. Music by William W. Furst.

CAST: Laura Clement (Ayesha), James O. Barrows (Leo Vincey), William West (Horace Holly), Tellula Evans (Ustane), Richard C. White (Job), H. W. Frillman (Mohomed), Al K. Freely (Azaf), J. Roberts (Achmet), M. Cornell (Billali), A. Messmer (Simballi), Mr. Fielding (Abdalli, a sentinel), F. Raabe (Olila, Chief Guard)

British actress-singer Laura Clement originated the role of Ayesha on stage, playing it in several venues over the years. She had begun her career by singing leads with the D'Oyley Carte Company in Gilbert and Sullivan productions. At one point in the 1890s, she appeared with stage legend Lillian Russell.

She

Lee Avenue Academy of Music, Brooklyn, N.Y., October 3, 1887. Dramatized by T. H. Glenny.

CAST: Prudence Cole (Ayesha)

She

Broad Street Theatre, Philadelphia, November 7, 1887. The Richard C. White Adaptation.

CAST: Alice Vincent (Ayesha)

This was a troubled production. A newspaper item stated that initial interest was poor and the play closed after one performance. Further, the players were never paid.

She

Niblo's Garden, New York, November 29, 1887. Three acts, six scenes. The David Belasco Adaptation.

CAST: Laura Clement (Ayesha), Wilton Lackaye (Leo Vincey), F. F. Mackay (Holly), Lois Fuller (Ustane), Howard Coveney (Job), Charles Brown (Clock seller), George D. Fawcett (Abdallah), F. Barnes (Mohammed), H.W. Frillman (Billali), E. Waters (Simballi), Fanny Addison (Dillyesha)

Miss Clement's appearance, acting and singing were singled out for praise by the critics, who found the male actors less than competent. Technical errors made for a number of unintentional laughs. The Flame of Life also proved less than inspired; instead of a revolving pillar of flame, a small fire in green limelight was utilized. In the climactic scene, Clement ducked behind a screen of rock and was replaced by Fanny Addison in the makeup of an ugly old woman.

New York Daily Tribune, November 30, 1887:

> … [L]ong, diffuse, turbulent, pictorial, prosy spectacle…. [It] wearied judicious part of a numerous audience and pleased the admirers of glare and tinsel.

New York Times, December 1, 1887:

> Three actresses impersonate "She," Laura Clement, whose name is on the bill, an unknown lady, and Miss Fanny Addison, whose vocal peculiarities are easily distinguished in the hysterical moaning of the dying hag…. *She* is full of music…. It is commonplace, irritative and at best merely academic.

She

Hollis St. Theater, Boston, January 16–21, 1888. The David Belasco Adaptation.

CAST: Henry Aveling (Horace), William Faversham (Leo), Charles Bowser (Martin Brown), Howard Coveney (Job), N. M. Fawcett (Abdullah), F. Barnes (Mohammed), H. W. Frillman (Billali), E. Waters (Simbali), F. Clare (First Sentinel), Laura Clement (Ayesha ["She"]), Lois Fuller (Ustane), Fanny Addison (Dillyesha), Molly Brown (Attendant)

Opening night was very well attended and well received. It was noted that the dramatist had not followed the novel faithfully, but as drama, the adaptation worked.

William Faversham (1868–1940), who played Leo, was near the beginning of his career with this production. Though London-born, he achieved his fame on the American stage, in roles ranging from Romeo to Jeeter Lester. He also appeared in a few silent and a few sound films.

Boston Advertiser and Record:

> Some tableaux ... were extremely well presented ... as a lurid scenic play, *She* is an undoubted success.... Miss Laura Clement was a fair She in every way, and her singing fully deserved the applause which it received. Ustane ... was impersonated by Miss Lois Fuller with an earnestness and simple abandon....

Boston Sunday Time:

> *She* is ... the most coherent, consistent, and interesting romantic melodrama of many seasons. It is played in a very excellent manner by a more than competent company.

She

Gaiety Theatre, London, September 6, 1888. Five acts and seven scenes. Dramatized by permission from the popular novel of H. Rider Haggard by Edward Rose and rewritten and adapted for Miss Sophie Eyre by William Sydney and Clo Graves. The whole produced under the direction of Mr. William Sydney. Scenery by Walter Emden, E. G. Banns. Original music by Edward Solomon, Hamilton Clarke. Characteristic dances arranged by John D'Auban. Wigs by Clarkson. Dresses by J. A. Harrison. Special costumes worn by Miss Eyre designed by A. Chasemore and executed by Miss Fisher.

CAST: *Prologue* Edmund Maurice (Kallikrates), Glyn Wynn (Junis), Enid Leslie (Seta), Fanny Enson (Amenartas), Sophie Eyre (Ayesha)

An interval of two thousand years is supposed to elapse between the Prologue and the opening of the play.

Julian Cross (Horace Holly), Edmund Maurice (Leo Vincey), Mary Rorke (Ustane), James East (Job Round), E. Cleary (Mohammed), H. Maxwell (Billali), Edmund Gurney (Ugogo), George Aubrey (Selim), Charles Seymour (Ibrahim), William Holl (Barifi), Charlotte Elliott (Masrar), Lily Wilson (Boyane), Edith Vyse (Kayali), Maud Graves (Utala), and, Sophie Eyre (She)

Haggard himself was present on opening night. From the front of a proscenium box he gave "a rhetorical address" which was "frequently interrupted." He spoke of the certainty that the play would be considered an excellent dramatic work; the response was shouts of laughter and cries to leave that up to the press. Part of the problem was apparently the small size of the stage, which proved inadequate for such a spectacle.

She

Grand Opera House, San Francisco, March 18–24, 1889. The William Gillette Adaptation.

"SHE," AT THE GAIETY THEATRE.

Magazine page illlustrating 1888 London staging of *She*.

CAST: M. E. Heisey (Horace Holly), William S. Harkins (Leo), Charles Bowser (Martin Brown), Maurice Pike (Job), W. B. Barnes (Abdullah), J. Buckland (Mohammed), H. W. Frillman (Billali), F. Schuster (First Sentinel), J. Walton (Second Sentinel), Tellula Evans (Ayesha ["She"]), Evlyn Tattey (Ustane), Jennie Reeves (Dillyesha), Alice Maitland (Attendant), Arab sailors, Male and Female Amahagger, Choristers, Guards, Mutes, Attendants, etc.

She

14th Street Theatre, New York. September 9, 1889. The William Gillette Adaptation.

CAST: Laura Clement (Ayesha), Will Harkins (Leo Vincey), Matt Snyder (Holly), George Parkhurst (Job), Charles Bowser (Martin Brown), Tellula Evans (Ustane), W. B. Barnes (Mohammed), H. W. Frillman (Billali), E. Waters (Simballi), Fanny Snyder (Dillyesha), F. Schoester (First Sentinel), Molly Brown (Attendant)

New York Tribune, Sept. 10, 1889:

The piece as presented was an improvement on last season in many respects. A stronger element of comedy was introduced as a relief to the somber weirdness of the scenes depicting the mysterious power of the mighty Ayesha, and a greater dramatic intensity was shown throughout.... [T]he spectacular and scenic effects, except in one instance were more attractive than heretofore.... The women in the chorus were about as poor a looking lot as could be found, and the cast generally was weak. Miss Laura Clement renewed her former success as She, combining as she did a musical and well-trained voice with no small degree of dramatic power and a liberal allowance of good looks.... Matt Snyder looked and acted Holly acceptably.

She

H. C. Miner's People's Theatre, New York, September 9, 1889. Prologue and five acts. Dramatized by William A. Brady.

CAST: George P. Webster (Horace Holly), Jean H. Williams (Vincey, Father of Leo), C. A. Ferguson (John), Ida Raymond (Mary), Jean H. Williams (Leo Vincey), Murray Woods (Job), Marie René (Ayesha — She), Helen Corlette (Ustane), Belle Douglass (Buena, an Old Hag), B. J. Murphy (Billali), F. J. Fraser (Mohammed), Frank Belmont (First Amahagger), F. Car. Shiner (Second Amahagger), Ed. Burgess (Capt. of Dhow), O. P. Howland (First Sailor), Thomas Williams (Second Sailor), Fred Starr (Guard)

Harry Miner was a man of many hats who devised the idea of the theater chain. At first, he had holdings within a certain area of New York, so that a production could be readily moved from one venue to another. He later expanded his operations, but his base remained the People's Theatre on the Bowery.

She

Empire Theatre, Providence, Rhode Island, August 26, 1894. Adapted by Edwin Barbour. Produced by A. Y. Pearsons.

CAST: Ethel Raynes (Ayesha), Edwin Brown (Leo Vincey), Maud Durand (Ustane), Fred Summerfield (Roma), William Lee (Billali), Mart Stephens (Job), Dan Williams (Ted)

One review included the following observations: "The story ... is developed in every particular. The mechanical effects are startling; showing a real live person slipping into a roaring volcanic flame and in an instant ... is shriveled into a mummy. The scenery used in the play covers some 16,000 feet of canvas."

She

Seattle, May 10, 1907. Prologue and four acts. Adapted by Charles A. Taylor.

CAST: Laurette Taylor (Ayesha), Frederic Clarke (Kallikrates), Susie Howard (Amenartes), Verne Layton (Romba), Chas. E. Dale (Alka), Frederic Clarke (Leo Vincey), James S. Morton (Mr. Horace Holly), Willard R. Feeley (Jeo Lumpkins, Leo's servant), Richard T. Love (Teddy Donovan, Holly's servant), Nell Gibson (Mother Rummet), Jos. A. Carroll (Prof. Deep), Susie Howard (Eustan)

Laurette Taylor (1884–1946) was a stage actress of note in the early years of the twentieth century. In 1912 she would create her most famous characterization, the title role of Peg in *Peg O' My Heart*, which she would reprise in the 1925 film version.

For this role, Taylor had her fingers wired so that when she touched her shoe, sparks would result. On the second night, something went wrong with the circuitry as she was about to go on stage. It failed to function, but was repaired in time. When she got on stage, however, she was so upset by the incident she became entangled in her costume and then passed out. She was replaced by her sister Bessie, who was her understudy.

She

Buenos Aires, Argentina. Théatre expérimental de L'Industrie Torcuato Di Tella, June 1968. Adapted by Marcos Arocena. A dance interpretation.

CAST: Marcela Ruiz (Ayesha), Marcus Arocena (Leo)

OTHER PRODUCTIONS

An unauthorized ballet version of *She* was performed at the Royal Opera House in Budapest, Hungary, in 1898. When Rider Haggard heard of it, he wrote the manager, asking for photographs and programmes, since he was the author of the novel. His request was turned down because he was believed dead. The writer then sent a refutation, to be printed in Hungarian newspapers, but was refused because the editors thought it was some crackpot's scheme to make money.

A dramatization of part of *Cleopatra* entitled "The Overthrow of Harmachis" was written by Clara B. McIntosh and Emma Sheridan Fry and published in the July 1900 issue of *Women's Magazine* in the United States.

Rudyard Kipling
Radio Adaptations

Radio, with its infinite power of suggestion, would seem to be an ideal medium for the works of our two authors, yet precious little was ever presented over American airwaves, and not a lot more over British ones.

A note regarding the British adaptations is necessary. The BBC does not loan or make copies of programs, so that it is necessary to visit their archive if one wishes to listen to any. Those programs listed herein are the only ones which have been preserved, and there is no index as yet for earlier programming. So while there may have been earlier adaptations made from the works of our two authors, the only record of them lies in old issues of *Radio Times* magazine. Since this writer could not afford a trip to Britain, the task is left to some wealthier, more adventurous soul.

Mr. Kipling himself was heard over the British airwaves on two occasions. The first time was on July 12, 1933, at a luncheon given by the Royal Society of Literature for the visiting members of the Canadian Authors' Association. The second was on May 6, 1935, during King George V's Silver Jubilee, when he gave a speech, relayed from the Connaught Rooms, at the Annual Banquet of the Royal Society of St. George.

The Drums of the Fore and Aft

Escape, April 11, 1948. 30 minutes.
CAST: Gill Stratton

The Drums of the Fore and Aft

Escape, July 14, 1949. 30 minutes.
CAST: Wilms Herbert

The Jungle Book

Rainbow House with Bob Emery, 1942. Mutual Network, 15 minutes.
CAST: Sabu

The Jungle Book

BBC (Great Britain), July 17, 1980.

A sequence of scenes set to music by Charles Koechlin.

Performed by soloists and ladies of the Netherland Vocal Ensemble and Rotterdam Philharmonic conducted by David Zinman at the 1979 Holland Festival.

Kim

BBC (Great Britain), May 6, 1972. Abridged in 15 parts by E. P. Thorne. Read by Joss Ackland.

Kipling's English History

BBC (Great Britain), March 27–March 30, 1973. 5 episodes. Read by Marghanita Laski.

Kipling in Love

BBC Radio Four (Great Britain), October 19–December 7, 1994.

Eight plays adapted by Ed Thomason from short stories.

(1) His Wedded Wife (2) Lispeth (3) Venus Annodomini (4) The Courting of Dinah Shadd (5) In the Pride of His Youth (6) Love o' Women (7) Beyond the Pale (8) On Greenbow Hill

The Maltese Cat

BBC Radio Four (Great Britain), November 25, 1976. Directed by Colyn Dearman.

The Man Who Would Be King

Escape (CBS), July 25, 1948. 30 minutes. Produced and directed by Norm MacDonald. Adapted for radio by Les Crutchfield. Editorial supervision by John Dunkeld. Special music by Ivan Ditmars.

CAST: Ben Wright, Wilms Herbert, John Dehner, Peggy Webber, Jack Kruschen

This is a faithful version treating the main points of the narrative. The only variations are the name of the girl, here called Maram, and having Peachey go off alone, without mention of his passing.

Mrs. Hauksbee

BBC (Great Britain), October 1, 1970. Adapted for radio by A. C. Rawlinson from two short stories. Produced by John Tydeman.

The Wish House

BBC (Great Britain), October 20, 1984. Play based on short stories by Rudyard Kipling adapted for radio by Sue Glover. Produced by James Runcie.

CAST: Jane Wenham, Mary Wimbush

H. Rider Haggard Radio Adaptations

Only one of H. Rider Haggard's novels has ever been adapted for radio, and that only once in Britain and once in America. One can speculate that Britons had lost their taste for fantasy or perceived Haggard's stories as outmoded. Perhaps Haggard's passing at the birth of radio broadcasting meant that he was quickly forgotten. Perhaps the political climate precluded airing of Haggard works since they lacked any patriotic slant. Maybe there were no Haggard aficionados among radio producers or writers. Whatever the case, the once popular author has been largely neglected on radio.

She

Escape (CBS), July 11, 1948. 30 minutes. Produced and directed by Norm MacDonald. Adapted for radio by Les Crutchfield. Editorial supervision by John Dunkeld. Special music by Ivan Ditmars.

CAST: Berry Kroeger, Larry Dobkin, Kay Brinker, Ben Wright, Wilms Herbert

Given the limited time allowance, this production presented only the highlights of the novel. Differences, therefore, are mainly omissions, such as the "hot-pot," the trial and death of the Amahagger who attack the outsiders, no Ustane and no tour of Kor. Both Holly and Leo are present when Ayesha unveils and when she shows the body of Kallikrates. Job is killed in the Amahagger attack, rather than dying after watching Ayesha perish in the Flame of Life. The mood is faithfully captured with sound effects.

She

BBC (Great Britain), April 6, 1979. Dramatized by Victor Pemberton. Produced by David Spenser. Music by Anthony Smith-Masters.

Rudyard Kipling
Television Adaptations

Only Kipling has been adapted for television. With the limited technology of its "live" days, television had no hope of producing any of Sir Henry Rider Haggard's romances, but it could have handled such titles as *Beatrice, Dawn,* or *Stella Fregelius.* However, apparently no one made any attempt to transfer his works to the small screen, most likely because even by the early 1950s they had become dated. Extensive research has turned up not even a single adaptation of a Haggard work for television.

On the other hand, Kipling's canon offered a wealth of material due to its inclusion of many short works, which held more appeal for early television producers. Sadly, though, only one novel and two short stories were ever tackled by American companies.

The Light That Failed

Studio One (CBS-TV), October 10, 1949. 30 minutes

CAST: Felicia Montealegre, Richard Hart.

An unintentional *faux pas* occurred when the ad agency handling Westinghouse, manufacturer of light bulbs and other products, scheduled this production for the sponsor. The company was incensed, undecided whether to have the title changed or another of their products substituted. Following a verbal donnybrook between agency and sponsor, the latter course was chosen.

The Light That Failed
(retitled *The Gathering Night*)

Studio One Summer Theatre (CBS-TV), August 24, 1953. PRODUCER: John Haggot. 30 minutes

CAST: Christopher Plummer (Dick Heldar), Gaby Rodgers (Bessie), Martyn Green (Torpenhow), Margaret Phillips (Maisie), Melville Cooper

Variety:

The Light That Failed was cut sufficiently ... to have a drastic effect on the continuity.... [It features] a jumpy characterization by a newcomer, Christopher Plummer.... Melville Cooper did a couple of solid bits and Martyn Green was polished....

This time around, the station decided to change the title of the episode rather than have its sponsor feature a different product.

The Light That Failed

Family Classics (CBS-TV), March 16, 1961. PRODUCER: Jacqueline Babbin; DIRECTOR: Marc Daniels; TELEPLAY: Walter Bernstein. 60 minutes

CAST: Richard Basehart (Dick Heldar), Lois Nettleton (Maisie), Helena deCrespo (Bessie), Edward Atienza, George Turner, Eric Berry

VARIETY:

Richard Basehart gave a sterling performance.... Helena deCrespo ... carried off her performance with force, bite and humor ... in full command of her role.... [I]t looked as if the fortress locale had been made of papier maché. Once the setting switched to more civilized surroundings ... the production values shone.... Marc Daniels directed in fine style....

The Man Who Would Be King

Suspense (CBS-TV), October 17, 1950.

CAST: Francis Sullivan

The Phantom Rickshaw

Favorite Story (syndicated), February 8, 1953. 30 minutes. DIRECTOR: Sobey Martin; TELEPLAY: Robert Yale Libott, from the story by Rudyard Kipling; PHOTOGRAPHY: Curt Fetters; EDITOR: Martin G. Cohn; SOUND: Herbert Norsch

CAST: Edward Norris, Ann Kimbell, Forrest Taylor, Gertrude Michael, Bruce Payne, R. Lal Singh, Peter Brocco

VARIETY:

Norris plays it straight down the middle as the handsome heel.... Gertrude Michael is a capable haunt.... Ann Kimbell vivacious and competent as the current girl friend.... Sobey Martin's direction has a lazy tempo.... Robert Yale Libott's adaptation ... is well done.

Kipling

BBC-TV (Great Britain); 25 episodes, 50 minutes each; 1964

July 26, 1964: "Private Learoyd's Story." DIRECTOR: Peter Cregeen; TELEPLAY: Anthony Reed

August 30, 1964: "The Madness of Private Ortheris." DIRECTOR: Shaun Sutton; TELEPLAY: A. R. Rawlinson

September 20, 1964: "Black Jack." DIRECTOR: Peter Cregeen; TELEPLAY: Pat Dunlop

October 11, 1964: "Watches of the Night." DIRECTOR: Max Varnel; TELEPLAY: William Emms

November 1, 1964: "Love o' Women." DIRECTOR: Max Varnel; TELEPLAY: William Emms

November 22, 1964: "His Private Honour." DIRECTOR: Lionel Harris; TELEPLAY: William Emms

There were two regular characters in this series, newspaper editor William Stevens (Joss Ackland) and his assistant James Lockwood (Kenneth Fortescue). Six of the episodes featured "The Soldiers Three."

In all the episodes, Private Ortheris was played by Harry Landis, Private Learoyd by Douglas Livingstone, and Private Mulvaney by David Burke.

Bibliography

Bowers, Q. David, *Thanhouser Films: An Encyclopedia and History*, Library of Congress, Washington DC, 1997.

Brown, Hilton, *Rudyard Kipling*, Harper and Brothers, New York, 1945.

Caine, Michael, *What's It All About?*, Century, London, 1992.

Carr, John Dickson, *The Life of Sir Arthur Conan Doyle*, Carrol & Graf, New York, 1990.

Carrington, C.E., *The Life of Rudyard Kipling*, Doubleday & Co., Garden City NY, 1955.

Cohen, Morton, ed., *Rudyard Kipling to Rider Haggard — The Record of a Friendship*, Hutchinson & Co., Ltd., London, 1965.

Courtney, Margaret, *Laurette*, Limelight, New York, 1984.

D'Agostino, Annette M., *An Index to Short and Feature Film Reviews in "The Moving Picture World,"* Greenwood Press, Westport CT, 1995.

_____, *Filmmakers in "The Moving Picture World,"* McFarland, Jefferson NC, 1997.

Eames, John Douglas, *The M-G-M Story*, Crown Publishers, New York, 1983.

Etherington, Norman, *Rider Haggard*, Twayne Publishers, Boston, 1984.

Fairbanks, Douglas, *The Salad Days*, Doubleday, New York, 1988.

Gianakos, Larry James, *Television Drama Series Programming, 1947-1959*, Scarecrow Press, Metuchen NJ, 1980.

Golden, Eve, *Vamp, The Rise and Fall of Theda Bara*, Emprise Publishing, Vestal, New York, 1996.

Higgins, D.S., *Rider Haggard, A Biography*, Stein and Day, Briarcliff Manor NY, 1981.

Huston, John, *An Open Book*, Ballantine Books, New York, 1981.

Jewell, Richard B., with Vernon Harbin, *The RKO Story*, Arlington House, New York, 1982.

Katz, Wendy R., *Rider Haggard and the Fiction of Empire*, Cambridge University Press, Cambridge MA, 1987.

Lahue, Kalton C., *Gentlemen to the Rescue*, A.S. Barnes & Co., New York, 1972.

Laski, Marghanita, *From Palm to Pine — Rudyard Kipling Abroad and At Home*, Facts on File, New York, 1987.

McKay, George J., *A Bibliography of the Writings of Sir Rider Haggard*, The Bookman's Journal, London, 1930.

Marill, Alvin H., *Movies Made for Television*, Baseline/Zoetrope, New York, 1987.

Parish, James R., and Don E. Stanke, *The Swashbucklers*, Arlington House, New Rochelle NY, 1976.

Scherle, Victor, and William Turner Levy, *The Complete Films of Frank Capra*, Citadel Press, New York and Secaucus NJ, 1992.

Scott, James Edward, *A Bibliography of the Works of Sir Henry Rider Haggard*, Elkin Mathews, Ltd., Takeley, Bishop's Stratford, Herts, 1947.

Sellers, Robert, *The Films of Sean Connery*, Vision Press, London, 1990.

Slide, Anthony, *The American Film Industry*, Limelight Editions, New York, 1990.

Smith, R. Dixon, *Ronald Colman — Gentleman of the Cinema*, McFarland, Jefferson NC, 1991.

Taylor, Ina, *Victorian Sisters*, Adler & Adler, Bethesda MD, 1987.

Thomas, Tony, *The Great Adventure Films*, Citadel Press, Secaucus NJ, 1980.

Thompson, Frank T., *William Wellman*, Scarecrow Press, Metuchen NJ, 1983.

Vahimagi, Tise, *British Television — An Illustrated Guide*, Oxford University Press, Oxford, 1996.

Vardac, A. Nicholas, *Stage to Screen*, Harvard University Press, Cambridge MA, 1949.

Vazzana, Eugene Michael, *Silent Film Necrology*, McFarland, Jefferson NC, 1995.

Wilson, Angus, *The Strange Ride of Rudyard Kipling*, The Viking Press, New York, 1977.

Articles

Bodeen, De Witt, "Antonio Moreno," *Films in Review*, June-July 1967.

Davis, Henry R., "Clara Kimball Young," *Films in Review*, August-September 1961.

Dumont, Herve, "Ayesha & Antinea," *L'ecran Fantastique*, June 1985.

Leibfr[i]ed, Philip, "Kipling on Film," *Films in Review*, January-February 1994.

Leibfr[i]ed, Philip, "H. Rider Haggard on the Screen," *Films in Review*, September-October, 1995.

Lodge, Jack, "The Career of Herbert Brenon," *Griffithiana 57/58*, October 1996.

Manvell, Roger, "The British Film Academy," *Films in Review*, January 1952.

Redi, Riccardo, "Brenon in Italy," *Griffithiana 57/58*, October 1996.

Turner, George E., "The Making of Gunga Din," *American Cinematographer*, September 1982.

Index

Abbey Theatre (Dublin) 195
"About Fiction" 7
Ackland, Joss 206
Actions and Reactions 73
Addison, Fanny 197
The Adventures of Robin Hood (1938) 146
African Film Productions 129
A. H. Wheeler and Co. 3
Allan and the Ice Gods (novel) 8, 9
Allan Quatermain (novel) 7, 8, 95–98, 138
Allan Quatermain (1919) 98, 99, 128
Allan Quatermain (play) 195
Allan Quatermain and the Lost City of Gold (1987) 99–101
Allison, May 83
Andress, Ursula 178
Auer, Florence 160

Balestier, Beatty 4
Balestier, Caroline 3
Balestier, Wolcott 3
"The Ballad of Fisher's Boarding House" 13
Bara, Theda 83–85, 107–109, 124, 166
Baratollo, Guiseppe 104
Barkas, Geoffrey 130
Barker, William H. 163
Barrack Room Ballads 3
Barrymore, Lionel 22
Bartholomew, Freddie 19, 46
BBC 202
Beatrice (novel) 101–104, 205
Beatrice (1922) 104
Beery, Wallace 76
Belasco, David 195
Bell, Monta 78
Belshazzar (novel) 8
"The Big Drunk Draf" 74, 76
The Birth of a Nation (1915) 109
"Black Jack" 74
Blackwell, Carlyle 168

Blythe, Betty 168
Boers 5
Bogart, Humphrey 64
Borradaile, Osmond 78
Bow, Clara 72
Bradenham, Norfolk 5
Brattleboro (Vt.) 9, 16
Brenon, Herbert 104
Bringing Up Baby (1938) 28
Briskin, Sam 38
Brown, Bryan 51
Browne, Porter Emerson 83
Bruce, Nigel 172
Bulwer, Sir Henry 6
Bulwer-Lytton, Edward 6
Burke, David 206
Burne-Jones, Philip 4, 81
Burroughs, Edgar Rice 2

Caesar Film 104
Caine, Michael 64–66, 70
Caine, Shakira 65
Campbell, Mrs. Patrick 82
Canadian Authors' Association 202
Cannon International 29
Capra, Frank 13
Captains Courageous (novel) 4, 14–16
Captains Courageous (1937) 16, 18, 19
Captains Courageous (1977) 19
Captains Courageous (1996) 22
Captains Courageous (play) 191
Carew, James 83
Casablanca (1942) 146
Cetwayo and His White Neighbours 6
Chadwick, Helene 73
Chamberlain, Richard 101
Churchill, Winston 7
Ciannelli, Eduardo 25
"The City of Dreadful Night" 22
The City of Terrible Night (1915) 23

Civil and Military Gazette 2
Clarke, Harry Corson 92
Clary, Charles 81
Clement, Laura 197
Cleopatra (novel) 105–107, 201
Cleopatra (1917) 108–113
Cleopatra (play) 195
The Cloak That I Left 8
Collier, John 78
Colman, Ronald 56, 57
Columbia Pictures 65
Comedy Theatre (London) 196
Conan Doyle, Arthur 1
Conland, Dr. James 16
Connery, Sean 29, 64–66
Cooper, Gary 56
Cooper, Merian C. 171
Costello, Dolores 60
Costello, Helene 60
Costello, Maurice 60
"The Courting of Dinah Shadd" 73
The Covered Wagon (1923) 120
Cruze, James 120, 161
Curry, Charles 232
Curtiz, Michael 146
Cushing, Peter 178

d'Alcy, Jeanne 160
La Danse de Feu/Le Colonne de Feu (1899) 160
"The Daughter of the Regiment" 73
Dawn (novel) 6, 113–116, 205
Dawn (1917) 116
Dawn (play) 196
The Days of My Life 8
Debits and Credits 191
deCordova, Leander 166
Dee, Frances 172
Delysia, Alice 163
DeMille, Cecil B. 146
Devil Caresfoot (play) 196
Disney, Walt 36
Ditchingham 6, 8
Doraldina 73
Doro, Marie 104
D'Oyley Carte Co. 197
Dracula 175
The Drum (1938) 26
Drums of Africa (1963) 138–140
"The Drums of the Fore and Aft" 202

East Lynne (1913) 163
Eclectic Film Co. 10
Elephant Boy (1937) 78

Elliott, Gertrude 194
Essex Productions 10

Fairbanks, Douglas, Jr. 26
Fairbrother, Sydney 132
Faire, Virginia Brown 92
Faulkner, William 27
Faversham, William 198
Film Supply Company of America 119
Fireside Productions 13
Flaherty, Roberty 78, 80
Flynn, Errol 47, 51
The Fool (1913) 82
A Fool There Was (1915) 83–85
A Fool There Was (1922) 85
A Fool There Was (play) 192, 193
Ford, John 91
Ford's Theater 192
Forterscue, Kenneth 206
Fox, William 83, 84
Frankenstein 175
Friese-Greene, William 163
Fultah Fisher's Boarding House (1922) 13

Gable, Clark 64, 76
Gahagan, Helen 172
Garbo, Greta 72
A Gardener's Year 8
"Garm — A Hostage" 73
"The Gathering Night" (TV) 205
The Ghost Kings (novel) 9
Gielgud Theatre (London) 196
Gillette, William 195, 196
Gilmore, Wendy 181
Globe Theatre (London) 196
Gloucester (Mass.) 22
"The God from the Machine" 73
Goetz, Harry 27
Gow's Watch (play) 191
Granger, Stewart 134
Grant, Cary 26, 28
The Grasp of Greed (1916) 152
The Great Train Robbery (1903) 160
Griffith, D.W. 109
Grimes, Steve 64, 65
Guiol, Fred 28
Gunga Din (1911) 23, 24
Gunga Din (1939) 10, 24–29, 65, 69, 75
Gunga Din (poem) 3, 5

Haggard, Henry Rider 1, 3, 4, 5–11, 99, 107, 130, 134, 135, 138, 160–163, 168, 171, 175, 195, 196, 198, 201, 204, 205

Haggard, Lilias Rider 8
Haggard Glacier 8
Hammer Films 175
The Harbour Watch (play) 191
Hart, William S. 19 6
Hawks, Howard 28
He (novel) 7
Heart and Soul (1917) 124, 125
Hecht, Ben 10, 28
Henry VIII (1911) 163
Henty, G.A. 1
Hepburn, Katharine 28
Herman, Alfred 171
Hidden Valley (1917) 11
Hill, Gladys 64
Hilliard, Robert 191, 192
His Egyptian Affinity (1915) 163
"His Private Honour" 73
HMS Kipling 5
Hollywood (1923) 120
Holmquist, Sigrid 55
Hope, Anthony 1
"How Fear Came" 30–32
Huston, John 64, 65
Huston, Walter 56

"In the Matter of a Private" 74
"In the Rukh" 4
"The Incarnation of Krishna Mulvaney" 73
The Irish Guards in the Great War 5
It's a Wonderful Life (1946) 13

Jaffe, Sam 26
Jess (novel) 116–119
Jess (1912) 119, 120–123, 161
Jess (1914) 123, 124
José, Edward 83
Junge, Alfred 133
The Jungle Book (novel) 2, 4, 30, 40, 202
Jungle Book (1942) 31, 32, 34
The Jungle Book (1967) 35, 36
The Jungle Book — Mowgli's Story (1998) 40
J.W. Lovell and Co. 3

"Kaa's Hunting" 30
Kalem 168
Kidnapped 1
Kim (novel) 4, 40–44, 191, 203
Kim (1950) 45, 47, 75
Kim (1984) 49, 51
King Kong (1933) 171
King Solomon's Mines (novel) 6, 7, 125–129, 133
King Solomon's Mines (1918) 129

King Solomon's Mines (1937) 130–132
King Solomon's Mines (1950) 47, 134–136
King Solomon's Mines (1985) 99, 140–143
King Solomon's Treasure (1978) 99
King Solomon's Wives (novel) 7
"The King's Ankus" 30, 31
"Kipling" (TV) 206
Kipling, Caroline 4
Kipling, Elsie 5, 191
Kipling, John 5
Kipling, [Joseph] Rudyard 1, 3, 4, 5, 7–10, 16, 25, 27, 29, 31, 34, 36–38, 40, 61–63, 65, 77, 81, 83, 85, 92, 191, 193, 195, 202
"Kipling in Love" (TV) 203
"Kipling's English History" (TV) 203
Koechlin, Charles 202
Korda, Alexander 26, 31, 32, 78
Korda, Vincent 32
Korda, Zoltan 32, 78, 80
Korngold, Erich Wolfgang 27

Landis, Harry 206
Lang, Andrew 7, 8
Larrinaga, Mario 171
Lasky Co. 166
Lean, David 76
Lee, Jason Scott 37, 38
Leigh, Vivien 56
"Letting in the Jungle" 30, 31
Liberty League 9
Life's Handicap 73
The Light That Failed (novel) 3, 52–54
The Light That Failed (1912) 11
The Light That Failed (1916) 54, 83
The Light That Failed (1923) 55, 56
The Light That Failed (1939) 56–58, 60, 69
The Light That Failed (plays) 193, 194
The Light That Failed (TV) 205, 206
Livingstone, Douglas 206
Lloyds of London 27
London Films 26, 32
Lone Pine (Cal.) 29, 47
Loos, Battle of 5
"Love-o'-Women" 73
Lucoque, Horace Lisle 10, 163, 166, 195
Lucoque Ltd. 163
Lukas, Paul 47
Lumière brothers 60
Lupino, Ida 56

Ma (novel) 7
MacArthur, Charles 10, 28
Mack, Helen 172
Mackenzie, Aeneas 64

The Mackintosh Man (1973) 64
"A Madonna of the Trenches" 5
Maharajah of Jodhpur 51
A Maid of Mandalay (1913) 60, 61
Malika Salomi (1953) 174
"The Maltese Cat" 203
Mameena (play) 196
Man of Aran (1934) 78
"The Man Who Would Be King" 3, 61, 63
The Man Who Would Be King (1975)
      63–69
The Man Who Would Be King (radio) 203
The Man Who Would Be King (TV) 206
"Mandalay" 3, 60
Many Inventions 4, 73
Margitson, Major 6
Margitson, Mariana Louisa 6
Mary of Marion Isle (novel) 8
Méliès, Georges 160
Milland, Ray 56
Miner, Harry 200
The Misfits (1961) 64
Mr. Meeson's Will (novel) 149–151, 166
Mr. Meeson's Will (1915) 151
Mr. Smith Goes to Washington (1939) 13
Mitchell, Thomas 56
Monteros, Rosenda 178
Montezuma's Daughter (novel) 8
Moore, Roger 29
Moreno, Antonio 72
Morning Star (novel) 195
Mother Maturin 4
Motion Picture Distribution and Sales Co.
      119
Moving Picture World 10
"Mowgli's Brothers" 30
"Mrs. Hauksbee" 203
Mutual Network 34
"My Lord the Elephant" 73
My Official Wife (1914) 60

Nada the Lily (novel) 4
The Naulahka (novel) 3, 16, 70–72
The Naulahka (1918) 72
Negri, Pola 72
Netherland Vocal Ensemble 202
Nethersole, Olga 194
Newman, Alfred 27
Newman, Paul 64
Newton, Robert 76
Nichols, Dudley 171
"Night of the Long Knives" 65

Oland, Warner 73

Old Ironsides (1926) 120
Oliver Twist (1949) 76
"On Greenbow Hill" 73
O'Toole, Peter 51
"The Overthrow of Harmachis" 201

Pa (novel) 7
Pathé 11, 83
Pathé Exchange 10, 83
Pathé Frères 10, 13
Pearson, George 83
Pearson, Virginia 84
People's Theater (New York) 200
"The Phantom Rickshaw" (TV) 206
Pioneer 2
Plain Tales from the Hills 2, 3, 73
Plummer, Christopher 65
Polglase, Van Nest 171
Porter, Edwin S. 160
Powell, Frank 83
Powell, Michael 133
Pressburger, Emeric 133
Previn, André 49
Princess Anne 70
The Prisoner of Zenda (novel) 1
"Private Learoyd's Story" 74
The Public Enemy (1931) 57

Quatermain, William 6
The Queen of Sheba (1921) 168
Queen Sheba's Ring (novel) 195
Queen's Theatre (London) 192

Radio Times 202
Raiders of the Lost Ark (1981) 140
Rainbow House with Bob Emery 34, 202
Rathbone, Basil 46
"Red Dog" 31
Red Eve (novel) 9
Redford, Robert 64
Reeve, Christopher 29
Reliance Pictures 27
Rhys-Davies, John 51, 140
RKO 10, 27, 29
Robert Brunton Studios 10
Robertson, Forbes 191, 193, 194
Rooney, Mickey 46
Roosevelt, Theodore 8
Rose, Ruth 171
Rosza, Miklos 34
Rotterdam Philharmonic 202
Royal Opera House (Budapest) 201
Royal Society of Literature 202
Royal Society of St. George 202

Royalty Theatre (London) 191
Rudyard Kipling's "The Jungle Book" (1994) 37, 38
Rudyard Kipling's "The Second Jungle Book — Mowgli and Baloo" (1997) 38
Rural England 8
Russell, Lillian 197

Sabu 26, 31, 32, 34
Sampson Low 3
Savile Club (London) 3, 9
Sayre, Joel 28
Schoedsack, Ernest B. 171
Scott, Randolph 172
The Second Jungle Book 4, 30
Selig Polyscope Co. 31
Sergeants Three (1961) 10
Shaik, Selar (Sabu) 78
Shaw, Harold 129
She (novel) 5, 7, 10, 11, 153–160, 166, 195
She (1908) 160, 161
She (1911) 120, 161–163
She (1916) 163
She (1917) 166
She (1925) 166
She (1935) 170–174
She (1965) 175–178
She (1980) 181
She (1982) 181
She (plays) 196–198, 200, 201
She (radio) 204
She and Allan (novel) 10
Sheffield, Reginald 29, 65
Sheridan, Emma 201
Sheth, Ravi 51
Sir Rider Mtn. 8
Die Sklavenkonigin 146–148
Small, Edward 27
Smith, C. Aubrey 87
Snow, Marguerite 120, 161, 162
Soldiers Three 2, 3, 28, 73, 74
Soldiers Three (1911) 11
Soldiers Three (1913) 11
Soldiers Three (1951) 74
"The Solid Muldoon" 74
South African National Film, Video and Sound Archive 130
"The Spring Running" 31
The Stain (1914) 84
Stallings, Laurence 31
Stella (1921) 184
Stella Fregelius (novel) 182–184, 205
Stephen, J.K. 9
Stevens, George 28

Stevenson, Robert 130
Stevenson, Robert Louis 1
Strand Theatre (London) 196
The Stronger Passion see *Beatrice*
"A Study in Scarlet" 1
Suratt, Valeska 83, 166
Swallow (novel) 184–188
Swallow (1922) 188, 189
Swanson, Gloria 172

"The Taking of Lungtungpen" 73
Taylor, Laurette 201
Taylor, Robert 46
Tearle, Geoffrey 83
Temple, Shirley 87, 91
The Ten Commandments (1923) 148
Terry, Ellen 83
Thanhouser 118–121, 161, 162
The Thief of Bagdad (1924) 26
"The Three Musketeers" 73
Thy Servant–A Dog (1935) 10
"Tiger! Tiger!" 30, 31, 32
The Time Tunnel 65
Tolkien, J.R.R. 2
"Toomai of the Elephants" 30, 77, 78
Tracy, Spencer 18, 76
Traffics and Discoveries 191
Transvaal 6
Traverse, Madeline 83
Treasure Island (novel) 1, 6
The Treasure of the Lake (novel) 8
Tree, Sir Herbert Beerbohm 163

Ufa 133
Urich, Robert 22

"The Vampire" 4, 5, 81, 83
The Vampire (1910) 81
The Vampire of the Desert (1913) 82
Vancouver, B.C. 22
Veidt, Conrad 46
Veiller, Tony 64
The Vengeance of She (1968) 178–181
Venice Film Festival 80
Victor, Henry 163
Vidor, King 28
The Virgin Goddess (1975) 11
Vitagraph 168

Watson, David 65
Watusi (1959) 136
"Wee Willie Winkie" 3, 86, 87
Wee Willie Winkie (1937) 87–91
Weekly News 2

Wellman, William 56, 57
Westminster Abbey 5
Westward Ho 2
What Price Glory? (play) 31
What's It All About? 64
White, Pearl 72
Whitman, Stuart 29
Wild Boys of the Road (1933) 57
Williams, Jamie 38
Wings (1927) 57
"The Wish House" 203
The Witch's Head (novel) 6
"With the Main Guard" 74, 76

"Without Benefit of Clergy" 10, 91, 92
Without Benefit of Clergy (1921) 92 94
Women's Magazine 201
World Pictures 168
The World's Desire (novel) 7

Yeats, William Butler 195
Young, Clara Kimball 60
Young, James 60

Zaza (1924) 172
Zemach, Benjamin 171
Zinman, David 202